ARE YOU TWO SISTERS?

ARE YOU TWO
SISTERS?

The Journey of a Lesbian Couple

Susan Krieger

TEMPLE UNIVERSITY PRESS
Philadelphia • Rome • Tokyo

TEMPLE UNIVERSITY PRESS
Philadelphia, Pennsylvania 19122
tupress.temple.edu

Library of Congress Cataloging-in-Publication Data

Names: Krieger, Susan, author.
Title: Are you two sisters? : the journey of a lesbian couple / Susan
   Krieger.
Description: Philadelphia : Temple University Press, 2022. | Includes
   bibliographical references. | Summary: "Utilizing an autoethnographic
   approach, this book probes the nature of female intimacy in contemporary
   society by tracing the life of a lesbian couple over a forty year
   period"—Provided by publisher.
Identifiers: LCCN 2021032119 (print) | LCCN 2021032120 (ebook) |
   ISBN 9781439922125 (cloth) | ISBN 9781439922132 (paperback) |
   ISBN 9781439922149 (pdf)
Subjects: LCSH: Krieger, Susan | Lesbian couples—United States. |
   Lesbians—Identity. | Women with disabilities—United States. | Intimacy
   (Psychology)—United States. | Sociology—Biographical methods. |
   Sociologists—United States—Biography.
Classification: LCC HQ75.6.U5 K729 2022 (print) | LCC HQ75.6.U5 (ebook) |
   DDC 306.76/630973—dc23/eng/20211022
LC record available at https://lccn.loc.gov/2021032119
LC ebook record available at https://lccn.loc.gov/2021032120

Printed in the United States of America

9 8 7 6 5 4 3 2 1

For Estelle

Contents

Preface

In these pages, I speak intimately about a lesbian relationship I have had with my partner "Hannah" for the past forty years. In writing these narratives to tell our story, I often turned inward, exploring interactions between us over time—how we met, how our relationship evolved, how I sought to come to terms with the twoness of us, with our individual differences, and with how together we moved through the world. Because my reflections were so often introspective, I was extremely grateful for the support and encouragement I received from others when I turned outward. I thank the Clayman Institute for Gender Research and the Program in Feminist, Gender, and Sexuality Studies at Stanford University for providing a scholarly home for me as I worked on *Are You Two Sisters?* I am grateful, as well, to Guide Dogs for the Blind for the gifts of Teela and Fresco, my two guide dogs, who have kept me safe and who have managed to wiggle their way onto many of these pages.

A core set of friends and colleagues have given me invaluable suggestions and support. I thank Paola Gianturco for encouraging me to take the risk of probing an intimate lesbian relationship and then carefully reading my drafts and helping me clarify my meanings, for assuring me that I was also speaking about self-other relationships more broadly, and for her abiding belief in me. I thank Zoe Becker for reading my chapters over and over and telling me, with a broad smile, that she felt this book was a contribution to "our lesbian herstory" as well as of potential interest for others. Susan Christopher reviewed the manuscript with an editor's eye, advising me about proper usage and giving me feedback about how the narratives felt emotionally. Ilene Levitt and Kathe Morse provided insightful responses on selected chapters.

I am profoundly grateful to Carmen de Monteflores both for reading selected chapters and for ensuring that Hannah and I know that our love for each other is more important than any problems we might face. I thank Marny Hall for earlier encouraging us as a couple, Esther Rothblum for her commitment to lesbian studies and for her belief in this project, and Donna Levitt for marrying us.

Several sets of people provided hospitality for Hannah and me as we traveled in the desert Southwest: I thank Phoebe Wood and Phil Norton for a home near the Bosque del Apache National Wildlife Refuge; Shirley, Marty, and Bryan Mize for their cottage in the Mimbres Valley; and Glen Surbey and Michelle Simpler for a lodging among the mountains near the New Mexico–Arizona border.

In many of the narratives in this book, Hannah and I cross paths with others who have been part of significant moments in our joint life. Although their presence in these stories may be brief and they appear here under pseudonyms, I deeply appreciate their contributing in vital ways to our journey and their support of us individually and as a couple. Hannah's and my journey was not taken alone.

I am delighted that Temple University Press has chosen to publish *Are You Two Sisters?*, carrying on the tradition of *The Mir-*

ror Dance. Especially, I am grateful to Shaun Vigil, my thoughtful and astute editor; Mary Rose Muccie, Temple Director; Carolyn Ellis and Leila Rupp, who provided invaluable reader reports and suggestions; copy editor Heather Wilcox; and Art Manager Kate Nichols.

Most of all, I thank Estelle Freedman, who has brought joy to me daily and been a model for how to share a life. Estelle has improved my prose in all of these narratives while encouraging me to be faithful to our reality. She has generously granted me permission to draw from our joint life in telling these stories, despite her concern about public exposure of what for us has been a very private experience. I hope that she may find in this book much that makes the exposure feel worthwhile. I thank her for our forty years together and for her wisdom, her patience, and her love.

ARE YOU TWO SISTERS?

Introduction

Several years ago, as I stepped out of a bar in a small desert town in New Mexico, a man followed me out and called after me, "Are you two sisters?" He had seen me with my partner Hannah inside the bar where she was now settling our lunch bill. As I walked with my guide dog toward our car across a dusty parking lot, the man tagged after me and called again in a challenging tone, "Are you two sisters?" I felt unnerved and did not respond, but his question stayed with me. Why did he ask? Why did he need to know? And why was it so hard for me to answer him?

When Hannah came out and we drove off, I told her what the man had said. "What did you tell him?" she asked.

"I didn't say."

She assured me that was all right. But I was uncertain. I knew I had felt a need to protect myself in this isolated town surrounded only by dry desert fields and mountains. But I also felt, "I should have had the nerve to speak."

I had, by then, been working on this book for some time, exploring the intimacies of a lesbian couple. The man's question called my attention to how lesbians were viewed in the outside world—that just as Hannah and I were always relating to each other, we were also constantly navigating our boundaries with others around us, needing to protect ourselves and often not knowing quite how to do it.

I subsequently decided to title this book *Are You Two Sisters?* because that is a question lesbians are often asked when others seek to know us, and because it suggests our own intimate self-questioning: Who are we? How am I different from others, and how am I the same? It also suggests feelings of vulnerability about our boundaries—the sense that one can easily be assaulted simply walking out the door.

Are You Two Sisters? traces the life of a lesbian couple over time, beginning in the 1980s with a meeting on a university campus, and through the several decades that follow as the two women become increasingly intimate with each other and share adventures in the larger world. Throughout, I raise the question: What difference does it make that the two women are lesbian? What makes them similar to others? What makes them different? What can be learned from following in the steps of these two women and considering their self-other dilemmas? Especially, I ask, why does lesbianism remain so often invisible?

I first examined issues of lesbian identity in my 1980s study, *The Mirror Dance: Identity in a Women's Community.* In that ethnography, I focused on a sixty-member social group in which individuals sought a sense of themselves apart from the straight world. In *Are You Two Sisters?* I explore similar dilemmas of self and other, but this time, I focus on a lesbian couple. Like *The Mirror Dance*, this book is innovative in its narrative style. It draws from interior reflections to probe the often hidden world of a lesbian intimacy, as well as to suggest broader themes concerning self and society.

In a previous work, *Social Science and the Self,* I argued for the value of an autoethnographic method of investigating social realities, one that recognizes the first-person experiences of the researcher as a legitimate source of broader insights. In my subsequent studies, I applied this approach to explore experiences of gender, identity, and disability. *Are You Two Sisters?* extends my method in new ways. This book is intended both for the general reader and as a contribution to the academic fields of gender, sexuality, and disability studies. A bibliography placing the current work in the context of literature in these fields appears at the end, along with an Afterword, "On Writing *Are You Two Sisters?*," that discusses the book's method and underlying themes.

While issues of invisibility and identity have run through all my previous work, *Are You Two Sisters?* is the most intimate of my books. It takes the reader along not only on my singular adventures but into the heart of a relationship I have had with another woman for the past forty years. Written in a candid personal style, it describes how I first met Hannah in 1980 when I stopped by her office, ostensibly to ask her advice on my new lesbian community study, but really to get to know her. It follows us as we move in together after three years of living apart and leads the reader along with us as we visit places and lovers of our past, travel in the New Mexico desert and along the California coast, nurture a home full of dogs and cats, come to terms with differences in our personalities and habits, and eventually get married, even though we did not view that institution in the most positive light.

In these pages, I tell the story of our journey in a manner both introspective and novelistic, often describing situations between Hannah and myself through dialog and evocative suggestion of scenes. I wish to enable the reader to feel "right there" with us in our life together, to experience things as we did, to see us and, at the same time, to reflect on the journey along with me.

"Hannah" in these tales is a stand-in for the real-life woman with whom I have shared my life intimately for the past forty years. I use a pseudonym for her, as in my prior work, because my writing is a version of experience unavoidably from my point of view.

When others appear in my accounts, they are figures of my imagination, no matter how accurately I seek to represent them. Were Hannah to tell our story, I am sure there would be much similarity, but it would be her version and her perspective would be articulated more fully.

I use the term "lesbian" in these narratives to refer to relationships of intimacy between women, often including shared sexuality. I am aware that others may use different terms, but this word resonates the most deeply for me, perhaps because it was in common use when I came of age seeking close, loving relationships with other women. I hope that readers may identify with some of the experiences I describe no matter the name assigned, and that this new book, like *The Mirror Dance*, may have a mirroring function.

When I began this ethnography, I did not know where my inquiries would lead. I knew only that I wished to explore the pivotal relationship in my life as I had once explored the many intimacies of a lesbian community. I wanted to do it justice, and I wanted Hannah to be pleased. As the chapters unfolded, I thought intently about some of the themes that I had first become aware of in writing *The Mirror Dance*: What did it mean to be a lesbian in a nonlesbian world and to be similar to each other as women yet very different? How can I be with another woman and not lose my sense of self to who she is? The deep feelings and idealistic expectations raised by lesbian relationships struck me—particularly the desires for mutual nurturance and acceptance. I noticed patterns of separateness and boundaries; of vulnerability or openness, of one to the other; of a life without a predetermined course, and without the usual heterosexual roles and protections. And very importantly—always lurking in the background—was the search for security and the need to protect one's lesbian intimacies from the outside world.

While I was working on this study, during 2015–2020, the vision loss I had been experiencing for many years intensified. The words swam on the computer screen before me to such an extent that, increasingly, I had to rely on my computer's voice to speak my words aloud to me. I listened to my prose as I wrote it, playing back my paragraphs repeatedly, sitting away from the computer monitor, eyes cast down, feeling the flow, feeling and thinking, over and over again—what am I expressing? How will it affect the reader? Am I capturing the emotional sense that is right for this remembrance, this incident—for when we first shared a bed, or took that trip to the desert, or drove across the golden California hills toward the beaches? Because I was listening as I wrote, I felt that, more than ever before, I was paying attention to the lyrical feel of my narratives and to using my inner voice as a way to convey outer experience as well.

In a way, *Are You Two Sisters?* may be for the reader, as it was for me, a challenge in the art of listening. Each chapter is a tale told from the inside out about a couple relationship. Each is a story about part of our journey, designed to stand alone as well as to fit with the rest. Each describes an experience Hannah and I shared and reflects back on our life together up to that time. The book is organized in thematic sections, in which the different stories fall: "Formalities of Attachment," "Our Formative Years," "The Sweep of Time," and "Who We Are." This organization seemed to me most fitting to the nature of the individual reflections, each written in pursuit of insights into a lesbian relationship and its self-other dilemmas.

Rather than a book that begins with the time I first met Hannah and moves forward in a strict chronological fashion, in *Are You Two Sisters?* many small journeys cumulatively fill out the shape of the whole. Some chapters are more deliberately retrospective than others, but all have that somewhat wistful quality of intermingling the present with the past, as occurs in real life. Some are literally travels along back roads in which Hannah and I face new challenges and reflect on our past life together. Others are journeys in a more figurative sense—journeys in getting to know each other, or in moving in together, or in seeing a couples therapist over time and learning new ways to relate to each other.

One of the themes that has struck me most as we travel is that Hannah and I lead a life that is often "under the radar," not easily seen by others. We blend in with a background of heterosexuality so that it is often hard to tell that we are lesbians. We are protective of our privacy with each other and move carefully in an outside world that may not be friendly to women who do not choose intimacies with men. Yet we take for granted the naturalness of our bond, the subtle pleasures that tie us together. I invite the reader to join us as the book opens with a story of our taking a major step not available when we started out, that of getting married. We are in San Francisco City Hall saying our vows, reflecting back on what has come before and ahead to what may yet unfold. That afternoon, for our "honeymoon," we take a trip down the coast with our dogs, again remembering times past when we traveled the same coast—visiting the beaches, getting acquainted, dealing with the challenges of our relationship, braving new roads and adventures.

Here, then, is *Are You Two Sisters?*—because issues of lesbian intimacy have long fascinated me and I wished to probe them further, and in answer to a man's question outside a desert bar. I hope the reader will enjoy my tales and share the excitement I have long felt in braving life with Hannah. I remain grateful to her real-life counterpart who, many years ago, opened her office door when a stranger knocked on it one fall afternoon, inquiring about her willingness to talk about a nascent lesbian community study. With this new book, I thank her for that conversation and for enriching my life ever since.

Part I

Formalities of Attachment

One

Our Marriage Day

I had rolled over in bed earlier that morning and given Hannah a kiss, as I do every morning before getting up. But this day was going to be different. "Happy Marriage Day," Hannah said from out of her sleep, returning my kiss softly, lingering with it more than usual. "Happy Marriage Day," I said, feeling an awkwardness about how the day would go, the high expectations, fearing what might be different after the big event. What would it do to us? I wondered. We had been okay as a couple so far. We had come a long way. We'd learned how to get on lovingly with each other, sometimes with pain and effort, but we were doing all right. Now, after thirty-two years together, we were going to change things. Why mess with it? I thought. I had visions of couples who build a new house so they can live happily ever after, and then when it is done, they break up. I did not want that to happen to Hannah and me.

"Do you think we'll be okay?" I asked my love as she lay beside me in the warm bed.

"Of course. Don't worry. It's just City Hall. I'm going back to sleep," she said.

Leaving her comfortably under the covers and stepping out of the room to get dressed, I thought about the first time I had been married, back when I was in graduate school in the 1970s. The man I married would later choose to be gay, and I would choose lesbianism, but we did not know that then. At the time, I think we did what was conventionally expected of us—fulfilling dreams for how we ought to be, for the next step we should each take in life. I did not, even then, believe in the necessity of marriage. It seemed to me too full of expectations about how two people ought to behave together, and it seemed to confer a higher status than that which would befall me as an individual unmarried woman. But only after we got married did the momentousness of it hit me. I looked down at my gold wedding band and suddenly thought, "This should not be." I should not be getting extra privileges because I am now married. People should not be looking at me differently—as a more desirable woman, perhaps, because I am married to a man, because someone wants me. But most of all, it was the extra rights and privileges that bothered me—the legal and financial advantages, the sense that it was viewed as better to be in a couple than alone. I thought that all the same advantages should be given to persons as individuals. The couple should not be the more valued unit. Thus, as I looked at the ring on my finger, although I liked it—a classic thin, gold band like my mother had—I did not like what it stood for, even as I wore it proudly, basking in the social acceptance it offered.

Joel and I were married in my parents' backyard. I wore a white dress with a short skirt and a lacy top with a high neck, and purple shoes. Joel wore a boldly colored flowered tie and a pinstriped blue suit. After we had said our vows beneath a chupah under tall trees, standing across from the rabbi, Joel smashed the traditional glass and the family and friends made sounds of approval, calling out "Mazel Tov" and clapping for us as we walked back toward the house while a string quartet played. We had stepped just out of earshot when Joel turned to me. "We can

break up at any time," he said. "This doesn't have to be forever."
I felt relieved. Those were my sentiments exactly, knowing what
often happened with couples. I then went back to mingling with
the guests.

It was going to be quite different now, I thought—no white
dress or flowered tie, no man, no audience, no reception in the
yard. Thank goodness. But it still was a ceremony, a charade in
some sense of that word—a performance that might have little
relation to my inner reality. Hannah and I would have to go to
City Hall. We would have to sign papers. I was not looking forward to that—though I was looking forward to going to the
beach afterward with our dogs.

I deeply loved Hannah and I wanted to keep being with her.
But there was something about the romanticization surrounding
marriage, the sentimentality, the sense of forever—as if a statement of vows could make that happen. There was something
about the unconventionality of everything Hannah and I had
experienced together. Not only were we lesbians, but I was me—
not quite fitting in, not like everyone else, uncomfortable often
in my own skin. Would marriage make me more comfortable,
more secure? Would it make us happier? I wondered.

That morning, after feeding our two dogs and three cats, I
went downstairs into our basement where I keep the harness my
guide dog Teela wears when she leads me. Nearby, beside the
sink, I had some white freesias waiting in water. Carrying the
flowers to a table, I carefully attached them to the harness with
gardening wire. Teela, my Golden Retriever–yellow Labrador
guide, was going to be our flower girl today. Behind the table on
which the decorated harness now rested were stacks of boxes
containing papers and valuables from my past. In one of those
boxes was my wedding dress from many years before. Or was it?
I thought maybe I had given it away. I had a memory of going
through my boxes once, finding the wedding dress, and feeling
I should not part with it. It didn't have much meaning for me in

the present, and I wasn't going to hand it down to anyone, but it was simply the kind of thing you keep. Probably it was in one of those boxes, I thought. Maybe now I could part with it.

"Good morning," I said back upstairs in the kitchen as Hannah came in for breakfast.

"It's our marriage day," she said with a smile.

I knew she liked to call it that, rather than our "wedding day," because weddings suggested a big formal ceremony to her, whereas all we were doing was getting legally married. I did not feel a need to avoid the term "wedding," but I knew what she meant.

"It's a big day," I said. "I hope it goes well."

"Do you know what you're going to wear?" she asked.

"The cream-colored shirt that goes with the white shirt you are wearing—the one you suggested."

"Good," she said.

Hannah likes to be my arbiter of dress, for which I am often grateful.

She, I knew, had a special shirt she had bought recently for the occasion—a white overshirt that looked crisp and clean and softened her, casting a gentle glow on her face as a wedding shirt should.

I felt I would not be dressed up enough, not as elegant in style as Hannah. I hoped I wouldn't make our marriage day feel less special because of the plainness of my attire. But Hannah had approved of it, and that was the important thing.

Standing in the kitchen beside her, I was aware that Hannah had not been married before. "You have to be especially nice to her," I told myself, resting my hand, for a moment, on her shoulder. "This day may mean more to her than you. You know how she likes sentimental things. I don't think she is as afraid of it as you are. Remember that marriage is something new for her. You are the one with wedding presents in the kitchen cabinet—all those large serving dishes. She hasn't had this kind of experience before, with people making a fuss over her. She isn't as jaded about it as you, not as skeptical about marriage."

Yet I knew that Hannah, like me, was critical of marriage. She saw it as a heritage from patriarchal institutions in which the woman was originally the property of the husband. And she knew we did not need it to be together. We had waited through all the years when lesbian marriage was not a legal alternative, and through the years afterward when many people around us were getting married, wanting to affirm their relationships, the legitimacy of their desires, to feel accepted and equal and like everyone else. But we had waited until marriage became legal to take this step.

"We don't need it," Hannah had always said to me. But after the 2013 Supreme Court decision, we consulted with a financial advisor and a lawyer and decided it was to our financial advantage to get married. Sitting with Hannah in her study at her computer one evening, I had looked over her shoulder as she scrolled through the City Hall listings searching for an available date. The financial advisor had suggested getting married as soon as possible. We chose a date two weeks later, July 16, at 11:25 A.M.

This morning, the date having arrived, we each dressed quietly, the feeling between us somber, as if the seriousness of the day loomed large. I was nervous, unsure what would happen at City Hall, other than that Julia, the sister of Hannah's oldest friend, would meet us there, usher us through the process, and officiate the ceremony. She worked in the mayor's office in City Hall and liked marrying people when she had time.

Before we left the house, Hannah and I went out into our yard and took pictures of each other dressed in our white and cream-colored shirts and dark slacks. Hannah is smiling in those photos when I look at them now. She glows with an inner happiness, a sense of confidence, a sense that this is a special and important day and that she is looking forward to it. In the pictures, I look more tense, I think. I remember that as we took the pho-

tos, Hannah kept asking me to relax. "You're not smiling normally," she said. "It's too forced. Relax. Turn your head sideways,
but not too far."

Leaving the house through the basement, I lifted Teela's decorated harness from the table and placed it across her golden
back. Hannah had in her bag some papers we might need. I
slung my camera bag over my shoulder. We got in the car and
drove downtown.

We parked not far from City Hall, where, when we got out,
Hannah took a photo of Teela with her freesia corsage and me
kneeling beside her on the sidewalk. But what Hannah really
wanted was a picture of the three of us. In front of City Hall, she
found a tourist who took our picture with the imposing gray
dome and broad steps of the building in the background. We
were properly posed—Hannah, me, and Teela—in memory of
this special day.

I stood there at the moment of the picture-taking, feeling
glad to be with Hannah, and glad to have Teela beside me—my
guide, my grounding when things got too extreme or unsettling,
too much not in my world. "I love Hannah," I kept thinking. "I
want to be married to her. But in City Hall!" This was too urban
a place for me. The city was my home, but not my home in an
underlying emotional sense, a sense of comfort and fit. But it was
Hannah's home—a place she liked—the place I had moved to
long ago in order to be with her. It made sense that, because we
lived here, this is where we would get married. But if I had my
way, if it were only me—and there's the rub: it wasn't. It was me
and Hannah together, sometimes doing things her way, sometimes mine. And, I reminded myself, this was the first time Hannah had gotten married. She had made the arrangements—with
our friend Julia, with City Hall, organizing us. I had simply gone
to get the flowers for Teela and was bringing my new camera to
record the event.

Julia met us just inside the entrance to the grand building, her hand outstretched with a large corsage of pastel-colored flowers formed into a lavish puffy ball. She had run to the florist a few blocks away and was out of breath. She handed the flowers to Hannah, who, startled by the surprise gift, quickly handed them off to me.

I handed them back to Hannah. "You take it," I said. "I have a dog and my camera. It's awkward for me."

"I don't want to carry it," she whispered to me in an emphatic tone while Julia had stepped away to check on our place in line for the registration.

"The flowers look nice on you. Why don't you want to carry them?" I asked.

"Isn't it obvious? I don't want to be the bride. You take it."

I knew what she meant. Both Hannah and I did not like the term "wife," or the sense of being a "bride"—the traditional division of gender roles. These terms reflected a time when the woman was chattel, property, not commanding of independent resources or an independent life, when a woman was seen in relation to a man. We wanted to be seen as apart from that mold, as two individuals—getting married perhaps, but not in the old way.

"It's okay to carry them," I said to Hannah. "It's different with us. It doesn't make you the bride."

I am not sure who carried that lovely floral bouquet upstairs. I think we handed it back and forth between us.

After registering, Hannah, Teela, and I followed as Julia led us through the magnificent, high, inner rotunda of the San Francisco City Hall. She had a private space in mind under the arches upstairs where we could have our ceremony. As we climbed the main stairway and followed a walkway along the perimeter of the broad central atrium, I looked around in the grayness of the esteemed place. It was reassuring to know that we were going somewhere more secluded, because the scale of the space was overwhelming. But then I thought it was fitting. We were not getting married in just any place—at the beach, or in my parents' backyard. We were getting married here, where the formality suggested that something important was about to happen.

Arriving finally in a corner of the mezzanine under the eaves near an archway softly lit with light from windows high above, Hannah took my hand. She led us to a balcony overlooking the great hall, where on staircases and under other archways, other people were getting married. Lifting her arm, gesturing forward, she described for me what she saw: "The woman over there on the nearby staircase has on a white wedding dress. The man is in a tux. They have a large party of people with them." "Across the way is another couple, looks like two gay men in suits."

"Are most of the couples gay?"

"It looks mixed."

Hannah then left to make arrangements with Julia for how we would proceed. I stepped back under the eaves and settled Teela on the ground at my feet, where she looked up at me expectantly, glowing golden under the ceiling lamps, the corsage of white flowers gently decorating her. I took out my camera and snapped a picture of her, glad for her familiarity in this unfamiliar place. I lay the generous bouquet from Julia down on the ground next to her beside my camera case.

Julia soon returned with Hannah to report that Steve, a friend of hers from the mayor's office, was going to be our witness. In our preparations for this day, Hannah and I had overlooked bringing a witness of our own, so much were we imagining the event to be only the two of us, not a big to-do.

When Steve arrived, I handed him my camera so he could take pictures of us, not knowing, at the time, how important that might be. For later, those pictures would become, to a surprising degree, the reality of the wedding ceremony for me—as if it all faded once it was done, as if it was fading even during. It was so unusual, so much not anything I might have conceived of before.

But with the pictures, after the ceremony, I could look back at them, and we could send them to our friends and family—"our wedding pictures"—just like people ordinarily did.

At the moment when I handed Steve my camera, however, I did so with misgiving. This was my brand-new camera, purchased only a few months before for our upcoming trip to New Mexico—to take those other pictures that I so valued when I got them home. For then I could enlarge them on my computer screen and could see what I was not able to see at the time with my limited eyesight. My pictures had helped me in prior trips to the desert to bring pieces of it home, to save images that mattered to me. Wouldn't they also help me remember this wedding day, this marriage ceremony between us? But at the time, it felt like such a brave act to hand my camera over. What if it broke or was damaged, what would I do? "If it's damaged," I told myself, "I will deal with it. This is what a person does in my position. You bring your good camera. You let someone take pictures with it."

I was so hesitant with my emotions, with the degree to which I would let myself feel, let myself invest in this day. "It was for Hannah," I had told myself all along. "It's for the money. It's a thing we should do after all these years. It doesn't matter that much." If it had mattered, maybe I would have suggested that we have our ceremony at the beach or in some natural spot Hannah and I especially liked—like under the redwood trees near the beach down in Pescadero. But I didn't advocate for that or offer it as an alternative for us back when we were planning our wedding day. The convenient, the easiest route, seemed the best. Go to City Hall and sign papers. Get it over with. Ignore the details, except for making it legal.

In the pictures that Steve took of us that day, I am always smiling. I look happy, as does Hannah. But I know, in looking at them, that we always smile for our pictures. I was aware of smiling all the time in City Hall that day, especially during the ceremony and after—as if to show the outside world that I was happy, as if to be happy, as if that was required. You were happy on your marriage day—happy to be with your beloved at this significant event, a culmination of your life together. In the end when we left City Hall and walked down the wide front steps, I realized that I had been smiling so much that my jaw was tired. My teeth hurt.

Was my smile for the outside world only, or was it for the inside too, I wondered—the inside that had such a hard time believing that Hannah and I were a couple, a couple as we should be, a couple committed to each other. But were we also romantically intertwined in that sense of being swept away by one another, enraptured when the other person walked into a room, such that you could not pull yourself away? All that sentimentality, the mythology of love and marriage, of being "in love"—was it true of us, or had it escaped me?

Hannah and I, we are just two people, I thought. We had fallen into being together, then stayed together. We worked things out, mostly because Hannah is so practical. She was willing to work things out with me—because she wanted to, because, she said, she loved me. She wanted to be with me. Maybe I was some kind of romantic figure for her, but I did not know. Was she a romantic figure for me? Was she the "love of my life," my shining star, my most special friend? Did it take my breath away when she walked into a room? How would I know?

I had spent such a long time denying it, not viewing our relationship in those other terms—those swept away, heart-throbbing, losing yourself, caught up in the maelstrom of love terms. I had doubted that those terms applied to me when it came to Hannah. She simply was "the one"—the woman, who, soon after I met her, my heart sunk. It did not soar, it sunk, that day when, in her secluded apartment in San Francisco, I stepped into the living room and looked back toward her in the kitchen and somehow grasped that she was the one for me, that we would be tied, that this was my fate. I think Hannah reminded me too much of my past, my family back East that I wished to escape. I had felt a deep inner dread at that moment—Hannah, the city, the walls of her apartment, they felt like they were closing in on me.

Yet it had happened—in spite of my defenses—from the very beginning, in her apartment, when I felt suddenly that my life was about to change. And it had happened every day since— when I walked into a room in our house and she was there, when I saw her getting dressed in the morning, her soft breasts—larger than mine even though she is a smaller woman—those breasts she would not let me touch when she was choosing her clothes for the day. I'd offered to kiss them, but she held up her hand. When she comes home at the end of a day and walks in through our kitchen door, my breath is caught, my heart skips a beat. I am so surprised that she is there. When we are out in public and she walks away from me—such as when we are on the campus—my lifeline leaves. I watch her go, her figure merging into the crowd.

I remembered the first time I had seen her in an airport when I went to meet her after a trip she took back East, when I was initially getting to know her. All the people had come out from the plane and were milling around, but I couldn't find her. I couldn't see her at first. Then I looked down below the level of the other heads and there she was—my Hannah, a small woman, shorter than the others. But when she was with me, when she was standing by my side, she has never seemed small. She was big, bigger than me—more judgmental and sensible, more caring, definitely caring of me. That day in the airport, my heart had soared. Surely that was testament to the love that now I sought to assess, to determine whether, in fact, it was true, whether it lived up to all the glamorous romantic expectations surrounding marriage—and maybe not the old, traditional marriage—but our marriage, the justification for our being a couple seeming somehow at issue on this day.

I know that when I look at the pictures of Hannah and me taken during our marriage ceremony and immediately afterward, I see myself as a gentle person, and as happy, as if the happiness is on the inside. I am looking over at Hannah with devotion as if I adore her, reflecting the care I also see in her eyes. When I look at those pictures and see my external smile, maybe I am seeing my inner emotions too, I thought. I am an actress, but not that good. Maybe some of my inner self was shining through—the care I felt for Hannah, and she for me, the joy I felt in her presence.

Hannah walked over now in our corner of City Hall and took my hands in hers. "Are you ready to get married?" she asked.

"Yes. Are you?"

She nodded, smiling.

We stepped forward in that gray space that was softened with a touch of gold, the lamps above us casting a welcoming glow all around us. Julia came and stood before us, announcing that the ceremony was about to begin, holding a cardboard plaque printed with the words she would read. Steve stood a distance to the side with my camera, which occasionally flashed, though fading into the background. Hannah held the bouquet. I held Teela's leash firmly in my left hand, my right gently resting across Hannah's shoulder. The time had come.

Julia began: "We are gathered here for the purpose of uniting in matrimony Hannah Golden and Susan Krieger. The contract of marriage is most solemn and is not to be entered into lightly, but thoughtfully and seriously with a deep realization of its obligations and responsibilities. Please remember that love, loyalty, and understanding are the foundations of a happy and enduring home.

"No other human ties are more tender and no other vows more important than those you are about to pledge. Please face each other and join hands.

"Do you, Hannah, take Susan to be your lawful wedded spouse? To have and to hold from this day forward, for better or for worse, for richer or for poorer, in sickness and in health, to love and to cherish as long as you both shall live?"

"I do," Hannah said, looking into my eyes with a directness that pierced right through me, challenging me to look back at her in the same way.

"Do you, Susan, take Hannah to be your lawful wedded spouse . . . ?"

"I do." I said, returning her gaze, almost flinching with the intensity of it, the open sincerity of the moment.

"Now that you have joined yourselves in matrimony," Julia continued, "may you strive all your lives to meet this commitment with the same love and devotion that you now possess. By virtue of the authority vested in me by the State of California, I now pronounce you 'spouses for life.'"

I kissed Hannah, and she kissed me, as together we held the flowers in our joined hands. We belonged together, I suddenly felt. We had come a long way, Hannah and I. The gentleness, the understatement of it all, the fact that it was Hannah's oldest friend's sister marrying us, that Teela was there with us, and that Hannah positively glowed in her white shirt, suggesting a purity—I took it all in. I felt more relaxed now than before, glad that the ceremony was over. Yet, to my surprise, it had moved me. I had not expected the realness, the seriousness of the vows. I had not ex-pected any vows at all, nor such a churchlike ceremony, so tradi-tional, with so many words. I had expected a signing of docu-ments, something more legal and perfunctory, strictly on paper. And here we were standing in a puddle of sentiment amid much that had deeper meaning—dressed for the occasion—we had even each worn "something borrowed, something blue." We had brought a flower girl.

Did Hannah cry when we said our vows? Did I? I don't think I did. But I remember that I was extremely moved—drawn into that world of honoring marriage that I so often refused to enter.

The ceremony—the words—were more sobering than I expect-ed. They were not the "swept away with love" words that I had been thinking about earlier, but I was glad I had had those thoughts, consulted those feelings. These words were equally moving—even more true of us perhaps—and yet I wanted us to be those fantasy people—the two lesbians in love, the two lesbi-ans who dared it all—who had no roadmap, no guide, no tem-plate for how to be—and yet who had made it, who had merged their two households not so long ago, and perhaps we were, in fact, those two. It was actually quite a while ago that we had merged our homes. But it did not feel that way. It felt like we had just met. Just yesterday I found her. Only yesterday, I did not know her, and then I did. Every day, every single day, I looked at her and thought, "She is a stranger. She is not my sister. She was not brought up the same way as me. She is someone else, some-one foreign to me—the way she brushes her teeth, drinks her tea, has her breakfast in the morning. She is a very different person from me, walks at a different pace, has a different life."

Yet we were together, together still—working it out, the kinks, the snags. We were here in San Francisco City Hall getting mar-ried where the arches glowed golden and we stood in front of one of them looking at each other with adoration, with gentle happi-ness, with relief. We had made it, we had come here, we had been officiated, we had been given flowers, we had gotten along. We had done what we were supposed to do.

After the ceremony, Hannah and I posed for a few more pho-tos—in front of the high, picturesque archway, looking at each other with heads tilted toward one another, framed perfectly for the day, for an official wedding photo by our witness photogra-pher. Steve did a good job with the pictures, and Julia took some too—Hannah and me by the balcony holding the flowers, Han-nah alone looking joyous, Teela with us sitting at my feet. Teela posed, sometimes distractedly, her head turned away from the camera, but there with us, a part of our family. She lent an air of naturalness, a suggestion of our broader life, and she, like us, was anxious to leave.

But in the end, it was hard to tear ourselves away. At least it was hard for me—to leave that protected corner upstairs where Hannah and I, in the company of my guide dog, had finally gotten married.

Julia and Steve signed the papers, and we headed back around the atrium to go downstairs. Across from the elevator was a statue of Harvey Milk, and Hannah asked that we pose for a picture beside it. This wasn't an image with which I wanted to remember our wedding day—it felt too male and political to me—but I understood that it had meaning for her, and so it is one of our treasured pictures.

In the elevator on the way down, Hannah suggested we say the "Shehecheyanu," the Jewish prayer for the first time experiencing a joyous occasion. Then she led as she, Julia, and I recited the Hebrew for: "Blessed art Thou Lord our God, Ruler of the Universe who has given us life, sustained us, and allowed us to reach this day."

At a counter in the main lobby, we waited for a long time to receive our marriage certificate. We could have come back for it two weeks later, but I wanted us to walk away with proof. The glossy marriage certificate the clerk handed to me was not ornate, but it did have an official seal at the bottom, a decorative border, and our names up top. Papers in hand, Hannah, Teela, and I then walked down the steps of City Hall and out into the open air.

The fresh air felt invigorating, the sun breaking through the fog that had been omnipresent when we arrived only two hours before.

"How did you feel about the ceremony?" I asked Hannah.

"I felt good," she said, putting her arm around my waist as we walked toward our car. We got in, sat in the car for a while and relaxed, then headed for a bakery where we hoped to buy two jumbo-sized, vegan brownies to use later as our wedding cake.

But when we arrived, the bakery was closed. "What should we do for a cake?" I asked Hannah, thinking that maybe later when we went down the coast, we would find one there.

"We don't really need a wedding cake," she said. "It's enough that we are going to take the dogs to the beach."

"We need a wedding cake," I said. "We'll find one."

Back at home, Esperanza, our small black poodle, greeted us excitedly as we stepped into the kitchen. While we stood having a bite to eat, the front doorbell rang. Upon opening it, I was handed a large arrangement of brightly colored flowers—so elaborate it could only have been sent by someone for our marriage day.

I brought the flowers back into the kitchen. "My sister sent these," I said, holding them out to Hannah. "Look, they are very good flowers, really something special." We then took pictures of each other holding the cascading profusion of vivid blooms, as well as the original corsage given to us by Julia.

I called my sister to thank her. "How did it go?" she asked. "I thought about you this morning."

Julia's older sister called. Several other friends began checking in. There were phone messages for each of us.

This had been such a private day in my mind—go to City Hall, no big to-do, the two of us heading for the beach afterward. Now all of a sudden, there were flowers and calls, people who wanted to know how it went. That Hannah and I had gotten married seemed a big deal, something to be celebrated and enjoyed.

"Are you ready," I asked Hannah, "ready to go to the beach?"

"Let me change my shirt. I'll be ready soon."

Two

Down the Coast

That afternoon when Hannah and I went down the coast after our marriage ceremony merges, in my mind, with all those other times she and I have gone to the beach—to celebrate an event, to get away, to see the green or gold of the hills, to see the vast ocean that stretches at the horizon all the way to China. It's as if seeing that ocean, the unfettered expanse, feeling the breeze, walking along the shore frees us, gives us something in common, reconfirms our bond. More than any formal ceremony might— in a city hall, in a church, or in a synagogue—going to the coast is our way, I think, of celebrating us. It stirs memories of the first time we went to the beach together back when I had just met Hannah and we did not know how we would get along—when we parked behind a Day-Glo-decorated hippie school bus in a gas station across from the ocean and imagined that one day, we, too, might be hippies traveling the coast in our bus. We never did get a VW van as I hoped. By the time I might have bought one, I was losing so much of my eyesight that I would not be able to drive it, and Hannah liked smaller cars, so we got a Prius.

But we always came here. When we could not go to the desert, second best was a trip to the coast. It represented a melding of each of our lives, each of our pasts. We always talked on our drives as we looked out on the ocean—discussing our recent experiences, problems we each wanted to solve. We would look forward to the trip every time—to going somewhere together, to a time when we would sit close in the car, have no distractions, be able to converse. And from the beginning, we had brought dogs. At first it was Geronimo, the small black terrier-poodle I had when I first met Hannah, and who was with us for the next eighteen years. It was a shame to go to the beach, I felt, without bringing your dog. It was as if that deprived the dog of a chance for life, for freedom, for a new beginning. That was what the beach—what "going down the coast"—stood for to me, and perhaps for us—a chance for a new life, for feeling unspoiled, for having horizons that stretched all the way to foreign and unknown lands.

Yet a trip down the coast was also very familiar. Often, especially in our early years, we went up the coast to the Point Reyes National Seashore and beyond. But the coast south, for about an hour below San Francisco, was the home stretch increasingly—with the glittering ocean spreading before us as soon as we circled west and hit Route 1. This coast was so familiar that it was now hard for me to separate out the trip we took on our marriage day from all those others we had taken before and since.

That afternoon after we married, we packed the dogs into the car along with food for their dinner, their dishes, water, treats, and extra towels, and headed south. With us were Esperanza, our lively black poodle whom we got after Geronimo died, and Teela, my golden guide dog, also playful and loving the beach.

I took no pictures of our time at the coast that day. I doubt that I took my good camera with me, afraid probably of getting it covered with salt spray and sand. But, fortunately, Hannah took pictures and a few videos with her cell phone. They bring back, for me, the feel of that day, of our walk on the beach with our dogs.

Esperanza, our furry, black, little girl, is gone now. She died only ten months ago. So looking at the photos of me walking with her and Teela along the shore, and of my holding Esperanza in my arms, makes me want to cry. I miss her so. But the pictures bring her alive again. They remind me of the reality of that day—the sun, the glistening sand, and us.

The waves are breaking ahead of us as we walk, Teela on my left, Esperanza on my right. Hannah is behind us taking the photos. The beach is quiet, very private; it's one we come to often because we can sneak our dogs onto the sand. There is a sign at the entrance beside the path from the parking lot to the beach that says "No dogs," not even on leashes. But the state has not had enough money to patrol all the beaches, so we have been coming here with our dogs for some time. It's a small alcove of a beach, tucked away off to the side, while the main state beach in this area extends to the south on the other side of a central bluff. That is where most of the people go. They do not realize that if you walk onto the smaller part of the beach and circle around farther to the right, tall sandstone cliffs stretch up to the azure blue sky, keeping the highway and the interior land at bay. There, you can walk seemingly for miles, in privacy, unobserved. Or that used to be so—before the coastline changed in the years between when we got married and now. Back then, if we walked in the shadow of the cliffs, between them and the ocean, a vast new beach soon opened out on which we could take our dogs or walk alone, sheltered from the rest of the world, the Highway Patrol on Route 1, the people sitting on their blankets elsewhere. Today, the ocean, even at low tide, nips at the base of the sandstone cliffs, so the sequestered stretch of endless beach is gone. But on our marriage day, it was there.

No people were around when we arrived at our end of the parking lot that afternoon. Hannah took Esperanza, I took Teela, and we hurried from the lot to the sandy path leading to the shore. There we skirted the back edge of the beach where the vegetation begins to climb a craggy hillside between the beach and the road. We wanted to get the dogs quickly out of sight of any park rangers or police who might be driving by, spot them from above, and come to tell us no dogs were allowed. Teela, a guide dog, could go anywhere, but Esperanza could not. I always had a sob story in mind in which I explained to the roaming officer that it would be cruel to leave little Esperanza in the car, given that she was sick and I was blind. But it never came to that.

Esperanza was pulling at her leash, leading Hannah, and Teela was half guiding me as the two dogs nosed the driftwood and succulent plants, excited to realize they were at the ocean and no longer at home. Ever since we got Esperanza, and then Teela—and later my second guide dog Fresco—we have brought them to the beach, wanting them to feel this was a special place for dogs. Circling the perimeter of the crescent-shaped beach, we approached a large rock outcrop that juts up from the sand at the edge of the ocean, where the waves sometimes break through between it and the cliffs. But today the tide was low. We turned right past the rock, at the edge of the first cliff, entering that stretch of shore where we could walk unobserved.

There, in the bright sunlight, with the waves pounding with a ferocity that felt like a protective background, Hannah and I knew we were where we belonged—somewhere private, that stretched forever, together in the sun with each other and our dogs. The sky above the sandstone cliffs was a deep blue, which was unusual for this foggy coast at this time of year and could not be counted on for long. But for now, the winds stayed at bay, the air was cool but not cold, a gentle breeze coming up as we walked, invigorated, along the broad stretch of hidden beach. I looked back and could even see our footsteps—two lines of people's boot prints and two jagged lines of paw prints leaving a trail behind us yet to be swept away by a rising tide.

We continued in the shadow of the cliffs until I thought that Esperanza's little legs would be too tired for our walk back and that I would have to carry her the whole way. I turned to Hannah. "Have we come far enough?" I asked.

"Soon," she said. Then she spotted an area ahead where the sand extended back toward the cliffs, forming a cavelike opening at their base. In front of the opening, out on the beach, was a large rock bench, a piece of the cliffs that had fallen off, or that had once been part of the cliffs at the bottom, that now beckoned to us as a resting place. I took a seat beside Hannah on the rough-hewn bench and looked out at the ocean, our dogs, lying beside us in the sand, also looking toward the sea.

This was a wild place, I thought, between the two huge elements of nature—the cliffs and the ocean. A rogue wave could come up at any time and sweep us away. No one could see us here, but then no one could save us. "Do you think we are safe?" I asked Hannah.

"I do," she said, reassuring me as she has done so many times, that I will be safe—safe with her.

"The tide won't be high for a while," she said. "We'll be able to get back."

"Do you know how many times we have come to this beach?" I asked her.

"It's too many to count," she said. "You have walked on this part of the beach more than me. Usually you walk with Teela while I lie on the sand back at the other beach with Esperanza, and, all the time you are gone, she is crying for you."

"But today we're all here."

"Yes, we are."

"Are you glad we got married?" I asked.

"I am."

"Isn't this better than City Hall?"

"I like them both. But this is more 'us,'" she said.

"Do you remember the first time we went to a beach when I first met you?"

"I do. It was farther down than here. You made chicken sandwiches."

"I don't remember the sandwiches."

"I thought it was very caring. I was impressed."

Then in my mind, I saw a time that I did not mention—back toward the end of the third year I knew Hannah when we had a memorable walk on a beach farther south—a walk during which we talked about having children. I told Hannah that I did not want to have children. Up until then, it was part of her fantasy for her future, I think, that, in a couple relationship with another woman, she would have kids. But I had often been involved with women who had children in my past, and I knew they were a lot of work. I felt I would be the one to do the work, that I would be more the "wife" while Hannah went off to prepare for classes or give talks, that more of the physical caring would fall to me.

"It changes your life," I said to her. "It becomes centered on kids."

"I know," she said. "But that might be nice."

"I thought about it even before I was a lesbian," I told her, "back when I was married. I thought, and I still do, that I have too many internal problems, so I would not be good for kids. I have enough on my hands taking care of myself."

"What if there were only one child? Could you do that?" she asked.

"No," I said, looking at her searchingly as we stood together talking on that other beach down near where the elephant seals played. It was a bright sunny day. The sand was glistening.

I had planned that we would talk about children on our trip to the shore that day, so it was not a surprise for me, but I think it was for Hannah.

"I always thought I would have kids," she said wistfully.

"It's a condition," I told her. "You can have a relationship with me. Or you can have kids and I won't be there."

I am amazed now that I could have done that—been willing to give her up, to make that choice. But that is what happened.

"I have to think about it," Hannah said. "I hadn't thought of all those things. It's true, I was thinking that you would do more of the work."

"And you would come home and the kids would be nicely tucked in bed."

"Something like that, yes. But I would do my share."

It was not long afterward that Hannah and I started searching for a house in which we could live together. But first, I think, we had to get over that hump, that difference between us that blocked the way, and our pivotal discussion had occurred on a beach not far from where we now sat.

Now, many years later, on a similar beach, we were surrounded not by children but by dogs. The dogs are not a substitute for children for Hannah and me, I think. They are far less complicated and they do not live as long. But they are similar in that they show a way we care. Especially, the dogs are a way that Hannah shows she cares for me. She probably would not have had dogs on her own, but she has welcomed them into our life together because, I think, she knows I can be lonely and that the companionship is good for me. Caring for the dogs, and for our cats, grounds me, though sometimes Hannah will feel overlooked if I pay too much attention to them. We will be standing in the kitchen and I will be feeding the cats or refilling the water bowl, intent on my tasks. "What about me?" she will ask when I seem not to hear her or when I bump into her while moving about. "Aren't I important to you too?"

Then I reassure her. "Sorry, I forgot."

"You forget sometimes that I am here."

But today, we were not forgetting each other. We were focused on our life together, on what it meant to have been married this morning and now to be at the beach with our dogs. Looking at the ocean, sitting beside Hannah, my mind wandered to the trunk of the car where, under protective covering, was a chocolate cake. I hoped the frosting was not melting. We had picked it up at a local grocery store on our way down.

"Let's stop," I had said to Hannah as we approached the store. "Maybe they will have a cake."

"We don't have to stop," she said. "It's enough that we're together."

Why did she so often say that? I wondered. She tended to push away the importance of material things. She was supposed to be the sentimental one when it came to us. I was the one who didn't like to stand on ceremony or engage in the same rituals as everyone else. But on this day, I thought we should have a wedding cake. I had actually been planning, for some time, what we would put on top of it, though I had not told Hannah about that. I had made some calls, seen pictures online of little figures that people put on their cakes. What if the two were not a bride and groom, but two brides? Did the figures look androgynous enough so that the one in the tux who was supposed to be the man might be mistaken for a woman? Where would I get two women figures not wearing dresses, but pants? I had given up my search, in the end, because these were specialty items I would have had to order well in advance.

Still, in my mind, I saw a wedding cake—tall and white with multilayers, the bride and groom up top, just like in all the heterosexual pictures.

"Let's stop," Hannah finally said.

Entering the store, we went over to the bakery counter, where we stood eyeing the cakes on display on shelves. Teela, at my side, her nose raised, sniffed the air, ready to help us choose. Then there it was. It wasn't white and it was only one layer, but it was something Hannah reached for immediately.

"I see it," she said. "It's chocolate, with shaved chocolate on top." Lifting the cake in its box, she read the label. "It says it's made with flax. It's gluten-free and dairy-free."

Hannah had recently gone on a gluten-free diet, I knew, and she could not tolerate dairy.

"Let's get it," she said, looking toward me, then gently placing the cake in our basket. I almost cried. We were going to have a wedding cake after all, and Hannah seemed pleased.

I am always glad when Hannah seems pleased—when she seems surprised and delighted to do something that was originally my idea that initially she did not think necessary. It pleases me to please her, especially by surprise. I wanted her to feel that I cared about the sentimental side of our relationship. This cake would help do that.

"We can put something on top," I offered.

"It's not necessary," she said. "What would you put there anyway?"

"Something."

"Maybe we should come back for it later," she added. "The frosting might melt in the car."

"No," I said. "Take it now," remembering how, fifteen years earlier, Hannah and I had gone up north to check out a puppy who had been advertised in a paper—a little black dog to succeed Geronimo. I had been longing for a new dog and we had spent many months searching. A friend said, before we left, "If you like the puppy when you meet her, take her right then. Don't leave her there. Someone else might come in the meantime and take her. That happened to a friend of mine."

We arrived at the home in Sonoma County, met Esperanza, who was the runt of a litter of seven black poodle puppies, liked her immediately, pushed away all doubt, and took her home with us. Forever after, that was a lesson for us: "If you see a thing, especially a dog, and you want it, get it right then. Don't risk that she won't be there when you return."

"Esperanza," I said to Hannah as we stood in the store, and she knew what I meant.

I carried the cake back out to the car where Esperanza was waiting, eager for us to get to the beach. Seeing her lively, black shape, I remembered a time soon after we got her that had also been a lesson for Hannah and me. When Esperanza was a puppy, she used to like to take tee shirts and shake them with her teeth hard, as if they were prey that she was seriously killing by breaking their necks. She had been doing this for some time with tee shirts we gave her when, one day when Hannah and I were in a supermarket, I saw, on a high shelf, a big, tan, stuffed dog with floppy ears and tail that I thought might substitute for the tee shirts for her.

"For Esperanza," I said to Hannah as I reached for the floppy, tan dog and brought it to our cart.

"It's too big," she said. "We don't need it. She is happy with tee shirts."

"I know," I said. "But this is the right size. She likes to shake things that are bigger than her."

"You can get it," Hannah said. "But she won't use it. It's not needed. You always want to get her things."

"We can bring it back if she doesn't like it," I offered, fully expecting that I would not be doing that, because the tan dog would soon be covered with slobber.

"Okay," Hannah said finally, "if you want to."

Then out we walked with the big, tan dog. It had a red and green cloth collar, I think because this stuffed animal was left over from Christmas and now being recycled for Valentine's Day, which may have explained why it was on a top shelf and on sale.

Esperanza loved her gift. She loved it so much that we soon had to sew up the places where she had bitten out the eyes. The new dog, whom I named "Esperita," then became "Blind Esperita." She was followed by a second identical, tan dog, "Esperita's Sister"; by a smaller version of the same dog, "Esperiti"; and then by a series of Teddies, one of whom spent much time in the emergency room being sewn up in places where Esperanza repeatedly grabbed him with her teeth to shake him.

The three Teddies and Esperita's Sister now sit in a chair in our living room, the Teddies surrounding Esperita's Sister, guarding her protectively, reminding us of the little black dog who once had played with them so fiercely.

When not long ago, I asked Hannah if it might be time to take the Teddies and Esperita's Sister out of the chair: "Not yet," she said. "Let them be there a while longer. No one sits there anyway."

This was a far cry from that time in the market when Hannah had doubted my intuition that the tan, stuffed dog on the high shelf would be a treat for Esperanza.

"Remember Esperita," I will say to Hannah, or she will say to me on many occasions since that time—when we have to make a decision and we are on opposite sides, each of us convinced she is right. Then Hannah will smile, as if entertaining the thought that there is the remote possibility that I might be right as I was about the tan dog. Usually, Hannah is right on practical matters because she thinks things through in advance, while I act more on feeling. I will often come around to her perspective in the end. But sometimes, like today with the cake, I will be right.

I still have the original Blind Esperita. She is tucked away on a high shelf in the back hall closet in our house where I keep items that need to stay protected and dry, not in danger of becoming mildewed. Like the Teddies and her sister, she reminds me not only of Esperanza, but of Hannah and me and all we have come through together, of all that we have loved and weathered that now seemed so inexpressible, yet that surrounded us, as we drove, on our marriage day, with our dogs toward the beach.

Sitting on the rock bench, looking toward the sea, Hannah beside me, the dogs at our feet, I felt overwhelmed by a sense of our past. I turned to Hannah, "Do you remember the time we had Thanksgiving dinner at Pomponio Beach?" I asked her, "I think we did that twice."

"Yes," she said somewhat painfully. Then I saw us again that first Thanksgiving when we had taken our dinner as a picnic to a beach past the stretch of cliffs behind where we now sat. If you kept walking, much farther than we had come, eventually, past many other cliffs, the ocean breaking in the background, the shore would open out closer to the road and there would be another beach, accessible to the public from the road, Pomponio. That Thanksgiving was during the second year I knew Hannah, before we lived together. We were in her apartment. We had made turkey and the trimmings, and we were alone. Hannah seemed sad. I was not then aware of how much Hannah wanted to have Thanksgiving with other people, to have a sense of family and friends. A friend of hers had died recently, and that was affecting her too.

"How about if we make a picnic?" I asked her, hoping to cheer her up. "We can spread the tablecloth on the living room floor and eat our dinner there rather than in the kitchen."

We took out the yellow tablecloth and laid it down, began bringing in the food. Hannah suddenly burst into tears. She was not happy as I had hoped.

"How about if we take our Thanksgiving down the coast?" I asked her.

"Okay," she said.

We packed up the food in a cooler, put it in the trunk of my car and headed south.

Route 1 was deserted as we drove, the quiet that comes from people being inside their houses having their dinners or preparing. Pampas grass waved their white plumes at us from hillsides we passed. The fog was lifting as we approached the beach. From the road, I saw three tables on a dune overlooking the ocean. "How's this for a spot?" I asked Hannah, pulling the car into the lot at Pomponio Beach.

We took our food out of the car, carried it to a table, spread the yellow cloth, wiped away the dirt left on the dark wooden benches, and looked toward the sea. Geronimo wasn't with us that day. I had left him back at the house where I was living. It was just Hannah and me. Somehow the haziness, the late afternoon sun breaking through, the stillness of the empty beach, the mild weather, even though it was November, the sense of specialness all around us spoke to Hannah's need to have something more happen on Thanksgiving Day than just the two of us alone in her apartment.

I think Hannah still harbored a desire for more company, more of a sharing with friends, but I think our picnic helped.

A few years later, there was a Thanksgiving Day when I had a bad headache and my mood was low. I didn't even want to have a Thanksgiving meal. By then, Hannah and I had moved in together and I was feeling the stresses of working things out between us. How could I live up to her expectations? How would I be myself with her? I felt I was losing my past, losing a sense of who I was. Hannah looked into my eyes, took me by the hand. "We're going down the coast," she said. "We will take our dinner to Pomponio like we did that other time." I was in tears and reluctant, but I followed her, and, at four in the afternoon, again the sun peeked through, though it was foggier and windier than that first time. I was still feeling like crying as we pulled the car into the lot and looked for our table, then unpacked the provisions. But I could not help but feel Hannah's caring, her desire to lift my spirits as once I had sought to lift hers. It made a difference. It cemented the image in my mind—the two of us, the table, the turkey coming out of the container.

"Would you like cranberry sauce and stuffing?" Hannah asks, dishing some out toward my plate.

"What would you like?"

"I prefer gravy," she says.

On later Thanksgivings, we would not come to the beach again to have our meal. We would have it with friends. But in succeeding years, we always made it a point to come down the coast on Thanksgiving Day, either before or after our other commitments. We would drive down, see the Pampas grass on the hillsides waving their white fronds welcoming us, feel the chill of fall, perhaps the start of rain, and feel special being together. After a while, more people seemed to go to the beaches on Thanksgiving Day, so it was a less private experience for Hannah and me, and we stopped going as regularly.

In more recent years, the beach at Pomponio, like the beach farther down, lost the stretch of shoreline available for walking on the other side of the cliffs, and a stream filled much of the central beach with a pond. But on the bluff overlooking the ocean the three wood tables remained. You can see them from the road. We see them every time we drive by, and always, for me, there is a memory of those two Thanksgiving meals that Hannah and I shared—looking toward the sea, trying to make each other feel better, taking out our turkey, cranberry sauce, and gravy.

"Do you want some wine?" I remember asking Hannah, reaching for the bottle.

"Not for me, not now," she says. "Being here with you is enough."

"Too bad we didn't bring Geronimo," I say. "He would have liked it here."

"It's okay to be just us," she says.

I see those three tables in the dunes in my mind, forever silhouetted against the gray sea, waiting for us, no one else sitting there. I see them in memory of our past. It is fall when Thanksgiving occurs. That is always an important time for Hannah and me, because it is the season in which we met.

But now it was summer, mid-July three decades later, and we were not alone but with our dogs. Esperanza was restless, pulling at her leash, "Will you pet me now? Will you give me a treat?" Teela, waving her head, indicated she wanted me to play Frisbee or, at least, to follow her to the base of the cliffs so she could nose around.

"Shall we go back now?" I asked Hannah.

"I think it's time," she said.

"But first, will you take a picture of the cliffs with the blue sky behind them?"

She took out her cell phone, pointed it toward the top of a yellow-tan sandstone cliff where it met the bright sky, then pointed it at the ocean, at the dogs, then at us.

"Smile," she said, switching to the front camera. She stopped the camera, then started it again.

That picture, a video, now in my computer, shows Hannah and me, our heads together, smiling, singing to each other—the cliffs in the background, the low roar of the ocean. "Happy Marriage Day," we are singing, "Happy Marriage Day to us!" We look toward each other, laugh, and sing on. "Happy Marriage Day, Susan," "Happy Marriage Day, Hannah," our voices overlapping when we say the names at once. Our mood is almost giddy, happy with the moment, the unexpected, the song. I think it was my idea for us to sing, knowing Hannah liked singing, feeling I could follow her tune. I think she thought it was silly, unnecessary perhaps. But that video so captures the time for me.

We walked back along the beach slowly, Esperanza leading the way. She always liked to speed when heading back to the car, but Hannah and me, we were savoring the experience—the sun, this outing, this trip to the beach in memory of all that had gone before, in celebration of us, of who we were now. All this lay unspoken beneath our feet as we followed our footprints from when we had started out, now deeper in the sand, being blown by the wind but still there.

"It always seems shorter walking back," Hannah said, stepping carefully among the footprints as if not to disturb them.

"Can you tell which footprints are yours?" I asked her.

"I can't," she said.

"Yours are smaller and your boots have a different imprint."

"You can't see that well," she turned to me with a smile.

"Yes, I can. The sun is very bright. There's a lot I can't see, but some things I can."

"Do you think we can play Frisbee with the dogs?" I asked her as we neared the main beach.

"I'd rather be safe," she said. "Just let them smell things today. They are older now. I don't want them to get hurt. We'll play Frisbee another time."

I scooped up Esperanza soon after that and carried her in my arms, handing Teela's leash to Hannah.

We climbed from the quiet beach basin to the parking lot and walked over to the car. In the trunk, the cake was still intact. The frosting had not melted.

After we gave the dogs water, they jumped into the car. By now it was nearly dinner time. Hannah was anxious to get us to the restaurant where I had made a reservation—a Japanese restaurant in a nearby town—to remind us of our first date soon after we had met. It was in that earlier Japanese restaurant that I had sat across from Hannah in the darkened interior and looked into her eyes, feeling the seriousness of our connection and that there was something special about her.

In the parking lot behind the Japanese restaurant on the coast, I now took out the dogs' bowls and filled them with food. First Esperanza ate from her bowl standing on the back seat of the car. Then Teela ate her meal standing beside it lapping up her delicious morsels. We then moved the car closer to the front window of the restaurant so Hannah would be able to see Esperanza from inside. I always worried, when we left Esperanza in the car, that someone might steal her because she was a small, cute poodle. Or she might become anxious and rambunctious and try to get out of the car to reach us, throwing herself at the windows or door. She had never done that, but Geronimo had. He once forced open the front window where I had left it open a crack and was working on removing the weather stripping when I found him.

"Should we take the cake inside with us?" I asked Hannah as we got out of the car and cracked the windows for Esperanza.

"Let's save it for later," she said.

Inside the restaurant, Hannah led us to a table in the window.

"Can you see Esperanza?" I asked her as we sat down.

"I can."

"What's she doing?"

"She's sitting in the driver's seat looking at the door where we came in."

"Can she see us?"

"I don't think so."

As Teela settled comfortably at my feet, I handed my menu to Hannah to read for us. "Pick something that you like that you would not ordinarily get," I said.

"Maybe something spicy for you?" she added.

Our dinner at the Japanese restaurant that early evening, when it was still light, was unremarkable, the food a disappointment. But that was perhaps as it should be. That first time back in the fall when I had just met Hannah and the night was dark and the dishes each perfect no matter what their taste—that was the Japanese dinner to remember. Now what mattered was that we were here, in honor of that earlier time, and with both our dogs—especially Esperanza, since she did not go with us everywhere like Teela did.

We left the restaurant when the night was still young and walked back to join Esperanza in the car. We drove north along Route 1 silently most of the way, although talking, here and there, about the other restaurant and how it had been the first time and how it had been this morning in City Hall.

"It was a good day," I said to Hannah, reaching my arm over to tousle her hair, massage her neck. "It was better than I expected."

"Me, too," she said.

"But I liked the afternoon best."

"I liked both, I told you."

"This afternoon going to the beach with our dogs was our honeymoon," I offered.

"Maybe that's not quite the word for it," Hannah mused.

I looked it up later: "Definition of honeymoon. 1: a period of harmony immediately following marriage. 2: a period of unusual harmony especially following the establishment of a new relationship. 3: a trip or vacation taken by a newly married couple."

"That was us," I thought, and yet we were different.

Today was much like all our other days, except it was taking a timeout. And usually a honeymoon was something people took after getting married when they were looking toward their future, when they did not have so many years of the past to be recalled at every step. The honeymoon was the period when the couple was new—before their real life began—the life with many ups and downs and challenges, hardships that made things less easy.

Our life together hadn't been easy, but, then again, it hadn't been hard. It just was—always the two of us working things out, trying to find ways to relate. It had worked today to take the dogs to the beach, to make that our "honeymoon," our equivalent of what was normally done. We had gotten married this morning, and now we were returning from our honeymoon, I thought.

"The flowers will be waiting for us back at home," Hannah said, reaching over and gently placing her hand on my thigh as if to make sure I was still there.

"And the cats."

"Yes, the cats will be hungry."

As Hannah pulled the car into the garage back at the house, I turned to her. "It's funny not hearing Esperanza crying upstairs," I said.

"Yes, this is much better."

Usually, when Esperanza was left at home, she would whimper excitedly when she heard the car arrive, eager to greet us. But taking her with us had given us a new freedom. We could go anywhere, not have to worry about how she was doing or about getting back. That freedom, was it only about Esperanza? I thought. Or was it also about us? Having the dogs with us gave us license, a freedom to wander and be more ourselves.

"I'll bring in the cake," Hannah said as she stepped out of the car and opened the trunk. She carried it carefully up the back stairs to the kitchen as the dogs bounded ahead of her and I followed.

Inside, I went to check on the flowers. They were still intact in their colorful arrangement in the living room where I had left them, carefully separated from the rest of the house by a closed glass door so our three cats would not nibble on them in our absence.

I fed the cats on their food spots in the kitchen as Hannah placed the cake on a serving plate. It wasn't a large cake, but a modest one, small and compact, made of chocolate mixed with flaxseed meal with swirled frosting and the shaved chocolate on top.

"Shall we put a candle in it?" I asked Hannah.

"It's not a birthday," she said.

"Keep the cake protected from the cats for a while, I have something to do," I murmured as I took a handful of Baggie ties from a drawer in the kitchen, put them in my pocket, and carried them back to my study.

There, as I had planned, I turned on the bright standing lamps on my desk and went to work fashioning the two figures I had envisioned as decorations for the top of our wedding cake. It didn't take long, some twisting of the wires, a few false starts— and soon I had two stick figures, maybe three inches tall, with arms held out with bent hands, and little stick figure legs with feet, and little rounded heads.

I brought my spritely figures of Hannah and me into the dining room. "Now, bring out the cake," I said to Hannah.

She put it on the dining room table, shooing away the cats.

I placed my decorations on top.

Hannah smiled broadly. "What a good idea," she said, clapping her hands. "Did you plan that all along?"

"Which one is you, and which is me?" she asked.

"I made one slightly shorter," I pointed.

It was a small cake and a small surprise, but it felt very big at the time—something I had made for Hannah to show I cared. I then explained about looking into real cake decorations—the kind with a bride and groom, or two brides, but I hadn't done it in time.

"This is better," Hannah said.

She was so nice about it. Hannah always can be counted on to praise the little things I do, my little acts of imagination.

The shaped wire figures of Hannah and me, which seemed almost lifelike, at first were lying down on the cake, placed flat on the top, where they glowed stark white in contrast to the dark chocolate frosting. I took out my camera and took photos of them, as if to make the sight memorable forever, before the cake was cut. Then finally I stood the two figures up, so that, in the pictures, they look like they are holding hands and dancing. When flat on the cake, the figures were also holding hands, but upright, they were definitely dancing.

"For you," I said to Hannah, and gave her a kiss.

"For us," she said. Then she went to get my grandmother's silver cake cutter that Hannah always liked to use to cut cakes or pies.

The cake, when cut, was rather dry. Hannah poured Kahlua over our pieces, though not before carefully lifting off the two interlocked figures of Hannah and me that had been dancing atop.

"Do you know," I said to her, "my mother kept a piece of her wedding cake in her top dresser drawer mixed in with her underwear. I would find it sometimes when I was looking through her drawers. It was dry and hard from being so old, but it was chocolate, like this cake."

"You never told me that," she paused.

"Will you keep these figures from our cake?" she asked.

In my file cabinet, in the folder where I keep a copy of our marriage certificate, I have, in a small plastic bag, safely kept the two dancing Baggie-tie brides.

That night, in bed, Hannah and I held each other and had a few laughs. The City Hall, the flowers, the beach, the dogs, the cake, it was all so unreal, and yet very real. We hadn't intended to get married, and then we had. I hadn't expected to be sentimental about it, to really care, and then I had. Teela lay beside me on the floor next to the bed on her foam pad. Esperanza was curled up at the foot of the bed on my side. The cats were in place—Katie, our senior calico, at my head, Shadow, the hunter, down near Esperanza, lying with her. Sienna, her fluffy sister, lay sleeping on the desk in my study nearby.

Though surrounded by those we loved, Hannah and I were still unto ourselves. Hannah reached deep into my heart and touched me, and I reached into her soul. "You make me happy," she said. "You are my dearest, sweet Susan."

"I love you," I said, "more every day, and not just because we got married. Do you think we'll be different now that we are married?"

"I don't know. We shouldn't be. Is there something you want to be different?" she asked.

"I want you to love me. I want you to always tell me how good I am. I want to be good to you."

"You are, and I love you all."

She said that so often: "I love you all," as if I should know what it meant. It seemed to mean "forever and always," but perhaps it meant that she loved all of me.

I reached over, put my arm around her, and drew her close.

Part II

Our Formative Years

Three

Early Memories

I met Hannah in the fall of 1980 when I arrived on the university campus to begin a postdoctoral fellowship in sociology. At a meeting of women in the gay community center, I asked who the lesbian faculty were. "Hannah Golden," one of the students said, was the only lesbian faculty member. I looked Hannah up in the university catalog and found that she taught courses on women that sounded clearly non-mainstream to me, that dealt with alternative sexualities and women's history and culture. Did they really allow this in a university? I thought. I had been teaching organizational sociology in the Midwest and the Southwest and was not then familiar with many of the fields beyond my own.

That week at the start of classes, I stopped by Professor Golden's office. Colorful flyers announcing events were posted on her door along with a signup sheet for her office hours. She was certainly a busy woman, I thought. Yet there seemed to be a slot available in her time schedule for the next day. I came back then and knocked on her door. It was opened by a small woman who acted friendly. She said she could see me in a few minutes and pointed to a chair in the hallway. A student soon came out of her office. Then a man walked in, a colleague of hers, with whom she had a long conversation, closing her thick, oak office door. I wondered why I was kept waiting. I had been there first. Later, Hannah told me the details of her need to speak with this man, and that she was unsure why I was there, but I knew nothing of that at the time. I knew there was no reason she would focus particularly on me, nor know the importance of our meeting. Nor did I.

Entering Professor Golden's office, I sat down on a chair across from her. I explained that I was an organizational sociologist doing a lesbian study, that I had interviewed members of a lesbian community in the Midwest where I had recently taught, and that I wanted to talk with her about how to write up my study. She listened intently. We must have discussed something appropriate to the study. But what I remember most is Hannah's speaking to me about how her "community" was in San Francisco, where she lived. I told her I was looking for a place to live closer to the university in a less urban area. I imagined that she lived in a commune in the city, or in a communal or cooperative house. All my stereotypes about lesbians living in groups set in, which was odd because I was one, but I had the stereotypes still. We talked for a while, semi-personally, about my study, some background on each of us, though I gleaned very little about Hannah right then. I know that my heart had sunk when she said her community was in the city, as if she was saying that her life would be forever apart from me.

When the time came for me to leave, I may have shaken Hannah's hand, but I think I just stood there. I know I was surprised that she did not say, "Let's have lunch," or make a date for lunch. In my brief time back at the university, I had found that people I met to get acquainted always said, at the end of our first meeting, "Let's have lunch." It seemed strange that Hannah did not want a follow-up. I assumed that it may have had to do with her ties to her community in the city. She had said she preferred living there because then she had a separation from the university and that she did not like living where it was so suburban. Maybe she did not have many social connections around here, I thought. Or maybe she had a lover in her community in the city.

I left Hannah's office feeling rebuffed because we were not going to have lunch. Fortunately, a week later, she called, leaving a message for me in the sociology department. I felt surprised and glad. We planned to meet. We went first to a lecture hall to listen to a guest speaker and then walked over for lunch at the student union, where we took our sandwiches outside. We sat on stone benches, some trees and a building behind us. As we talked, I remember, I focused on Hannah's eyeglasses. They were sunglasses. Yet she had not brought a bag in which she might be carrying this second pair of glasses. She had been wearing regular eyeglasses when we met. What happened to her regular glasses? I wondered as I looked closely at her pants for large pockets and found none, and as I studied her shirt and vest for pockets. It was a mystery to me. Where had her other glasses gone? I did not, at the time, know about eyeglasses that can tint to gray in the sunlight. It was an odd thing to focus on during a first get-acquainted lunch—the mystery of a person's disappearing eyeglasses, rather than the mystery of the person. Indeed Hannah was a mystery to me—a new person, a new woman in my life, unfamiliar, someone whom I was not sure about. Who was she? Who would she be to me? She was a lesbian, but too lesbian? Was I?

"Are you a lesbian?" I asked her that first day in her office. She had answered "yes" and then asked me if I was one. I thought it would be obvious from my telling her about my lesbian study. But you do not know for sure unless you ask. And the answer can leave so much unsaid. For me, lesbianism feels often tied to my sense of inner vulnerability. It is the part of myself that seeks nurturing from another woman, yet that fears consequences— from the outside world, or from within, that might thwart the sense of comfort and love I so wish for.

Hannah later joked with me about our initial meeting when I knocked on her office door. "You were trying to pick me up," she said. "I really thought you were there to discuss your study."

That she felt I had come for guidance on my work was hard for me to comprehend. I knew I did not want advice on my writing. I was there to meet her.

What if when the door opened, it had not been Hannah? What if she had been someone different? Would I still be with her now decades later? Would I have fallen for her in spite of my doubts, those many thoughts that ran through my head in the subsequent months as I tried to figure out if she was right for me? She reminded me of my father. She reminded me of my mother. She was serious, honest, down to earth, careful, not surrounded by fantasy romantic notions in my mind but very much about the here and now. She wanted everything on the up-and-up, everything good between us. No crooked ways, no indirection. She also wanted to have her life separate from me for a long time.

Hannah considers our anniversary to be the day of our first formal date, on Halloween. I think of it as three weeks earlier, the day we met. That is a difference between us. Hannah is more conventional, I think. I wish often to separate myself from convention. Hannah is also more sentimental than I am. She cries more easily. My sentimental feelings are more hidden beneath the surface. Yet they come up now when I think of us back then. On Halloween, for our first date, we went to dinner at a Japanese restaurant. Hannah ordered Katsu don, pork on rice, a favorite dish of hers. As we sat in the darkened restaurant carefully talking, I looked over at her and she seemed to glow, bathed in a soft light from a lamp above. She said she was impressed that I had made a reservation for us at a Japanese restaurant, which I did because she had told me she had spent time in Japan during college.

After dinner, we went to a party in the house of a close colleague of Hannah's, where people danced in a large, dark wood-paneled living room and one friend of Hannah's wrapped herself up in sheets that looked like bandages and that kept coming undone. This friend, a lesbian, was hurting from a recent loss of a lover. Hannah danced with her. I did not dance or go in costume. I felt that the way I normally dress was costume enough. Hannah told me, that evening, about a previous lover of hers to whom she had been introduced by the woman hosting the party. It was a straight party, but we were there together. It was Halloween, which made it feel like a good time to be gay, and Hannah was gently introducing me to her life.

Later that night, we went back to the house where I was living near the university. I was renting two back rooms in someone's home while I looked for a longer-term residence for myself, my dog Geronimo, and my cat Jenny. I had a bedroom, an adjoining small living room, and a bath, along with kitchen privileges. In the bedroom was a single bed and a desk. The challenge soon was, how should we sleep?

Hannah sat on the bed leaning up against pillows. I sat near her on a chair, and we discussed it. I told her that I would sleep on the floor, and that I wanted us to sleep separately because I wanted not to confuse things with sex. I wanted to be more sure of our relationship first. I explained that I was seeking a different kind of relationship than my previous one with a woman whom I had left back in New Mexico, and that I now had three rules, or guidelines, for myself about getting involved.

The first rule was that the other woman, this time, should be available—not be in a relationship with someone else, or not yet over a relationship—and she should not be straight. Second, she should be my equal, more of a peer than sometimes in my past. Third, I should not use sex as a way to get close to her, or as a way to lure her into a relationship with me. I should resist the urge to reach out physically, but instead, I should know more about her first in terms of my criteria. Then if they were met, we could become sexual.

I think my requirements were a lot for Hannah to take in. But she was good-natured about it. She made me feel she respected what I was saying and that she was impressed with my seriousness. She also offered to take the floor.

I slept on the floor that night, wanting Hannah to have my bed. We took two cushions off the narrow couch in the living room and laid them out on the bedroom floor perpendicular to the bed a few feet away. I felt honored to have Hannah staying with me, but what I remember most is how uncomfortable it was. The floor beneath the couch cushions was hard. I rolled off them easily, and my feet hung over the end, as I thought, all the while, about this new woman in my life—close to me yet still so foreign. We went to bed late and I got up early to go to a group therapy session, leaving Hannah to close up and return home to the city.

I don't know if one of us said they would call the other. I know it seemed like a very long time until I heard from Hannah again. She subsequently told me she had discussed the events of our night with a close friend and come to the conclusion that further contact with me was worth it. But it was, I think, a pretty strict introduction to my needs.

We next got together for a trip to the beach. Hannah called, then came over to my house on the weekend. We made sandwiches and took them in the car with us. We took my light blue Toyota, which I had driven not long before from New Mexico, from that time in my life that I was not yet over. I had come to California seeking new dreams. When I lived in New Mexico, I had had a vision of finding a woman with a house in California. In my vision, the house was large and dark, and the figure of the woman in it was hard to make out. Could Hannah be that woman, I wondered, someone emerging from out of the darkness, beckoning me into a world of new adventures? She seemed thoughtful and caring. We drove through straw-colored hills on winding roads on the way to the ocean, and as we did, we talked. We discussed the route, with which I was very familiar, having taken it many times in my past. Did I tell Hannah, then, about my past and those previous woman lovers, our walks on the beaches? I must have. I know we shared that the beach was a special place for each of us.

We got out of the car at a low-lying, sunlit beach down the coast near a creek—a small, secluded stretch of sand surrounded by grassy dunes. I took out a Frisbee and tossed it to Hannah. She tossed it back, a bright orange Frisbee. I was delighted that she liked playing Frisbee and knew how. It was as if one of my criteria had been met. Before leaving, we got gas across the road, waiting in line behind a hippie school bus—painted with swirling Day-Glo designs—in which people seemed to be living, carrying their belongings happily with them on the road. Hannah and I talked about our fantasies of doing something similar, bumming around up and down the California coast. I felt good knowing we had this same fantasy, as if it released something carefree in me much to be desired.

It was not long before I slept over at Hannah's. I drove up to the city for a weekend, eager to see her, but then was surprised as I stepped into her apartment, for I immediately felt claustrophobic, as if the walls were closing in on me. The apartment was narrow, and being in the city reminded me too much of my past growing up in Brooklyn, New York—the smell of asphalt, the closeness of houses and people, the many things I had tried for much of my life to escape. I liked living in greener places. I liked the country, I liked getting away from people, feeling I had room to be myself, seeing vastness, not feeling pent up. And here I was visiting my new love, my new friend, in just such a place as I wished to avoid.

Hannah took my hand and promptly showed me around her apartment. There was a couch in a small living room, a bedroom, a study. In her study, she showed me her file cabinet, the darkroom she had made in her closet, the historical documents she had on her desk, her bulletin board and posters. She was interested in history, in social movements, and she had a fondness for old books and pictures. This reminded me very much of my father, who was a student of labor history and had file cabinets full of old pictures and documents. He had been a stable, guiding force in my life, and very different from my mother, who was volatile in her temperament, seductive and attractive, but difficult for me emotionally. For my previous lesbian relationships, I had sought out women more like my mother with whom to be close. That Hannah reminded me of my father came as a jolt, a disappointment—as if I was being taken back into my past, a constraining past that I wished to escape. I stood in the narrow hallway of Hannah's apartment leading, at one end, to her study, and, at the other, to her bedroom and felt my heart sink, my tears almost come, felt an inner deadness much like depression.

It mattered not that out Hannah's front window was a view of the Bay Bridge, the open sky, expansive for a city landscape. It mattered not that Hannah had invited me and was showing me her yard, the spaces she so valued, her life, welcoming me in. I was back and stuck and I did not know what to make of it. This will never work out, I thought. I can't stand this. I am not looking for my father. I am looking for my mother. Hannah simply is not the kind of woman who can provide me with support for the inner strength in myself that I so need, that inner valuing of myself. She is not the stereotypical heterosexual female, I felt, the paper doll, the myth of the nurturing, caring, exciting, romantic woman with the blond hair and the need for me—a mannish, or more male-related, woman in style. She was like me, too like me, butch lesbian, though a very cute butch. How could we ever be together? I felt caught. I did not know how to get out.

At that moment, I was also aware that Hannah was Jewish, as was I, and that the only person I had previously married was a man who was Jewish. This was going to be the end of my life, I felt suddenly. It was determined. It was all over. I also felt sad. If this is what falling in love feels like, why do it? I felt left out of the fantasy. I was not aware of all those inner gears in myself that had come to a halt that I would have to learn to mesh in a new way. But I was aware of the momentousness of it—that Hannah was the one for me, at least for now, perhaps for a long time to come. Our future was hard for me to imagine though. My present was standing in my way. I felt like I was a windup toy that had suddenly come to a stop.

Standing in the hallway in Hannah's apartment, I looked toward her bathroom across the way, where the door was ajar. I could see that she had put candles around the tub that might light a comforting bath. She was a woman who lit candles, I thought. She liked to make things special.

That night, I slept on the living room floor. Hannah offered to share her bed, but I insisted on the floor, wishing to follow the guidelines I had laid out just weeks earlier. I did not know Hannah well enough yet, I thought. The cushions we took off Hannah's couch to make my bed were thin, so this night's sleep was more uncomfortable than it had been back in my house. I can still feel the hard, wooden floor coming up through the worn padding and hurting my hips. Hannah slept in her bedroom with her Siamese cat Mocha. I slept in the living room with my dog Geronimo. I must have complained about the floor. Hannah offered again that I join her in her bed, with no expectations of anything sexual. But I did not trust myself. I needed to do it the old-fashioned, strict way.

A few weeks later, I again visited Hannah and again I asked to take the floor, but it felt so hard that I finally took Hannah up on her offer of sharing her bed. The thick mattress felt like such a relief, and I ached with a wish to be intimate with Hannah, but I was not yet ready for sex.

A friend said to me, "I think people do this. They put it off. They say they will wait. But eventually they give in."

The next weekend when I visited, as we climbed into bed, "Don't worry," Hannah said. "You don't have to do anything you

don't want to." We resolved to lie apart. But soon we were together. I could feel Hannah's soft body, her breasts, all the curves
in the right places, so reassuring, so close to me. She was, as I had
seen when we undressed, a perfect figure of a woman, though
small, and I had worried, would small be okay? Would I feel surrounded enough by her in bed? I had always thought that I needed a woman as large as myself as a sexual partner, because only
then would I feel engulfed enough, not wanting, smothered
enough by her love, her reassurance. How could a small woman
do that? I doubted it possible. I was so wrong.

During that initial period, one evening when I was in my
apartment near the university, I called Hannah to discuss several
chapters of my lesbian study that I had just written and given to
her to read. After some minor compliments, she politely criticized
the style. I had no narrator, she said. I was not presenting events
in historical order, this was not the way a community study should
be written, and my grammar was not correct. She had also looked
at my previous book, *Hip Capitalism*, and told me that the grammar was wrong in far too many places there too. Someone should
have told me about that and fixed it before the book came out.

I was shocked. I had never paid much attention to my grammar before. The way I wrote, the form was very natural. I described experiences in detail, and wrote in a stream-of-conscious-
ness fashion—in this case using the multiple voices of the women
of the lesbian community whom I had interviewed. I liked speaking in a somewhat imperfect inner voice. And here was Hannah,
so proper and organized, as formal in her expectations about
style as she was practical. She knew how writing should be presented. She knew the molds, the acceptable practices, the conven-
tions. She used them to make her own unconventional content
clear in the academic monographs she wrote.

"You can't do it this way," she said to me patiently.

"You don't understand," I told her. "This is what I want to do.
I don't want to do the conventional thing in terms of form."

"Well, people won't understand it. No one will publish it."

Our conversation that evening was the beginning of an exchange between us that would last a lifetime, for Hannah would later become my number-one reader, my cheering squad, my biggest fan. She would help me with my writing without destroying my originality. But back then I could know nothing of that. I simply knew that we were in two different worlds. How they might come together was going to be a challenge. Would she ever understand me?

I soon found a new place to live, again a back room in someone's house, but this time a place where my cat as well as my dog could happily settle in with me. Why I sought a room in someone else's house was partly economic, but it was also my sense of my place in the world—not yet setting up an apartment or house of my own. I was more comfortable living in someone else's home, as if it provided a reassurance I needed.

The house was south of the university in a quiet residential area, not in the wooded hills as I might have wished, where I had once had a relationship living with another woman for the first time, and afterwards I always sought that sense of intimacy, of the adventure and romance of living apart from things. This new house was not far from the hills, with tall trees and a large fenced backyard for Geronimo. My room, with its adjoining bath, was in a separate wing of the house with a door opening onto the yard. The house was owned by a woman with two children, a boy and a girl, which gave it a warm family feel. To reach the kitchen, I had to walk through the living room to the other wing of the house, which had me walking through the life of the family, and, though somewhat awkward, I got used to it.

In my room, I had my desk set up in the middle, an alcove with a music system, a big closet, a comfortable chair, a rug on the floor, a rocking chair for Hannah to sit in when she visited. My double bed was in the corner under broad windows that looked out on the yard. This might seem a small space for a woman, her dog and her cat and her lover, but for me, it was fine. It was to become my home base for the next three years.

When I first looked at the room, I had told the woman of the household that I was a lesbian and asked if that would make a difference to her renting to me. "It's the law. I have to," she said with a smile. I don't think she minded. But for me, most important was the fact that I felt I had to ask, to be considerate, because I did not want to live where I was resented because I was a lesbian. When Hannah came, it would be obvious, I felt. I had to announce it at the start.

I still see clearly in my mind that first time Hannah visited me in my new home. As she walked the length of the backyard to reach the door to my room, I was aware that the people in the kitchen looking out the window were seeing her for the first time. What did they think of Hannah? I wondered. What did they think of me? Did they think we were a good couple? Was Hannah right for me? I was so unsure. I also wondered, how did they feel about two women in bed together in their house?

I moved into my new place on my birthday in late December. Hannah and I had known each other, by then, for two-and-a-half months. We soon began commuting—one weekend at Hannah's house, one at mine. The outstanding fact of that arrangement for me was that I began getting headaches almost every weekend, particularly on the weekends I went up to the city. It was as if the tension of the change from being alone to being together was too much. I was packing so much into a short time—packing up to get ready to go to Hannah's, then dealing with the city, the urban environment, and with the relationship between us, which was full of working things out—what Hannah liked, what I liked, how could we combine the two? How could I best relate to this new woman, to her very busy world, and she to mine?

One day when I was driving from the university to my house, following Hannah's car in mine, I noticed that on the back bumper of her white Honda Civic hatchback was a sticker that said

"Susan B. Lives" beside an image of a woman with a raised fist. "Oh my," I thought, this is too close to home. I knew that I had been named for Susan B. Anthony by my father, with the optimistic expectation that I might become the first woman president of the United States. That was a legacy that I had tried to live down, because it was too high an expectation. But there it was on Hannah's back bumper. When we stopped for gas I could hardly wait to tell her, though I was afraid that it would lock me in, make our relationship seem too destined. Would I be able to live up to that name with her? I thought. I also thought this sticker made our togetherness seem more natural, and I hoped it would make Hannah like me more.

A few months later, Hannah's friend Kevin came to visit. She had known him since their days in graduate school. He was a gay man, yet they had been lovers. He had helped her move out here from the East when she first took her job at the university. They had driven across the country together. They were very close, still good friends, although they each had moved on to lovers of the same gender. I, too, had once had a sexual relationship with a gay man, the one I married, though I did not know he was gay at the time. We were both fulfilling conventional expectations in getting heterosexually married, only later to find that we each wanted a primary intimacy with someone of the same gender.

But the coincidence of Hannah's and my both having had previous formative relationships with gay men was now overshadowed by the fact that Kevin was about to arrive for the first time since I had met Hannah. She was about to go off to spend a long weekend with him in the Big Sur coastal hills in a creek-side cabin. They were accustomed to going away on a retreat when they got together so that they could reconnect after being apart, since he lived back East. I knew of Hannah's past with Kevin, and she reassured me that nothing sexual would happen between them—that was years ago, back when they had their sexual relationship, she said. But despite her reassurance about their current relationship, which I believed, I was worried deep down. She was going away from me. I did not know what would happen. In the innermost place where I had grave anxiety, I did not know. More basically than being worried about sex, I was afraid that I would lose her, that I would be abandoned, or feel abandoned.

My fears occupied a large space in my emotional life in that period just before they were to leave. It had happened at other times, too, I thought. I would experience a cold shudder, a sense of impending loss when Hannah was going off without me to do something of pivotal importance to her, particularly when she was going to do it at a time when we would ordinarily be together—a weekend, a dinnertime, or for an extended trip.

I knew, from what little I was learning about Hannah, that it was extremely important to her to be able to go away, to have a life apart from me. She needed my reassurance that, in our relationship, she could still have all the activities of her life that made her feel good as a separate person. She needed not to be overwhelmed or feel swallowed up by our relationship, or by who I was.

I wanted very much for Hannah to feel good being with me, so I knew I would have to provide her, in turn, with the reassurances she sought. I called a friend to talk about the upcoming trip. She said to me, "What you have to do is tell her to have a good time. No matter what you feel, just say it." We then practiced while talking on the phone. I belted out, "Have a good time." Then louder "Have a good time!" and again and again, until I felt those words could come forth from my lips toward Hannah without my thinking much about them.

"Have a good time," I said to Hannah the next day before they took off, and the next day, and the nights when we talked on the phone while she was gone. "I hope you have a good time." It felt like I was belting it out, almost yelling it, though probably it was more moderately said.

That phrase, "Have a good time," was to stick with me forever after. I soon began using it on many occasions when Hannah was going away from me, and she began saying to me, "I'll be back. I won't abandon you."

"I am not abandoning you just because I am going off with Kevin," she had said before she left.

"How is that not abandonment?" I had thought. "Of course, you are abandoning me. This is a weekend we would be spending together. You are not going off with me to Big Sur. You are going off with him." But I did not say that. I simply said, "Have a good time," grateful that I had practiced it, and grateful for the advice from my friend, for I would not have known to say this on my own because it was not the same reassurance I needed for myself.

When Hannah came back from her trip, she seemed to have missed me. It must have been those words, I thought, as she gave me a big hug. '

Hannah and I spoke on the phone often during that early period. I would be in my room near the university. Hannah would be in her house in the city or in her office on the campus. We would talk and then would schedule a next time to talk, a day we would go to the beach, which weekend we would spend at her house or mine, when we would see friends. We would almost schedule how we would act toward each other—wanting so much to reassure each other, to keep our relationship good. I was not used to this amount of structuring in my life. I soon began to feel boxed in. "You are putting me in boxes," I said to Hannah one night on the phone, not sure she would understand. But I know it felt like that, I think because Hannah was so good at being organized, problem solving, scheduling things between us so that they would work out well, so clear-cut in her thinking. And her habit of structuring ran up against my desires for freedom, to leave things open, to stay in the present, to be free of what anyone else might think. I also felt that night that it was about more than scheduling. I thought maybe Hannah did not understand me in the ways I wished, that she was putting me in boxes as a person, thinking about me in conventional terms that did not fit.

"Do you understand what I mean about boxes?" I asked her that night.

"I'm not sure," she said. "But I want to."

A further challenge for me as I was increasingly getting to know Hannah was the role of the university in her life. She was an excellent citizen, active in her department, exceptionally caring with students, a thoughtful colleague, a good friend. She was involved in the alternative culture in the university—made up of feminists, ethnic and racial minorities, and leftists—and she had recently co-founded the women's studies program. Soon after Hannah and I met, a colleague with whom she had been close died suddenly. I was with Hannah in her apartment when she heard the news. Then everything started getting hectic—much activity, phone calls and organizing, her talking with people, friends coming over, the introduction of many new people into my life. It was hard to keep them straight. Who was lesbian, who was not, who was related to whom, who was faculty, who was a student? Hannah was upset and tearful. She cried that night. I did not know how to comfort her. I was upset, too, I thought, but I did not want to be upset. I did not want to be distressed by her world—a world that still felt foreign to me. I felt that when Hannah was upset, it took her away from me. I lost her to an inner sadness, a fear, her grief. Suddenly it was as if we were no longer together. I felt undone, at sea without anchor.

I was simultaneously being introduced to Hannah's social world in the city. She was a member of a lesbian and gay history study group that met regularly and that I associated very much with San Francisco and with people who lived there. Her friends were comfortable in the urban environment, organizing, going on marches, having events, meeting in restaurants, living in houses on concrete and asphalt. And I was an outsider, not liking the urban setting, wanting to get away. The fact that it was history again reminded me of my father and the past that I wished to escape. The talk was often political, which was not something foreign to me, but my kind of political was more internal. I had strong left-wing beliefs that I learned from my family, so I never doubted I was as radical as anyone else. But I did not like to engage in political conversations or in working out my views in relation to other people. Suddenly, I was surrounded by that, wishing to hide, to be independently myself, to be back in my own world—my room, my writing, my life alone with my pets, and with the images from my past that kept floating back to me—images of other times and other places, and of women with whom I had once sought to be close. Those intimate relationships, though meaningful, had not endured. Would it be different with Hannah?

I remember the first gay march I went on with Hannah: the Pride parade in San Francisco in the summer of the first year that I knew her. The street was full of commotion, music, floats, people in bright clothing, men strutting by in leather pants. Again, I was overwhelmed by the city, wishing not to be here, yet wishing very much to be in the march, because I had marched all my life and believed in the value of demonstrations. Fortunately, Hannah and I had similar feelings about the parade being dominated by men, even if they were gay men. Similarly, we were excited to see the Dykes on Bikes leading the way with their motorcycle engines booming. We stood on the sidelines watching, fascinated, sharing the moment. Then spying her group striding by with their banner—"That's us," Hannah said, urging me to come with her.

As I followed her into the street to join her friends, it felt like a bold step—that I was stepping out of my element. It was not that I hadn't been on gay marches before. I had walked in this particular parade a few years earlier with the lesbian lover with whom I had lived in the hills. I had persuaded her to come with me, and I had made a sign I carried that said, "A couple of women." That was my speed, I thought: seemingly minimal, nothing overblown, just a statement in the midst of men that we were there, that there was power and huge significance in simply being a couple of women. She and I had not known where to enter the parade when we arrived. I had looked on at the floats from the bars, the men in drag, the many groups carrying identifying signs, and wondered where to join. There seemed no group I was naturally part of. Some people sped by on roller skates. One of the skaters flashed a smile at my sign. We stepped in right after them, though we did not stay long.

Now, though only five years later, it felt like much more time had passed, and here I was in a contingent, part of an organized group, without my having to do anything, even grant my permission. I had merely come along. I was suddenly part of things because of Hannah. She linked her arm in mine, encouraged me, at one point, to carry one end of their big, lavender banner as the lesbian and gay history group marched on. Her friends were welcoming and reached out to me. There were about a dozen of them. They threw beads and caught condoms others threw and walked proudly together, calling out to greet friends on the sidelines. All the while, I was shy, feeling people would notice me, feeling the hot asphalt at my feet, wondering what I was doing here—knowing why I was here: for the march, for gay power and gay pride. But what was I doing here with Hannah? This was not my life, my contingent; it was hers. I was in the threatening city and far from home. What if I had brought my dog Geronimo? I wondered. But it was not a place for a dog—too hot, too long a march. Still, he might have kept me company, made the world seem more mine. Hannah and I held hands as we walked. At that time, I was afraid of holding hands in public, particularly in the city where many people would see me. I was afraid someone—some little boy with a gun—would shoot us or throw rocks. Hannah knew of my fears as she took my hand. "I am happy to be here with you," she said.

Four

The Pull of the Past

At the end of my second year of knowing Hannah, I took her back with me to New Mexico for a visit. I wanted to introduce her to my past life, the people I had known and been close with, the desert landscape that remained so beautiful in my mind. I had lived in New Mexico for two years before I met Hannah. The relationships and experiences I had during that time felt still very present within me. It was time, I thought, to merge my two worlds, to take Hannah with me to this other place that I had left behind geographically when I moved to California but that lingered with me emotionally.

We drove off that summer morning from my house, heading south and inland past Gilroy, the garlic capital of the world, then down through the broad San Joaquin Valley and east up through the Tehachapi Mountain Pass. We took Hannah's car, her white Honda Civic hatchback with its standard shift and her Susan B. Anthony sticker on the rear bumper. It was August and hot as we started across the vast Mojave Desert. The sunbaked wind blew through the open windows of the small car. We had music on the stereo—Cris Williamson singing "I would go through a desert for you." I had told Hannah about the "hottest place in the United States," the town of Needles, where we would eat and stay the night, because it was a two-day trip. We passed through Boron first, the white borax dust coating the road, the heat shimmering in front of us. Only when we arrived at the motel in Needles did we realize that we had the heat on all the while in the car. It may not have made a big difference, because both the outside desert and the heater produced air of about the same temperature. But this mishap seemed to me like a cosmic joke, a commentary on the absurdities of life. It lightened my mood, made our trip feel like an adventure. Hannah, though, was a little worried. This was not an auspicious sign for what might later befall us on our trip. As we sat at dinner in the motel restaurant, she reached her hand across the small table and touched mine. "We have to be more careful," she said.

That night as I lay in bed beside her, feeling comforted by her softly breathing presence, I thought of the first time I had made this trip four years before. I had returned to California to gather my things after teaching for a year in the Midwest, and I was now driving from California to New Mexico to take a job at the university in Albuquerque. As I headed up through the Tehachapi Mountain Pass and over into the Mohave Desert, I sang to myself, aware that I was making the long drive alone, wondering how I would do it. Would I be too lonely? I knew I had to stay awake and keep my focus. My car's speedometer had died once a few years before, and I hoped it would not die now—that I would not have to estimate my speed by the speed of the cars I might be passing or tailing. The speedometer held out. In Needles, I stopped at a big family restaurant, proud of myself for making it there, and proud of my composure in asking for a table, as if I did this every day—drove through the desert alone stopping in strange places to eat. I stayed overnight somewhere, then drove on, leaving the Mohave finally behind, climbing up through Winslow, Arizona, thinking of the Eagles' song "Take It Easy," then on through eastern Arizona, the red cliffs spectacular, the landscape broad, and soon into New Mexico with its brown bluffs, through towns named Manuelito, Twin Buttes, Defiance. I saw signs that said "Last Gas for 100 miles," "Indian Trading Post, Souvenirs, Buy It Here." I felt awed by that drive through the desert, that push forward, the newness of it, the frighteningness of it.

I spent my second night on the road in the dusty town of Gallup in a motel lit up in bright red neon lights. The room had dark fake-wood paneling, a noisy air conditioner that made it impossible to sleep—then on into Albuquerque in the morning. Arriving on the campus at 10:30 A.M., I promptly locked my keys in my car and had to find a coat hanger to force open the front door. It was an unsettling arrival and I was excited and apprehensive. What would my future here be like? The air felt so clear, the spaces bare, the buildings low and creamy brown. I was alone, starting my life anew, looking forward to it, glad to be gone from the flat Midwest, wishing, in some basic way, to get back to California, and seeking a new and reassuring home.

And now I was with Hannah, no longer alone, not setting out on that same type of trip, not as anxious about what might befall me. Yet I was anxious about how things would go between us. We had never taken a long road trip like this before. On the drive from Needles through Arizona and New Mexico, I had pointed out the sights to Hannah, and told her about how I had felt the first time I made the trip. She told me about when she had driven across the country from the East to take her job in California. We exchanged stories as we played with the car radio, trying to get a station. We checked the heater, looked out the window, consulted the map to make sure we were still on the right road, occasionally held hands. I remember some of the details of our drive, but, most of all, I remember the feeling—Hannah close beside me, the sun on her shoulder, her presence physical and comforting, my greater calm with her near, my relief that she was doing half the driving, the sense of expectation we shared. At the same time, I was concerned: What would she think of my friends? What would she think of the place when we got there?

When I had first set out for New Mexico, I had asked people about what it would be like. Albuquerque, someone who had lived there told me, "It's a dustbowl town. The mountains behind it, the Sandias, are called 'watermelon mountains' because they turn red at sunset. But other than that, it's a big dustbowl." Someone else said of the area, "It's a magical place, more like being in another country than anyplace in the United States."

I had spent two years in the magical dustbowl with the red watermelon mountains. I made friends, had one main love, took a job at the university that I wished to have continue, but they were not hiring people like me. I returned to California with much sadness, driving off one morning with my dog and my cat in the back seat of my car. As we crossed through the Tehachapi Mountain Pass, heading down into California's Central Valley— the coast as if in sight—I could not know that three weeks later, I would meet Hannah and look forward to a future with her. Or that I would be still caught in my past, bringing with me its remnants, unprepared for how they would continue to haunt me.

Now with Hannah beside me, I was anxious to introduce her to the world I had left, anxious to revisit my past, to relive what I had missed, to capture again the magic. I wanted Hannah to enjoy the desert landscape with me and to feel at home. I also hoped that her presence with me would ease my sense of loss.

"We're almost there," I said to Hannah as she sat at the wheel and we neared Albuquerque. We drove up to a low-lying, white house near the river and pulled into the driveway, where we knocked on the screen back door. "I'll get Bess," a friendly woman said, opening the door for us, extending her arm in welcome. Her partner Bess had been my other mother, my anchor, my near lover when I lived in the dustbowl town. She had encouraged me to get Jenny, my cat, and Geronimo, my dog. Bess and Marie's house was the place I had run to when things got hard between me and Ann, the woman with whom I had been primarily involved. They had lived in a different house then, an adobe in the older part of town. This house seemed more modern, more spread out, unfamiliar to me.

"Hello," Bess said, coming out to the kitchen to greet us, her voice cautious, her smile soft, her tall body bending gently toward me, her gray hair pulled back.

Marie and Bess offered us hot dogs, but we did not have dinner with them. They had already eaten and it was evening by the time we arrived. Still, I kept wondering why they did not offer us more food. The atmosphere was friendly but subdued as we sat around the kitchen table talking. Here I was coming back with my new love to meet my old friends. Couldn't they muster more enthusiasm? I thought. Still, they were polite and nice. As we talked, I stared at a tall wooden hutch in the kitchen that held dishes. I kept wondering why it was called a "hutch." Bess showed us to the room where we would stay, her "sewing room," she called it, though I had not remembered that she had sewn. Hannah and I put down our bags, looked at each other, came back out and visited some more.

We stayed with Bess and Marie for almost two weeks, going off from their house to visit places I had known, trying, in the evenings, to socialize with them, going out for dinner with them, yet feeling, all the while, that our efforts fell flat. Something was missing. I went into Bess's bedroom one night, seeking to be close with her, reaching my arm out to touch her, to rekindle the old spark, to know it was still there. But she pushed me away coldly.

I got the message, "You're with her now." And the further message, "I have moved on."

Why I would have thought everything should stay the same, I do not know. But I felt that way. Why couldn't they all be in love with me like they used to be?

I returned to Hannah, put my arms around her. "Bess is strange," I said.

"It's just our base here," Hannah said. "We can go out and have good times on our own. You have things to show me."

In the next two weeks, I took Hannah up to the crest of the dramatic mountain behind Albuquerque and looked out, despite my fear of heights. The desert lay below us, the open space, the city extending toward distant mesas and buttes. We drove through a nearby ranchland area past a field with buffalo grazing. Those buffalo were gone by the next time Hannah and I visited in the area three years later, but they stay in my mind as a reminder of that first trip, that earlier time when she and I were new. We drove on north to Santa Fe and Taos, where we visited the museums, the historical Kit Carson house. I showed Hannah where I had once camped in the mountains, taken hikes, gone places on my own near Taos.

We walked around Old Town Albuquerque, saw exhibits in the museum, looked into the shops. I drove Hannah by the big A-frame house near the university where I had once lived, then onto the university campus. There I showed her the low, tan building where I had worked, where I had a small corner office—and where I once brought back another lover, Jan, to be with me on a quiet weekend evening. Thankfully, I had lost track of that friend by now, so there was not another awkward introduction to make in order to familiarize Hannah with my past. I drove Hannah to the flea market at the big county fairgrounds where I used to go regularly on weekend mornings to see what good junk or jewelry I might find, and where Jan had often pulled up her big white Chevrolet Impala and sold painted dolls and knick-knack gift items from the top of her car trunk.

I took Hannah to the Full Circle women's bookstore, explaining to her how the shop used to be located a few blocks closer to the campus, and that it was originally owned by June Arnold's daughter. June Arnold, as Hannah and I both knew, was the lesbian author of *The Cook and the Carpenter*, a novel in which she used the pronoun "na" to make the genders of the characters ambiguous. I always thought that was a phenomenal thing to do, and it totally confused me as I read the book. But I knew it was important, something as it should be. Was the cook the female "na," or was it the carpenter? I wanted to know, and never knew.

Who was the "cook," who the "carpenter," with Hannah and me? I must be the carpenter, I thought. But that was not what mattered. It was that we both knew the book—though I think it meant more to me than to Hannah, because of my appreciation for the ingenuity of the author. I wished I could be capable of such daring.

The Full Circle bookstore was now owned by a woman who had once co-owned a women's bookstore in San Francisco. We discovered that Hannah knew her previous partner. This was old times for Hannah, I thought as we stood in the store talking with the new owner. I felt glad that Hannah and I had come upon this experience, because it offered familiarity for her in a strange place. It tied her to her life back home, rather than to mine. She was making so many adjustments to my life on this trip and was of such good nature about it—about my taking her through the hot desert, about meeting the people who had once meant so much to me. Fortunately, I could count on the historical angle to make things feel familiar to her as we traveled. I learned that she liked finding plaques by the roadside commemorating a former pueblo or battle and that she enjoyed seeing old photographs in museums.

At lunchtime, I introduced Hannah to green chile, always getting my sandwiches with green chile on them, offering her a bite. "It's not for me," she said. "But you enjoy it. I like to see you enjoying things."

I took her to visit a colleague who was chair of the women's studies program at the university. When we met her at her house, Sylvia turned to Hannah—"I thought you would be old and gray," she said. "It's not the image I had in mind. I think because you were so accomplished. I always wanted you to come and speak here." I felt glad she said that, because it recognized Hannah as having special value, not just as someone coming along with me. Sylvia's partner came home during our visit, with her dog, half coyote, half German Shepherd, whom she had gotten while working on a nearby reservation and who was difficult to restrain. We were at least in a lesbian world, I thought, which I assumed would be comforting to Hannah. Some of my friends from that time were not lesbian, but most were.

One night as we drove out to visit another friend, whom I had known from a therapy group I had attended, we passed a restaurant where I could vaguely see a large, darkened plate glass front window. Suddenly I was back in a time when I had first arrived in Albuquerque and had gone out to lunch there with a group of lesbians I was getting to know. I had ordered an egg salad sandwich while everyone else ordered Mexican food with green or red chile on it in various degrees of heat. "The waitress brought me a sandwich with lettuce, tomato, and a fried egg 'over easy' on toast," I told Hannah. "I was so unfamiliar with everything."

That evening, although it was nearby, I did not drive Hannah past the home of a woman who had been my first lesbian affair after I arrived in the area. But I did tell her about it: how I had loaned three thousand dollars to this woman, because I had it and she needed it. And then I had to ask for it back when I realized that I had given it with strings attached—the strings being my assumption that she would continue to be in a relationship with me. Luckily, she returned the money, though not without my learning a lesson about giving. Hannah seemed to understand. She told me about a prior lesbian relationship of hers in which she had been very giving and it was not reciprocated. This made me feel better about my past, for I felt she was not judging me but seeking to identify something we had in common.

I eagerly took Hannah to the two lesbian bars in town. We went first to the bar in the northeast heights where I had often gone to meet my friends. "I used to order White Russians," I told

Hannah as we sat in a booth off to the side. "I did too," she said. I looked around us into the darkened space—the wood tables, the bar with a mirror behind it lit up brightly at the far end—as scenes from my past came back to me—someone coming over asking me to dance, the jukebox playing "Moon River." I was lonely a lot during that time even with my involvements, I told Hannah.

"Would you like me to play something on the jukebox?" she asked, looking across the table at me thoughtfully.

"Moon River," I said, wishing not only to hear it again, but to hear it differently now with her.

A few nights later we went to the bar down near the river where the tougher dykes used to go. The room was empty; it was a weekday night. The only other person was the bartender behind the counter looking on. On one side was a large dance floor, its worn wooden surface glowing invitingly under soft lights. When the jukebox began playing a fast, polkalike dance, I turned to Hannah: "Do you want to learn the 'New Mexico two-step'?" I asked, offering her my hand. She came out onto the dance floor with me. I was glad, and self-conscious, because I knew she was a better dancer than I was. A natural dancer, she knew how to move her body in time with the music and enjoyed it. I was always worried about someone seeing me, that I looked too awkward.

"No one's here but us," Hannah murmured in my ear. She followed effortlessly as I led. "I'm glad to be dancing with you," she said, bringing me close, reminding me that it was worth it to take the risk—of being close with her, of feeling as one—as my feet slid easily across the floor.

As we danced—step-together-step, spinning and moving in broad turns—I hardly believed we were here so far from home. I was leading, and Hannah was following, but also leading me in her own quiet way.

There was so much that I wanted to show her. I took her to the Jemez mountain area, where I used to like to go in the fall to see the red hills and the cottonwood leaves turning gold. I took her on backroads and high roads and through tucked-away towns. Often on our excursions, the weather was muggy; it rained; the yellow flowering chamisa growing by the roadsides made Hannah sneeze from allergies. "This may not be the best time of the year," I said, apologizing, explaining, wishing not to put her off, wishing Hannah to like what I did.

We returned to Taos one day to visit a shop I used to frequent. It was owned by two women, one of whom sold pottery in the front section of the shop; the other, a woman with short gray hair, sold jewelry in the back of the long, trailerlike store. "I always thought they were a lesbian couple," I told Hannah. "I felt they had something special between them." But on this visit, the gray-haired woman was no longer there, nor was the jewelry section. I wondered what had happened to her and felt sad. It made me think about how, maybe back then, when I felt the specialness between the two women, it was something I was seeking for myself. "You know my blue stoneware dinner plates," I said to Hannah, "I got them here," feeling I was telling her about so much more—about the lesbian world I had been part of, about my desires for intimacy.

In Albuquerque, I took Hannah past the SPCA, where I had found my dog Geronimo. I took her up on the back side of the mountain where it was green, drove past the house in the northeast heights where I had lived briefly and where my cat Jenny had had her kittens. We visited the nearby pueblos, took walks, looked at the sky, and then, one day, we drove out to a small town north of Albuquerque.

The road ahead of us soon narrowed, following the winding turns of the Rio Grande, leading away from the city toward the open desert, leading us forward, and yet back to my past—to the heart of what was pulling me back here, making me think, "Why did I ever leave? What have I left behind? Do I still want it?"

As I drove, I focused intently on the road, wanting not to miss my turns. I looked out the window for glimpses of my past—for that dream, that wish, that sense of what once was, for the experiences I'd had here that had left me with so much longing.

The road curved sharply as we neared the town—a set of houses scattered on sandy hillsides that rose from near the river, many of the homes new, in mock-adobe style, with broad views of the mountain, the Sandia range and peak, white clouds hovering above it.

We passed a sign that said "Drive slow, see our village. Drive fast, see our judge." Across from it was the convenience store where I had stopped with Geronimo the day I brought him home from the pound. I put him down on the counter in front of me as I took out my money to pay for a newspaper. The woman behind the counter said, "He's so ugly, he's cute." I didn't like her saying that he was ugly. He was my new puppy, a small, black terrier-poodle. I quickly gathered him up in my arms and left, taking him home, taking him to the home that I shared, back then, with Ann, in whose arms I only sometimes found retreat.

Ours was a taut relationship, a close relationship touching deep chords, but never meant to be for long. Yet it was a relationship that had tided me through my time in the desert—that spare part of the country—that held me there, that made life meaningful, that gave me a positive sense of myself—despite the tensions, the difficulties, the sense that "it could never be." Ann was straight. I was a lesbian. I was lured by the dream of our union, as perhaps was she. Now Hannah was coming back with me to meet Ann—to see where I had come from, where I had left my dreams, to see where Geronimo first played on the hillsides—digging holes in the dusty tan earth, running around, chasing cars and rabbits—teaching me how to care for him.

As we turned off the main road by the river and headed uphill toward Ann's house, immediately after the turn, I saw a small kitten wandering lost by the roadside. I stopped the car and got out with Hannah to check out the kitten. No houses were nearby where it might have come from. It was tiny—a soft golden tan kitten that meowed and cuddled up in my arms. "We can't leave it here by the side of the road," I said to Hannah, thinking back to all those stranded animals I had ever heard of, thinking back to how I had gotten my cat Jenny, a calico-tortoise stray, whom somebody had let out near the university, hoping she would be taken in. "It's okay to take her," my friend Bess had advised me. "When cats get pregnant around here, people don't want them, so they leave them off."

I held the tan kitten close to my body and turned to Hannah. "You're not thinking of taking it," she said.

"Just for now," I said, though, in my mind, thinking I was taking her forever.

Back in the car, I handed the kitten to Hannah, who held it in her lap as the three of us drove on up to Ann's house, which was just as I had left it—a brown, low-lying adobe-style home with windows looking toward the mountain, a sprawling driveway in back into which we pulled up.

Coming around the side of the house, I knocked on the front door. Ann came out to greet us—a small woman with long, dark hair, her manner cordial, her eyes astute, taking us in, welcoming us. I introduced her to Hannah as we stepped inside the front hallway. We soon sat at the dining room table and talked. The table sat beside a broad picture window with a stunning view of the distant mountains. As we talked, I held the tan kitten in my lap, stroking her, glad for her comfort, remembering the time when I had first come to live with Ann. I had brought with me Jenny and her new litter of four kittens—my brood, my loved ones at that time—seeking a home for us. It was three years ago, but it felt like much more. Now as I held the tan kitten, I felt I was holding onto a piece of my past.

I saw, in my mind, that past, the warmth, the sense of having found a home, the intimacy we shared, and so was surprised that, as Hannah and I sat at the table visiting with Ann, I felt surrounded by an emptiness. Much had happened in this house since I had left that had replaced me: Ann's grown children had lived with her for a while, other people had come. The intensity of what had happened between us seemed fading, disappearing into the recesses of the house around me. Ann offered us tea. We talked, exchanged pleasantries. Hannah and I told Ann about our trip, about finding the kitten down the road. Ann told us about her life, some troubles she had. I remember feeling her openness, but I did not feel a warmth from her. I felt a distance, a strangeness, a sense of disconnection. Ann seemed to be talking mostly about herself. She asked Hannah some questions, but she did not reach out to her in a way I thought Hannah could connect with, and I knew that, for Hannah, it was important for people to reach out to her, to show a genuine interest. It told her about the kind of person they were.

I showed Hannah around the house—the bedroom where I had slept and the desk where I wrote, the garage where Jenny had nursed her kittens, the yard where Geronimo had played. As I did so, I saw in my mind some of those moments when Ann and I had been close—in her bedroom, in the kitchen while we made dinner, sitting on the couch by the fire at night talking. I saw her seductiveness, saw my responsiveness, saw the old times, as if they were still there.

Then when Hannah and I drove off, after saying our goodbyes, I felt the loss, my dream undone, broken, left behind. The woman I had known, the woman I had once sought to be close with, was no longer there. The fantasy I had held had vanished into my past. I felt left as if bare, without protective clothing, only a car, a kitten, and a new love—a practical woman, Hannah, by my side—a judge of my past life and of what was good for me in the present, a woman insisting on integrity, on the truth of the moment, on seeing things for what they were. "She is very narcissistic," Hannah said of Ann as we drove away from the house, which was true, and obvious, and not something I had not known, but it was something that had once given life to me, provided for me, included me.

It seemed to me that Ann, like Bess, lost me as her narcissistic extension when I moved away and became involved with Hannah. I was included in their intimate worlds before, but now I was outside, at a distance, remote from a past that I so much wanted to return to—to experience again that hug, that embrace that I had long desired when I lived here—when my life depended on affection from these two women—on a deep sense of connection, respect, and love. And now it didn't anymore. It did not depend on them. It depended on Hannah, and, more, on me—on my ingenuity in finding a way to replace my past with the present, to move from the open expanse of desert, the possibilities of a fantasy of love and affection and of living with an inaccessible dream—to the possibility of living with a peer, a new lover, a woman like me.

Hannah was very sensitive, I knew. She wished to chart a path together with me that would incorporate both of our dreams. How could I leave my dreams that once were here? How could I leave them to go to her? The two seemed incommensurate. It felt not possible to merge my past with my present. Yet I wanted to do just that.

As Hannah and I headed down the hill with the tan kitten, I felt sad. I was driving away as I had done once before when I had left Ann for California—for the unknown, looking back toward my past, not knowing I would soon meet Hannah.

"There wasn't much there for you," Hannah said, reaching her arm over to comfort me as I drove.

Partway down the hill, I slowed the car to show her a spot where once, when I had first gotten Geronimo and taken him for a long walk down this dirt road, he was off leash and a car coming toward us ran right over him. It did not run over him with its wheels, but the little black dog rolled under the middle of the car from in front and then came out, unscathed, in the back. The tires had missed him. He was safe and sound. I picked him up in my arms, attached the leash, and got mad at him, wanting that never to happen again, wanting him never to be hurt.

Now I wanted never to be hurt—never to be hurt again in the same way as before, never again to lose a love, a dream.

At the foot of the hill, I stopped the car, pulled into a vacant lot, and turned off the motor. The tan kitten had been riding curled up in my lap.

"You want to keep her," Hannah said.

"Yes," I said tearfully. I could not imagine leaving her. "We could bring her home, take her with us in the car," I offered. But I knew it wasn't going to be. Hannah was too practical.

"She might be someone's kitten," she said. "They will miss her. This is her home."

"We could ask in the houses near where we got her. Maybe we can take her."

But I knew Hannah would not approve. We were just setting out, the two of us. Hannah had stretched herself to visit my past. It was enough that we were taking our experience back with us— that is how Hannah would think of it.

We got out of the car and walked down the road toward a house with a fenced yard, some children's playthings. It seemed a warm and inviting home. Maybe the kitten was from there, maybe they would take her in. I gently stroked the tan kitten in my arms, put my head to her soft body, held back a tear. "Be good, kitten. Have a good life. Know that I will miss you."

We left her off. We drove back to Albuquerque, then a few days later, started on the long drive home—retracing our route through Gallup, the red hills of Arizona, the Mohave, and the town of Needles, then on into Central California. As we drove through the western New Mexico desert and mesas, I kept wanting to get out of the car while Hannah drove. I wanted to pick shrubs from the roadside, take in the air, handle the dusty earth. I asked Hannah to stop the car several times so I could get out and gather my finds. I asked her to stop simply to stop: to halt time, to leave me in my past, to let me have my grief. I couldn't quite deal with continuing on.

"Just go on without me," I said to Hannah at one stop. "Just leave me here."

"You must be kidding," she said, moving the car a few lengths forward, then waiting for me to catch up.

Years later, Hannah would recall that time for me: "I wanted to leave you by the side of the road, I really did. We couldn't keep stopping the car. We had to get back. It was the desert. It was hot. I understand how you felt, but we had to go."

When I think back now on that trip, my adventure with Hannah, our driving, at first, with the heater on in her small car, with our openness to each other, and our dreams—when I think back on that time, I am amazed by what I put Hannah through, amazed that she still drove us back, that she picked me up from the side of the road, that she had a faith in us—a sense of our togetherness that carried us through, while I was torn, pulled into the past, then back into the present, and into the past once more. But I think it had to be. I had to go through that, with Hannah. I had to break away, be pulled, almost pulled, into my new life with her.

"Thank you for coming with me," I said to Hannah as I got back in the car with my finds—a rock and a piece of a desert plant. "I'm sorry."

"I know. Thank you for taking me," she said.

"Do you still love me?" I asked.

"I do. Do you love me?"

"I love you," I said as I leaned over and gave her a kiss.

Our life together would forever after be marked by that time—that venture into my past that allowed me to break free and enter more fully into my present with Hannah.

Five

Moving In

In my mind, my life with Hannah is divided into two parts: our life before we moved in together, and our life afterward. The first part lasted for three years, the second has lasted for over three decades, but those first three years cast a long shadow, presaging much that would come later.

"I think I have found a house for us," Hannah called me excitedly one fall morning. "It will remind you of the Southwest. It has wood floors, a rounded, white fireplace, and two bedrooms that can be our studies."

I went with her to visit the home that day, walked through the long house with the golden wood floors, saw the fireplace, the little niche for a statue up top, saw the back room that might be my study—next to the even smaller bedroom. It was a relief—something of my past here, something of my dreams. Feeling pleased, I agreed to visit the real estate agent to see if we could rent it.

On our moving day, we hired a man with a truck who brought my belongings up from forty miles away where I had been living in someone else's house for the past three years. Then he went to get Hannah's possessions from ten blocks away in the city. It was a foggy day at the start, threatening to rain. But the rain held off until Hannah's last file cabinet was carried into the room that would become her study, previously the master bedroom, across from the kitchen. This room would soon also become our gathering place, our den, where the dogs could lie down and the cats play—though I am sure Hannah has often wished that were not so, that her room stay more private, more just hers. At one point, she asked me to hang a sign on her door with a clock face. "Woman Working. Do Not Disturb until Noon," it said. For she knew of my tendency to want to visit her, even when she was occupied, always expecting that she would be glad to see me.

At first when we moved in, I kept boxes containing my belongings in the front room of the house that was to be our guest room. I had so many boxes piled there that there was no space for the bed, so I stood the mattress and box spring up against the outer wall. I was slow to move in, slow to unpack, as I am to this day. When we go on a trip, as when we go to New Mexico, I do not unpack for months after we get back. I feel I put so much effort into preparing to get there that I deserve not to have to unpack right away, while Hannah unpacks immediately, settles in. But more than that, my not unpacking, my leaving my boxes, my taking only tentatively some of my belongings at a time and moving them into my study or our kitchen—this betrayed my uncertainty, my fear, my desire not to be here, or to be here only hesitantly, gingerly, one item at a time. Maybe if I left my things in my boxes, I thought, it would indicate that I was not truly living in this new place, as I was not in my mind. I was, I think, still making up my mind: How could I be myself in a harsh urban environment full of more noise and cement than I had ever wanted to take on? How could I be myself with this change?

When several months later, feeling less afraid of the new space, I unpacked my last boxes and took down the mattress and box spring from the outer wall, the white wall behind them was pitch black. It was covered with mildew from where the full-sized mattress had been lying up against it. The mattress had been wrapped in plastic, so it was saved from the mildew, but the wall took much cleaning. After setting up the bed, I carefully pulled it out six inches from the wall. I subsequently did the same in all the rooms of the house—moved furniture and beds a respectful distance from the outer walls so they would not become mildewed or tainted with a bad smell. To this day, when I think of that time I moved in with Hannah, I always see that mattress lying up against our guest room wall. It reminds me of my fears of the outside: that it would seep in, damage my property, damage me, leave a mark.

Yet the house where I began to live with Hannah would, over time, become a refuge for me—a place where I have sought to make my own world, keep the external harshness out, do something apart. I have sought especially to do this in my writing: to create a world that is comforting for me and that captures some of my dreams. And I have sought to make a refuge with Hannah—to make a space for "just us"—though always there is the outside—and the fears within myself—that I must keep at bay.

When I first moved in with Hannah, we each kept our dishes in separate kitchen cabinets. We kept lists of how much we each spent on groceries. We came and went in separate cars, had separate friends, had our studies at opposite ends of a long hall, had separate storage spaces in the basement, separate pets. Still we were more together here than before. I began to get fewer headaches. I used to get headaches every weekend when we lived apart—tension from going to visit Hannah in the city, tension from her coming down to visit me. Now she was always around, at least always at night. There was a regularity to it that I needed, a reassurance I had long wanted.

But I still struggled with the question of what I was doing here. Was living in the city right for me? Was living with Hannah right? What had happened? How did I get here? I thought back on the three years before. I saw myself again in the back room of the family's house where I had lived with my dog Geronimo and my cat Jenny. I saw Hannah coming to stay over during the week because it was near the university, and, especially, I remembered the time she was denied tenure. The decision was handed down at the end of my first year of knowing her. Hannah called one morning to tell me that she had just heard she was being denied a more permanent place in her department.

She had received the same positive departmental vote as a male colleague who was approved with praise, but her department's recommendation had been overturned at a higher level in the university. There was a different standard when it came to someone like her, who studied women. "Call it trains," a senior colleague once said to her. "Do what you want in your courses, but call it 'trains,'" meaning she should use a more traditional title for her area of study. But Hannah had not called it trains. She called it "women's history," "feminist studies," "deviance," "alternative sexuality." She was a committed teacher and had won awards for her teaching and scholarship, I knew. But she also had worked on lesbianism and edited a women's studies journal. She was hardworking, conscientious. She had played by the rules. All her papers were in order, her national reputation outstanding.

Then down came the decision—no on her tenure. For a person who had striven so hard, done so much, it must have been a terrible jolt. I felt it could have been something that sent her reeling, that undid her, that caused her to be despairing, to feel "poor me." But I never felt that from Hannah. She came over to my house the next night and stayed over. Then in the morning, she sat on my bed, cross-legged, looking over at me with a steady gaze as I sat across from her in a chair. "I want us to be okay," she said. "Maybe we can go to the beach. Will you come up to my house this weekend?"

"Sure," I said, marveling at her calmness, her ability to carry on with what was normal between us.

What Hannah remembers best, however, is that on the day she was told of the denial, I drove up to her house carrying a small stuffed bear named "Kimmie Koala." Kimmie was holding a sign that said, "Congratulations! You wouldn't want to be one of them!" Trailing her were a few smaller bears. Tears come to Hannah's eyes when she reminds me of my giving her Kimmie. "It meant so much to me," she says. "You were telling me that I had not failed but succeeded."

Several nights later, we attended a gathering in the home of a woman where Hannah's female colleagues were discussing her tenure denial and what to do. The house felt dark inside. There was murmuring and much animated talk. Hannah spoke with her colleagues, explaining and getting their advice. I was introduced to individual faculty members I did not know. It was hard for me to see them in the darkness. But Hannah stood out to me—her resolve, her sense that you tried to understand how things worked, and then you figured out what to do.

Soon afterward, students and her colleagues started organizing and the "Tenure Hannah Golden" movement began. In our basement in a box that Hannah calls her "tee shirt collection," she still has some of the tee shirts that graduate students designed to help in fundraising for her legal fees. That spring, at the university graduation in a sunlit, outdoor amphitheater, the students stood up wearing their tee shirts and carrying placards that read, "Tenure Hannah Golden." A colleague from a neighboring university headed a broader national support effort, holding rallies, raising money, and soliciting letters. Hannah soon began meeting regularly with a lawyer in downtown San Francisco, working on a formal grievance, and then an appeal, to be presented to the university.

During the next months, Hannah's department twice resubmitted their recommendation that she be granted tenure, and, each time, the university rejected the recommendation at a higher level. Hannah then submitted a grievance, which, too, was rejected. The process seemed to me always to be going on in the background—new letters sought, a further rejection, more support, more working on legal drafts.

In the end, a year-and-a-half after the initial denial and an internal investigation, the university reversed its decision and granted tenure to Hannah. At a celebratory party on the campus attended by faculty who were happy for her, I stood with her as she received congratulations. Someone handed her a bottle of wine. She touched my shoulder and promptly handed it to me with a look I did not understand. Walking to my car afterward, she turned to me. "It was bittersweet," she said. "They were all celebrating, but I was very sad."

"Because of what you went through?"

"Yes. I felt I was not good enough."

When I think of Hannah's long tenure struggle—lasting from when she first submitted her papers two years earlier to the July when the denial was finally reversed—I think of how much it left a mark on her, and a mark on me because I was close to her. It made her feel she was not good enough, less smart, less deserving than others. She had to work doubly hard in the years afterward proving herself, I felt, seeking to get out from under the negative judgments, seeking to hold her head up high. She did that. But I know how hard it was. I would not wish it on anyone.

We moved in together a few months after Hannah received tenure. Sitting now among my boxes, thinking about this woman who had become so important in my life and about what had formed our bond, I saw again a moment I always see when Hannah's tenure case comes to mind for me. It's the day she is going in to meet with the provost of the university to discuss her case personally before his final review of the decision. Her formal appeal papers have been filed. We are in her apartment. She is getting dressed to go. She is wearing one of her hand-crafted ethnic vests and slacks. She looks, to me, very dykey. I feel afraid. Is she too dykey for the occasion? Will they deny her tenure because of how she is dressed? "Do you think you are dressed up enough?" I ask her.

"I like this vest. I'm going now," she says.

I was left to wait and worry. It turned out well. Still, I was amazed that someone so small and so apparently a lesbian could walk into the provost's office, have a matter-of-fact conversation, and, in the end, be granted tenure. It stays with me, too, that when the denial was finally reversed, the main reason given for the reversal was that Hannah's educational service to the university had been overlooked. No mention was made of the undervaluing of her scholarship, or of prejudice in that regard. This caused Hannah to have to bear further the weight of proving herself. It was as if she was hired for the woman's work of service, not for the male work of intellectual accomplishment. There was clearly a cost to not studying "trains."

The experience of Hannah's tenure case was formative for both of us, I feel. It drew me closer to her, made me feel part of a minority with her, made me see how much support she had from others, made me admire her resolve, but most of all, it helped me to know her. It also helped me now to understand better why she needed to live in the city, far from that place that had not wanted her, here where she felt more at home. I might have my difficulties braving this environment, but, at least, I would know it was where she belonged.

When I think of the period of Hannah's tenure case, I see, in my mind, the places where I worked. I see myself in classrooms in the university's business school completing my postdoctoral fellowship, listening to other postdocs talking about the sociology of corporate organizations and feeling odd because I was working on a study of a lesbian community—feeling odd, perhaps, because I was a lesbian and they were not. But Hannah seemed to approve of my interest in studying lesbians. She felt that having lesbianism in our work as well as in our personal lives was something important that we shared. While I had been studying a lesbian community, she had been doing research on lesbian history.

I see myself, too, during that time, in the back room of the house near the university where I lived, working on the manuscript of my new book, *The Mirror Dance*, taking out pages from the typewriter to give to Hannah to show her how I had improved my grammar by following her directions, then sending the manuscript off to members of the lesbian community I had studied and having them reject it as too revealing. "You are airing our dirty laundry out for the world to see. We will be the laughingstock of the whole U.S.," they said, and sent it back. I began sending the manuscript out to publishers, who also sent it back—"It's not really writing. It's just a presentation of raw data," they said, until one university press editor, who was also a playwright, saw value in the book's narrative style of interplaying the voices of the many community members.

To Hannah, I think, mine was a different world than that to which she was accustomed—more challenging of norms for how to do things. But I was enough like her in my basic values, I think, so that she could feel at ease with me. Like her, I was Eastern, Jewish, intellectual, raised on the value of social movements and social change. Different from her, perhaps, I was not as concerned with fitting in, with what other people would think. I needed, more, to measure up to my own standards, but she had some of that in common with me too.

When my postdoctoral term ended, I began looking for an academic job and did not find one. I then went to work as a "Kelly Girl," an office temp, in a Silicon Valley technology company, where I was handed a pile of reports and did not know what to do with them. I went into the restroom one day, looked at myself in the mirror and felt I could cry. Doing temporary work about the chemical production of silicon chips that I did not understand— killing the time of an eight-hour day—felt painful and wasteful to me, far from my own identity. I thought about how my writing and a tie to a university made my identity feel like mine, how important that was to me. One day, I received a blurb from a noted lesbian-feminist that might go on the cover of my new book now in press. I quit Kelly Girls the next afternoon, feeling back to a sense of my own identity, though what the future would hold was unclear. I started writing a novel. I looked around for more work.

At the start of my third year of knowing Hannah, I was driving up from the peninsula to teach at a college in San Francisco one day when the water heater in my car broke and the coolant spilled out all over the parking lot as soon as I arrived. I felt lucky to get there for my first day of classes and anxious about what might occur next. I stood up in the classroom before the students that day and felt strange. I saw myself as an itinerant teacher—teaching first in the Midwest, then the Southwest, then here—after making an arrangement with a department chair to cover whatever it seemed they might need, which, this semester, was a course on film criticism, because I had a degree in communication. I do not know how I got through it. Back then, it was before my many later discussions with Hannah about teaching: about how I ought to take it more seriously, not see teaching so much in terms of "me" versus "them," or of going through the motions, trying to fulfill a role that does not come naturally.

I was not as good a public citizen as Hannah, I felt, not as comfortable appearing before a group. I did not feel as rewarded from that as she did. Standing up before people, teaching, performing the role, made me feel too exposed, very vulnerable, as if others would see right through me and reject me. So I never have done it with ease. Back then, I had more of a sense that "this is really not me." I was less my true self with the students than I would be later in my career. I saw myself as primarily a researcher and writer, felt my contribution was mainly through the work I would do alone.

Hannah encouraged that work, but also, in small ways even then, began giving me tips on making teaching go more smoothly. And so we began—in those early years—to share our work lives as we did our personal intimacies, helping each other. I talked about my classes. She read and commented on my writing. She talked about her lectures, emphasizing the value of preparing, and I read and made suggestions on her writing and lectures as well. It was slow at first, more awkward than it would later become, but we were beginning to be a team.

Fortunately, my teaching that semester at the San Francisco college worked out well, perhaps because many of the students were older and accepting of my imperfections, and because the teacher part was deep in me, despite my self-doubts, but also because Hannah—with her keen eye for how to conform and how to live up to others' expectations—gave me suggestions that smoothed the way.

The next semester, on one rainy, dark morning, I drove over from Hannah's house in the city to a state college across the bay, my dog and my cat in the car with me. I had stayed over the night before at Hannah's and taken them along. I left them in my car when I went into the building for an interview with the department chair about teaching the following year. I hardly remember the interview, though I do remember the chair commenting on my jacket—a blue raincoat—that it looked like a good one. But what I remember best is coming back to my car afterward and finding the windows all clouded over from Geronimo's breathing, the inside of the car warm and damp—my cat and dog waiting for me. That was my homecoming then, my traveling family. I drove back down the peninsula to where I lived in the back room and let them each out, grateful for the continuity, for what felt like mine.

I see myself, later that spring, giving a talk in the local women's bookstore in San Francisco when *The Mirror Dance* came out. There was a small interested crowd. I am standing up before them, holding my book. Hannah later pointed out to me that one of the women in the audience was someone she had been involved with several years before. I looked around at the shelves of books lining the store's walls, looked over at Hannah, who was sitting in a middle row, and began to speak, buoyed by her presence. Afterward, a friend commented to me, "You shouldn't apologize for yourself," as I had done at the start. I had apologized, but totally unaware of it, something, I thought, that women do. Forever after that, when I have given talks, "Don't apologize for yourself," I tell myself at the start, and "Remember that Hannah is nearby." It began at that little talk in the women's bookstore not far from Hannah's house, while we were still living separately. But I felt very much at one with Hannah that night. I felt she was on my side. I felt she was proud of me.

I see us going to a bed and breakfast up in the wine country during that early period when we were still living apart. We are staying in a room on the second floor with antique dolls in shelves around us. The dolls, with their bald heads and vacant eyes, scare me. The floor creaks. We go to bed. In the morning, at breakfast at a big, round, wooden table in the kitchen, we are surrounded by heterosexual couples where the men work in business and one decorates downtown San Francisco department store windows. He is with a woman, but I wonder if he is gay. Hannah and I are quiet. We are out of our element.

Another weekend, we go to an inn in the wine country that is run by lesbians, and where lesbians are the guests for the most part. We stay in a room where we push two single beds together. I feel very nervous. This was because the bed and breakfast was run chaotically, but also because I often have trouble feeling a clear sense of myself when among other lesbians. I always feel I should be more like them, and I feel apart. But Hannah liked and felt more comfortable in the lesbian space. She has, I think, a more reliable sense of herself, is more psychologically bounded.

On both these trips, we were getting away from our usual life. We were doing what people newly involved with each other do— going off, exploring, as if the outer world explorations would substitute for the inner, though perhaps they did. Or perhaps it is that the outer explorations threw us together more, took us from our two separate worlds and made us one—on the road traveling, experiencing the same new bed and breakfast environments, looking at the ocean, the rolling hills of the inland valleys.

I see us in a room in a small motel overlooking the sea. There are big waves ahead. The room seems precariously perched on the edge of a cliff, as are we. It was an expensive motel. We stayed just one night, then went on up the coast. I see us in another bed and breakfast near the forest, the Fools Rush Inn, or perhaps we did not stay there, just thought about it. Hannah liked the possibility because it was run by two gay men.

I see myself driving up to the city often to stay with Hannah with my dog and my cat in the back of my car. My cat, Jenny, did not like the drive and always threw up, usually on the shelf behind the back seat. I got used to the fact that she would throw up once and then be okay. Geronimo did not like to be left when I visited Hannah. When I went away for the weekend and left him in my back room—with the family taking care of him, feeding and letting him out—he would always have a bowel movement on the rug, which I found when I returned. I began covering the entire floor and rug of the room with newspapers before leaving, seeking to discourage him, but he scratched the newspaper away and found a spot on the rug despite my efforts.

So it was with special appreciation that when I moved in with Hannah, I could have my dog and my cat with me. Jenny no longer had to throw up in the car, because her person was now not traveling between two homes. Geronimo could go outside with me and not be left. I could play ball with him in the middle of the street in front of the house. When Hannah and I went to the beach, we took him. He began becoming more ours.

I see myself in the front room of the new house after moving in with Hannah. I am sorting through my boxes, feeling it is an insurmountable task to unpack them. Where should things go, was I really here? Did I want to be here? How to merge our lives? I thought back on that day at the beach when I had told Hannah that if she wanted to have children, I would not continue to be in a relationship with her, because having children seemed too much for me, given the rest of my emotional life. She had thought about it and decided to be with me. After that reassurance, I had felt able to move in with her.

I felt overwhelmed by the move, surprised by my willingness to live in the city, whereas, before, I had hated the thought, felt so uncomfortable there, so out of my element. The sidewalks were too harsh, too many, there was too much cement. The place smelled like my Brooklyn childhood when the asphalt got hot. I wanted to get away, live in the country, be far from reminders of my past back East when growing up, which made me feel claustrophobic, without a freedom I needed.

But something about Hannah drew me toward her. If living in the city was what it would take to continue to be with her, I could do that, I thought. It was a time—perhaps it would have been at any time—when Hannah could not imagine moving down to the peninsula near the university. She had lived in that area, in a "suburb," she called it—back when she first moved to California to teach, about five years before I met her. She had not liked it. She felt it was not her "community," a gay and more ethnically diverse community, which she found in San Francisco and felt that, for her, was more like home. She felt more comfortable there than in a suburb where the people were white and wealthier. In addition, the experience of her tenure case had made her want to live far from the university—to live somewhere more her own.

We were sitting in my room down on the peninsula several months before moving in together. "We can just keep living in separate houses," I remember Hannah said thoughtfully, looking off into the air, then out the window, imagining, I thought, an eternal going back and forth, an arrangement that would let her have her separateness, that would keep things as they were. I looked at her, saw her ability to adapt, to stay the same, her calmness about it. "I'll move to the city," I said. "Would you like that?"

Why did I say that? Why did I offer it? I think it was because, deep down, I felt that Hannah, as she had told me, would not move to the area where I was living. She had made clear that she did not want to move anywhere in the vicinity, not even up in the hills, where my fantasies from the past lay—fantasies from a time before I knew Hannah when I had lived in those hills with my first serious lesbian lover and felt I had finally found happiness. That early relationship had not lasted, but my dreams and hopes remained. I wanted to find new dreams with Hannah.

"Maybe we could find something in the middle," Hannah offered as we talked, meaning, I felt, something closer to the city. We considered it, but I felt it was not really an option. In the middle of what? Between what and what, with nobody where they wanted to be? I thought it was just a fantasy that we could live in the middle. I felt very clearly, right then, that Hannah could not move to where I wanted to be. She simply could not do it emotionally. But I could do it even if I was afraid of it. "This is something you can do and she can't," I told myself. "She can't do it the other way around. She can't come to you that way."

I also thought, "It has been three years. It's about time. You can't go on living in separate houses forever." And the headaches, I told myself. My headaches will get better, because I won't be going back and forth every weekend. "I'll move to the city," I said. I do not think I said, "I'll move now because you agreed not to have children. You made a concession, so will I." I am not sure I felt it was in exchange. But I thought about it. At least it paved the way. I know I felt I could do it, so I would do it, where she could not. I agreed. I said, "I'll move to the city," and forever after, I have never let Hannah forget that I hate the city, did not like living there, that I did it for her.

I think it's been terrible of me to do that, to remind her of my sacrifice, of how miserable the city makes me feel very often, how deprived. But I think when I bring it up it lets the steam out, keeps the water from boiling over, releases that extra angst. Sometimes I tell myself, wishfully perhaps, that I am telling Hannah that I love her each time—love her enough to have moved here for her. But it is a backwards way of saying it. It seems to me a habit I had better drop. But I keep holding onto it. It relieves a constraint. It announces me to myself—"I am not this kind of person—I am not the kind of person who lives here. I live somewhere else. I am here for Hannah. I am here because Hannah could not move to where I was."

It is odd, perhaps, that the merging of the two of us has required such separation, such assertion of my individuality—of my reluctance to be here, to be who I seem to be—here in the city with Hannah. I am holding myself in reserve. I am somewhere else. Maybe I am always somewhere else in part. But where? Where is that somewhere else? Am I destined forever to be not quite at home, not quite where I want to be? I was missing my past—my old homes and loves. At the same time, I was attempting to share, to incorporate Hannah in my new dreams, hoping she was doing the same with me.

"Moving in together": it was so significant for us. There was our life before, and then this life afterward. Back then, there was a joke that when two lesbians met, one of them brought a U-Haul on their second date, because there was no way to be together enough without moving in. Soon they moved apart. The U-Haul came out again and they split up. The caution was not to do that too quickly. I prided myself, and perhaps we both did, on the fact that it had taken us three years.

Hannah and I moved in together three months after she received tenure; a year after we had traveled together to the desert and I had shared that part of my past with her; two years after I had met Hannah's mother; and a year-and-a-half after she had met mine. It was time to start over, to start living like two people who belonged together.

Hannah's mother had come to visit. I opened the front door and stepped into the living room of Hannah's apartment. "Susan, this is my mother, Vivian." I put out my hand. She offered hers to shake. She was a lively woman, a little jittery. I sat on the couch across from where she sat in a chair. It was late afternoon. We were visiting before dinner. I had just bought a new pair of shoes—orange clogs with wooden soles. I wasn't sure they were right for me. Opening the box, I held them out for Hannah to take a look. "What do you think?" I asked her, trying them on. "They look good. Keep them," she said as her mother looked on, then changed the subject back to tennis and life in Florida, which she had been talking about before. I learned that, earlier in the day, while walking in San Francisco in her high heels, Hannah's mother had stumbled and nearly fallen. This was not the kind of terrain for heels, too hilly. But Hannah's mother liked to have a glamorous appearance.

Later that evening, Hannah told me that her mother said of me, "She's too serious," referring, I think, to my concern about my shoes. I felt that her comment was a criticism. I felt it meant she did not think me right for her daughter.

That night, I noticed that when Hannah's mother washed the dishes, she used scalding hot water, holding the plates by their edges under the steaming stream. "She doesn't like to use soap," Hannah told me. "She uses very hot water instead. And she holds the plates by their edges so her nails don't break." I notice, to this day, that when Hannah washes dishes in our house, she uses very hot water. But she also uses soap, and she wears rubber gloves so that she does not have to hold the plates by their edges.

I think Hannah's mother thought I was a passing fad. But I stayed, and, on later visits, she was nice to me. I found I could joke with her. She had a sense of humor, more than Hannah, who is more literal-minded. Hannah does not take the same kind of delight in jokes that her mother did, or as some other people I meet do. Sometimes I miss that in her, but then I think, "It is

Hannah. You love her. This is why you chose her. She doesn't take things lightly."

When Hannah met my mother, the situation was different. Hannah had come back East with me to attend a sixtieth birthday party for my mother. I felt that when my mother and my other relatives met her, they thought she was perfect. They had no doubt. She was Jewish, smart, down to earth, spoke directly with people, could talk with anyone, was neat in her dress, and clearly caring of me. I had introduced my mother to two of my previous women lovers—the woman with whom I lived in the hills, and the woman back in New Mexico. She had not made much comment, kept her judgments to herself. But when it came to Hannah, there was a straightforward praise, a glowing, positive acceptance of who she was, that she fit in, that she was someone with whom my mother felt familiar. At the same time, I felt that my mother still stumbled over the fact that I was a lesbian. It was a hard "two of us" for her to accept in that respect, though it softened over the years.

After my mother met Hannah, I felt she liked her more than me, that Hannah was more how a person should be in my mother's eyes, that I was the awkward one—who did not wear a bra, who did not say things as directly, who had abandoned her for a different kind of life, abandoned values my mother was raised with, the norms, the heterosexuality. But none of that was on the surface. On the surface, Hannah was a welcome addition to our family and subsequently became like a lightning rod for me in grounding me in relation to the emotionality of my mother.

I can still see so clearly in my mind that time we first visited my mother. We are in the living room of my mother's house at a brunch we are giving for her close friends, mixing with them, talking. I am introducing Hannah. I am wearing a blue chambray work shirt and slacks, feeling underdressed, feeling terribly self-conscious, not sure of what to say to people, eager to discuss everything with Hannah later. How could my beautiful, sharp-minded mother be proud of me, her awkward daughter, who never wore the right clothes, who let her hair go wild, who stumbled and tried but did not conform. And there was Hannah beside me, the professor, the woman who knew everything, who had all the social skills, who emanated a straightforward warmth, a directness, a no-nonsense approach, who would in the future harbor me, take me away with her, yet bring me back—aware of the pull of family, the expectations, having come from a small town herself, aware of who people were, of sizing them up.

It was important for me that Hannah met and came to know my mother and her effect on me. I told Hannah about how I felt my mother often viewed me as a threat to herself and her control over her life, and how I felt that, ever since I was a child, my mother had needed to keep me at a distance. She would strike out at me with words or gestures so that I would not upset some inner balance she needed, some scaffolding of self-protection. My mother's aggressiveness might not be obvious, I told Hannah, but it was there beneath her more amiable appearance, and it had undermined my inner sense of self-worth and safety.

Often later, back at home, Hannah would say to me when I was particularly upset—she would brush her right hand over my left shoulder, as if brushing away crumbs—"That's your mother. Go away. Get off of Susan." She was brushing away my mother's hostility toward me that I often turned on myself, brushing it away like an unwanted guest.

Hannah and I began seeing a couples therapist at the end of our second year of knowing each other. We did not think we were breaking up. Rather, we wanted to be sure our relationship worked out well, that we did not develop bad habits. I think it was more Hannah than me who was behind this new adventure, for she had a deep distrust of the times when we would not get along or when I would become very upset about something, particularly if it was in response to the relationship between us. I think I had more of a tolerance for not getting along smoothly because that was common in my family. But Hannah thought that was not how things should be. She felt it was best if people always calmly said how they felt, without acting out or expressing their emotions in indirect ways.

We entered a small room on the second floor of a building in Hannah's neighborhood in San Francisco, where we met a therapist whom I liked—a lesbian who was quick with a joke and who took off her shoes while sitting and talking with us. She made me feel that she liked me, which was reassuring for me, since I had feared she would take Hannah's side in the therapy. She had us each talk about how we felt. One day, as I sat across the room from the therapist, Hannah in a chair to my right, the therapist turned to Hannah and said, "Why don't you view her like a storm, a beautiful storm, and let it pass?" This was in response to Hannah bringing up how terrible it was for her—how she hated and was frightened by those few times when I got so upset that I struck out and broke something. It had not occurred to Hannah to take a distance from such display, and it had not occurred to me that I could stop my outbursts once they began, or that I should. For I was trying to talk to Hannah back then, trying to tell her I was upset about something I could not bring myself to say in words— about her failing me perhaps, about my failing myself, about my losing her, losing a sense of anchor I might have needed. Whatever the cause, I could not spell it out, could not talk it out with Hannah, and so I threw a coffee mug into the kitchen sink, blurting out some incoherent words as I left the house slamming a door, only to return moments later to talk.

"A beautiful storm," Hannah said looking toward the therapist and then at me. That evening, on our way home, "I hadn't thought of it as watching a beautiful storm," she said. "I think that helps."

Once in another session, Hannah complained that often when she came to visit me in my back room, I would be vacuuming my rug, hardly noticing that she had arrived, asking her to step aside so I could finish, as if she was an annoyance, as if I didn't want her there.

"Her vacuuming is her way of telling you she's glad to see you," the therapist said. "It's her way of saying 'hello.'" I could hear Hannah smile. She had not thought of that, simply hadn't thought of it.

"You never thought of it that way?" I asked her on our walk home.

"Never. But I guess I can. When you are vacuuming, I'll think you are telling me how much I mean to you. You are getting ready to welcome me."

In our sessions, I felt that the therapist was often explaining me to Hannah. I felt she was on my side, although it seemed, on the surface, that she was talking more often to Hannah, addressing her concerns about me. I felt grateful that the therapist was alleviating what might be problems between us, tensions that made Hannah feel uncomfortable and that might make her doubt that it was good to be with me.

I remember, during that time, feeling increasingly appreciative of our relationship yet unable to take for granted that it would continue. Our togetherness felt so tentative, so precarious, so much something in the moment. Could I count on Hannah's still accepting me in the future, I wondered, her still wanting to be with me? I feared there might be something I would or would not do that would make her give up, feel the relationship was not right for her.

I never took for granted that we would continue to be together. I still do not. I feel that would do our relationship injustice, that it would be wrong. For me, every day, every step, is a proof of my deserving to be with Hannah, a showing that I care enough, am good enough to her, that I am making the life between us work out well, with enough rewards for her—as well as for me, of course. But it is "for her" that I am often thinking. I so much want to please her, to measure up. That began back in our early years and still it is there as an undercurrent within me.

We saw the therapist for ten months, with my coming up to the city each time and staying over with Hannah, always glad to see her, and anxious about how the therapy would go. The therapist was helpful to us in providing us with insights and encouraging us to understand each other better, but there was also a way that the therapy was confrontive that felt unsettling—as if it exposed us too much to our differences without a sufficient sense of resolution, without enough guidance for how we might be more connected. Often the session stirred up much raw emotion that was not easy for me to calm down afterward.

One evening after our session, as we climbed the hill to Hannah's house, the night dark and blustery, the wind blowing our clothes—I turned to Hannah. "Do you think we can stop now?" I asked her. "I feel the therapy is too harsh."

"Yes," she said. "I agree. I feel we have gotten enough from it."

"Do you think we'll be okay?" I asked her.

"I do."

We would go again to that therapist briefly two years later, and to another several years after that, and for the same reason—to help us continue to be together in a good way. At one point, when I feared that Hannah and I might break up, we started seeing a therapist who had a more gentle approach with us and who emphasized how much we cared for each other. I remember feeling, with that second therapist, that, as lesbians, there was so little support in the outside world for our being a couple that a therapist—in helping us with our difficulties—was providing a bulwark, a strengthening of us, an affirmation of our togetherness sorely lacking elsewhere.

To the outside world, as a couple, we might want to present a good face, I felt—to show happiness, to show we were getting along—and not only getting along, but getting along well. Then there is the inside, the struggles or conflicts, misgivings or fights, and these were hard to deal with between just the two of us. It made me wonder, especially back then, "What will hold us together? There seems so little there, the strings so thin and tenuous." Maybe we needed those three years before we moved in together in order to feel more secure as a couple. Maybe I needed those three years in order to know I could brave the city, in order to volunteer to do it. But, in fact, I think it was far too long a time. We should have done it sooner. I had too many headaches. There was so much back and forth, though that time slips by quickly in my mind now when I think back on it.

As I sat sorting through my boxes several months after moving in with Hannah, I was reflecting on our past, seeking to lay it to rest. I looked up at the wall where the mattress had lain, now wiped clean. Images from our first three years swum in my mind like scenes from a dream I had not yet finished living. Where was the hill Hannah and I had climbed while deciding that the initial couples therapy was too harsh for us, while deciding that we were two women who needed gentleness? We had climbed that hill and now we were here. The wooden floor of the room around me glowed golden as I focused on unpacking my last few boxes. Hannah came in to check on how I was doing. I had opened one carton containing several kitchen platters that had been given to me as wedding presents back when I was heterosexually married. I lifted one out, held it up to Hannah—"Do you like this plate?" I asked her.

"Yes," she nodded.

"Where should I put it?"

"In the kitchen, in the cabinet on your side."

That plate is there still, a reminder of all those times I was now leaving behind.

"I have these books." I pointed to a nearby box.

"We'll get bookshelves," Hannah said.

"Come," she took my hand. "Stand up. Come to the front window with me."

We walked over to the broad, front window in the living room, looked out at the street and up at the bright sky, then turned and looked back into the room.

"See that fireplace over there," Hannah said. "Look around at this house. I want you to feel warm and protected here. I want to protect you."

"I love you," I said.

"Do you mean it?"

"I do," I said, not knowing the full weight of it, not knowing then the strength of what Hannah would add to my life, knowing only that "I love" and "I do" were the things to say at that moment. How could she protect me, this woman for whom I had moved to the city, for whom I struggled to decide how to unpack my boxes, what to put where, how to sort it out? How could she protect me from all that had come before, from all that was going on inside me as I sought to reconcile my inner and my outer worlds? How could she do it? Could she do it? I was moving in, but into what? What would this new togetherness be like?

I held out my arm and she came to me, her presence reassuring, her body soft against mine. "We're together," she said. "That is what counts."

Part III

The Sweep of Time

Six

On the Road Again

Last December, Hannah and I returned to New Mexico for a visit. Much had happened in the thirty-three years since our first trip to the desert when I had taken Hannah back to my past and introduced her to people I once knew and to the countryside that had so delighted me. On our first trip, it was a new experience for us—part of my life, not yet fully part of Hannah's. I was very aware of my past, thinking of times from when I lived there, thinking of people with whom I had once been close.

Over the years, Hannah and I have taken many trips back, each time making the place more our own, making the past that was so present for me initially recede ever further into the mistiness of times gone, and making our present together emerge as something strong. But it has been with tiny steps, with each year a new unfolding of the value we place in each other. At home, we are caught in the everyday, often going our own ways, doing our separate work. But on the trip, we are more thrown together—together in the car, and at meals, together in reflecting on an experience that only we have had, making the most of things, figuring out our plans when something goes wrong. It is not that we fail to do this when at home, but it's more obvious when on the road, when it's just the two of us, and the car and the open air, and staying in strange places, seeking to enjoy the scenery, the food, the unexpected adventures.

Last year, I planned our trip as I always do, mapping out the weeks, the inns where we would stay, reserving a car—because ever since that first visit, we have flown. "Next time, let's fly," Hannah had announced at the end of our first trip—in view of the hours we had spent in driving, the hot desert, the problems in getting me to leave. Never again would she watch me walk off into the desert beside the highway as she sat in the car waiting for me to come to my senses and get back in so we could get home. Now a plane would whisk us away and I would sit next to her high above the ground, sad to leave, but unable to get out. In that space and time above the plains and mountains stretching below us, I would feel again my deep tie with her.

It has meant so much to me that Hannah has been willing to make this trip to New Mexico with me—first every few years, then every year. I had not believed it would work out that way at first. Each year, especially initially, I worried about whether she would have a good enough experience to want to return. There was so much in my past still emotionally present in the desert for me that would arise within me as soon as we landed—particularly in those first few years when we continued to see Ann, the woman with whom I had been intimate before, and a few other old friends. I would, I think, always yearn for a kind of mothering on our New Mexico trip, and it would be a gradual process, over time, in which I would turn to Hannah for that nurturing and protection, rather than imagining that some other woman with whom we might cross paths would provide it. I would have to learn that it would have to be us—the two of us alone on the road. It helped that, for many years, I could speak with my therapist back home as we traveled. But even then, it was Hannah—

the one who was with me, who lay with me close in bed—it was Hannah who was, and would increasingly be, my home.

Especially in the early years, I had much trouble adapting to each new place we went. The unfamiliarity would scare me at first. I didn't do well with the adjustments. I wanted each new place we visited or stayed the night to hold me, welcome me, be a very interesting or spectacular place, and, at the same time, a comforting one. I wanted each place to fulfill fantasies I had long before assigned to this part of the country. It was a big task for this little trip, a challenge each time: How could I make the environment more my own, as well as more our own? I think I have done better with that over the years, made it easier for me to find comfort in our experiences, and easier for Hannah to be with me and to enjoy the experiences in a relaxed way as well.

Last December when we returned to New Mexico, it was our twenty-fourth visit there together. Memories from the past filled my mind as we started out, and then all along on the trip. It was as if this adventure away from home was a barometer of sorts—as it has been each year—an occasion to look back and think about times past, what has changed, what has stayed the same, a time to assess who we are now together.

Upon arriving in the Albuquerque airport, I followed my guide dog Fresco down a long walkway toward the baggage claim area, Hannah a distance behind us, because Fresco walks unusually fast. I was still getting used to Fresco after ten years of walking with my first guide dog, Teela. I remembered embarking with her at this airport, hearing someone say at the baggage area on our first trip, "Oh, a Palomino dog!" I was so proud. She was tall and majestic. Fresco, though only somewhat smaller, is more like an ordinary dog in appearance, all Lab, and yet very lovable when people see him—a handsome, butterscotch-colored dog. At the baggage claim area, as Hannah, Fresco, and I waited for a sky cap to assist us with our bags, I felt more helpless than I like. I was standing around, unable to reach in and catch our bags or to push the cart to take them to the shuttle bus. I used to do all this when I had full sight and was not attached to a guide dog. But now I could not see well enough to grab a bag from the carousel before it quickly disappeared, spinning away from me, and if I could reach it and yank it back, I might hit a passenger standing beside me whom I would not see. In the confusion, I might drop the leash and lose connection with my dog. So Hannah commandeered our arrangements, pointing out our bags to the sky cap and lifting one on her own as Fresco and I stood by. Then wanting not to feel useless, I reached in toward the spinning bags.

"Don't," Hannah said. "It's getting away from you," noting that the bag I sought was moving along on the carousel beyond my sight.

I understood. I was the one who had suggested that we get help at airports because of my blindness. Still it was hard for me. I felt like a big mass of a person with no purpose, simply standing by, to be looked at by others—"there's a woman with a guide dog, a blind woman."

"We'll follow you," I said to Hannah as she glanced toward me before following the sky cap and his cart toward the shuttle bus.

I could have linked arms with Hannah right then, heeled Fresco by my side, and followed the sky cap together with her as we sometimes do. But I wanted to keep this vestige of my ability to be able to do something on my own. At least I could walk by myself, I thought, even if with Fresco. He was more an extension of me than Hannah, I felt, a sign of my ability to be independent, though independence was truly a fiction, I believed. It was all interdependence.

"There's no curb here. It's a curb cut," Hannah cautioned me as we approached the street outside the baggage claim area that we would have to cross to reach the bus stop.

At the bus, a driver loaded our bags inside—our two small suitcases and two blue duffels. Upon our arrival at the rental car terminal, Hannah quickly went and got a cart. This was the tricky part for us. I knew I could lift our bags onto the baggage cart, but since the cart was small, they would begin to fall off as we made our way along the sidewalk and then inside to the ticket counter. It was a heavy cart for Hannah to push because she has back troubles and must constantly be careful not to strain. The duffels kept slipping. I lifted them back. "Do you want me to push the cart instead of you?" I asked Hannah. "I can do it." "Let's just go slowly," she said. A suitcase fell. I put it back, feeling the precariousness of our mobility, the need for watchfulness.

At the ticket counter, I again felt useless as Hannah did the paperwork to sign up for the car. I had made the reservation. But physically I could not drive the car, which felt like the more significant job. I was now self-conscious not only about myself, but also about the two of us. What would people watching us think or see—two women with a guide dog who needed help, who kept checking with each other to determine how to navigate: "I'll take the dog." "I'll follow you." "Do you want my hand? Be careful." "Forward, Fresco!" Ours was a constant interchange of brief conversations, of concern with moving thoughtfully, not taking idle steps.

Out in the parking lot, a rental car agent showed us two cars she had put aside for us. I opened the back of the larger one and assessed the space to determine if it would be big enough for our luggage and groceries. The car, a small SUV, was more rundown than I had hoped. I began to worry, as I always do, about the car we would get for this trip. Would the driver's seat be supportive enough for Hannah's back and sufficiently adjustable? Would the passenger seat be firm enough for me? Would the back seat be wide enough so Fresco would not slip off when the car lurched? Would I be able to move things around to unload the vehicle easily given my lack of sight? How did the motor sound? I wished for some extras like a moon roof that might make our trip feel special.

But most of all I was concerned about the view. Would we be high enough so I could see out broadly, have a clear, panoramic view of the surrounding countryside as we drove? Would I feel as if floating on air—like a privileged stranger taking in the scenery, whisking through the desert as if in a travel movie? I was, I think, more aware of the possibilities for lack of vision than I might be if I had good eyesight. I wanted all the advantages that might make my vision more possible, more exhilarating than it easily could be when the darkness and blurriness of my eye condition interfered and marred my view.

As we drove out of the rental car parking lot toward the interstate, the wide sky greeted us, brightening the vast desert in all directions, the sun beginning to lower in the west above distant mountains.

"I have to concentrate," Hannah said. "I need to be sure we don't go north. They make it easier for you to go toward Santa Fe around here. It's as if nobody ever goes south."

I remembered the first time we had driven south from this airport. We had missed our turn and had to circle the airport several times. I knew Hannah did not like to be inefficient in her driving, so now she focused intently on finding our way.

We were soon out on the broad, straight flow of the highway heading south. Hannah adjusted the mirrors. I began getting a feel for the road. I wanted to see if we would have a smooth ride. "Do you feel bumps in the road?" I asked Hannah as we hit a rough patch of highway that I felt would be a good test of the car's suspension.

"I can't tell about that right now," she said, "I'm getting used to the controls. Check with me later."

The sun was now lower in the sky and beginning to shine into Hannah's eyes. "Can you pull down the visor on your side for me?" she asked.

As I did, I looked over at Hannah, then off into the distance at the hazy desert ranchlands, the blurry mountains. "The cot-tonwoods at the river look fuzzy to me," I said. "Do you feel it is very hazy today?"

"It's perfectly clear," Hannah answered. "Maybe you are see-ing the glare." She put on her sunglasses. But I did not want to put on mine, because my sunglasses would make everything too dark. They would take away what little definition in the land-scape I might be able to see. It was either glare or darkness. I chose the glare.

"I'm glad we're going south," Hannah said. "I know it will be a while until I'm not thinking about work, but I always feel good when we get to this part of the trip. I'm happy to be here." She reached her hand over and gently touched my arm, letting me know we were together. "Thank you for making all the arrange-ments," she said.

"I wish things were more clear," I mumbled a few minutes later. "But I'll get used to it. Thank you for driving."

I sat back, surveying the blurry scenery, feeling the sweep of the road, Hannah's presence beside me, Fresco behind me warm-ing the back seat. Looking out the window, I remembered how Hannah and I had not always driven south. Initially we went north—to Albuquerque, Santa Fe, Taos, and beyond—because I knew that area from before, and because it was spectacular: rich with Native American heritage, with high mountains, museums, the arts and crafts, and places I had explored in my past. But then there was a turning point and we began to head south to places more unknown. We had started out by visiting the wildlife refuge toward which we were now headed, because my friend Bess had told me about it back when I lived here—that she and her partner Marie liked going there for a week or two and up into the surrounding high mesas toward the west. It was a special place, I gathered. So I began taking Hannah to it, planning a trip in which we would drive south to check it out. Fortunately, we had both liked the refuge. We had made many visits back and were looking forward to it now, unsure of what would be different this year, what the same.

"Do you remember the first time we came this way?" I asked Hannah.

"I do. I was so glad to see the sun and sky."

I remembered that first time we had driven south. We had spent the night before up in Abiquiú at Ghost Ranch where Georgia O'Keefe had lived. It was so cold that night in our room without heat that we slept together in a single bed with all our clothes on. In the morning, we drove toward the warmth and sun. I remember how happy Hannah was when we reached this stretch of highway. "I like this," she had said. I was so glad to hear it. I wanted to please her, to have her feel relaxed and comfortable on the trip.

A few towns south of the airport, we now pulled into the parking lot of a Walmart so I could pick up a blanket for Fresco's bed. "I can't believe we're stopping at Walmart," Hannah said.

"It's what we do here," I said.

"I know."

I was aware that going into a Walmart was something Hannah did with much reluctance, especially initially, because she did not approve of the company's hiring policies. I almost had to drag her into Walmart the first time. I had to threaten to go in by myself, which would take much longer because my limited sight made it hard for me to find things.

"I'll go with you," she had said finally. "But I won't like it."

Since then, we had developed a habit of stopping at Walmart after getting off the plane and renting the car, and always there was that difference between us. I was not averse to Walmart on principle. I enjoyed having the experience. But I knew Hannah did not. There was a lot that she did for me to make the trip one I would like.

Back on the highway an hour farther south, we pulled into a rest area so I could feed Fresco. I poured his food into a plastic bag, adding water and holding it out for him like a makeshift bowl as he stood by the car lapping it up. Meanwhile, Hannah went in to use the restroom. When she came out, I walked up the ramp to go in but quickly came out to get her. "It's dark for me in there. Would you come with me?" I asked. She did, then held Fresco as I figured out the layout of the stall. It was darker for me this year than before. I would have to get used to that. Each year, it seemed, things got darker, harder for me to see. The start of a trip was always a test of that: would I manage, would I still be able to enjoy our experiences, to find comfort and excitement in what I had once prized?

Outside by the car again, I looked up at the sky, glad to see white clouds above the mountains in the west. It might mean a beautiful sunset.

As we drove on, Hannah turned to me. "Do you mind if I sing?" she asked. I knew Hannah liked singing in the car. It helps release her tension and makes her feel happy. She had told me they always sang in the car while driving when she was a kid. "We ain't got a barrel of money," she began, "but we'll travel along, singing this song, side by side." I knew Hannah wanted me to sing with her, but not being confident about carrying a tune, I joined in only on the "side by side" part.

Sometimes I have actually sung this song in full with Hannah. Once when we were in a park in the coastal redwoods of California, we walked into the woods to an overnight camping area where there was a small amphitheater with a wooden stage up front and split log seats in rows facing toward it. We got up on the stage with Teela and danced, pretending to tip our hats like hobos, and sang the song full blast, enjoying it, me free, like Hannah, to belt it out, verging on carrying a tune. Since then, I think we have considered this "our song," particularly the "side by side" part.

We also have a song we sing, or Hannah does, at certain moments when we are out driving in the desert that is a combination of "Don't fence me in" and "I want to be a real cowboy girl." It reminds us of who we are, not only because of the vast ranchlands "under starry skies above" that we travel through, but also, and especially, because of the dreams we each had when young of doing what the boys did, being adventuresome and capable, not being "just a girl."

We began talking after singing—where would we have dinner, what might the trip be like this time, how would things go for us—when the clouds to the west suddenly demanded attention. The row of fluffy white clouds above the mountains out my side window had begun to have yellow halos around them as the sun snuck behind them, then came out. These clouds seemed to be moving south with us, racing alongside our car as we drove— their billowing white shapes gliding above the dark mountain peaks and challenging us to chase them. If we could keep pace with these glorious clouds, then indeed we would have a spectacular sunset.

"It's beautiful, isn't it?" I asked Hannah. "Do you see any color in the sky yet?"

"I see a row of orange below the clouds," she said. "It's beginning to turn pink." She looked past me out my window and up through the front windshield toward the sky as the orange-tinged clouds rushed ahead of us, blown by strong winds, and we followed them.

We were driving fast, keeping up with the racing clouds, watching the light change overhead when I noticed an unfamiliarity in the scenery by the roadside. "I think we missed our turn," I said to Hannah. "We have passed the exit to the refuge."

"It couldn't be," she said. "I didn't see the exit. We haven't come to it yet."

That was Hannah—at least at times—doubting my eyes. Just because I was blind did not mean I couldn't see. True, often I miss things, but sometimes I don't. The next exit, I knew, would not be for a long time.

"You're right," Hannah finally said. "This is going on too long. We should be there by now."

"I feel terrible," she turned to me moments later. "I shouldn't have missed the turn. I hate it when I make a mistake like that. I think I am losing my mind. Will you still care for me when I get old, when my mind goes?"

"I will," I said. "But your mind didn't go. Your head was in the clouds!" I laughed. I thought it very funny.

But Hannah did not laugh. "Don't laugh," she said. "I'm serious."

Fourteen miles later, we came upon an exit, got off the highway, and headed along a back road in the reverse direction toward the refuge. The light became softer as we drove, the sun lowering, the tan and greenish earth, trees, and blue ponds of the sanctuary glowing a gentle ashen gold—the day receding but first cloaking everything in softness. I never liked this part of the day very much, when the light fades and I begin to see less and less. I like the morning when the sun begins to brighten the landscape subtly and my vision begins to emerge out of the darkness. But Hannah, I knew, liked the evening, when the moon begins to rise. "There's the moon, over there. I see a little bit of it." she said. "It's a crescent. Can you see it?"

"No," I said. "But you enjoy it. It's too faint for me. Where exactly do you see it?"

We drove on, taking in the scenery with a sense of privacy. No one else was on the road. To me, it was worth missing our exit to have this more secluded backroad excursion—a quiet time with more nature around us. But Hannah, I suspected, was probably still thinking about having missed the correct turn. What did it say about her? What did it say about us? Would she be able to care for us? Would I?

I recalled the first time we had made our trip to New Mexico, driving across the country from California in Hannah's small car with the heater accidentally on as we started through the Mojave Desert. I had thought that was a funny occurrence at the time—

the heater on in the car in the hot summer desert—a joke, something to be laughed at, a good story to tell. I don't think I was
aware, at that time, that it might feel very different to Hannah.
Maybe then, like now, she felt remiss, hard on herself for making
a mistake, was scared, or at least concerned about making such a
mistake again—one that might jeopardize the two of us. That was
perhaps a difference between us. We have so many, and some of
them keep recurring. I have to bear in mind always, though it's
hard to do, that I may experience things differently from Hannah. I have to allow room in myself to accept, or at least to see, the
difference and not insist that my way of seeing something is right
or the way Hannah also ought to see it. This is hard for me because I so often think I am right and cannot comprehend the
necessity of another perspective.

In this case, the lesson for me was that I should not laugh at
Hannah for having her head in the clouds. It wasn't funny to her.
It was serious. I shouldn't remind her of that time when she
missed our turn because she was a "dreamer," which is the kind
of person who normally has their head in clouds. Usually she was
the practical one who does not make mistakes. I think she prides
herself on that, takes her responsibilities very seriously, while I
pride myself on having a tolerance for getting lost and on seeing
the humor, which helps me deal with experiences that might
otherwise be unsettling.

We soon turned in at the bed and breakfast where we would be
staying, a few miles down the road from the refuge. The owner,
Jeannine, came out to greet us in the driveway beside the white
Territorial adobe house. Her partner, Max, was away, though he
was usually there when we arrived. They had not always been
together. At first when we stayed at Jeannine's, she was alone, a
single heterosexual woman recently out of a marriage. I was self-
conscious about our being a lesbian couple. How many other lesbian couples had stayed here? Did she know many? Over the years,
it seemed there were others, maybe increasingly so—lesbian cou-

ples who came down from Santa Fe or were traveling from Colorado or Utah and liked this special place. Sometimes two women arrived together about whom Hannah and I could not tell. Were they lesbian, or were they not? "The photographer," I once said to Hannah of a guest, "Do you think she is a lesbian?" "I don't know," she said. "But maybe the woman with her is. On second thought, maybe they both are. But they don't seem like a couple."

It was like that when we went places, when there seemed to be someone with dyke potential. I liked that expression, "dyke potential." It summarized the unsureness we often had, or that I had. I think Hannah is usually better at telling whether a woman is a lesbian. She is generally better at sizing up people than I am. She has a more clear sense of their overall psychology.

We had started staying at Jeannine's nineteen years ago, the second year we began visiting the refuge. At first, I was very much longing for the home I had left when I moved away from New Mexico. This generous, comfortable adobe with its three guest bedrooms and location in the farmland near the river, and with Jeannine's welcoming yet understated presence, had felt like just what Hannah and I needed. Still, traveling was so often a challenge for me—the threat of strange places, the newness of them, especially as day merges into night. I am not sure what I expect will happen—that the landscape, the environment, will swallow me up, not let me be free, not provide the comfort and protection I need, that it will bore me, leave too much empty space around me, leave me alone with the voices in my head. That last is at the heart of it, I think: that I fear being left alone with the inner voices that so often threaten to undermine me, that criticize and mock me and make me doubt my own ability to be safe. I look to the outside world to distract me from these negative voices, to help me banish them. I also, whether at home or on the road, must constantly talk back to the voices so that I can live a positive life. "Go away. Stop picking on me," I tell them, as I seek to reconstruct a sense of my own worth.

Hannah knows about these things. I am amazed always that she is still with me, that she has taken trips, lived with me for so long, not been scared off by the inner challenges I confront, that she does not reduce me to them.

She has, I think, a remarkably healthy personality, a problem-solving personality, which is not to say she doesn't have her worries. But she greets the world with an openness, a confidence in her own resourcefulness. On our last visit, for instance, when we arrived at the bed and breakfast, Hannah walked into the house and announced happily, "We're here!" in a big voice, plainly comfortable. I was shocked. How could she possibly believe that anyone else would be happy to see us? I am such a shrinker—I tend to withdraw to protect myself, fearing people will not want to see me and feeling awkward. But Hannah, more self-accepting, can walk into someone's house and announce happily, "We're here."

That night, we went out to dinner, came back, unpacked, and went to bed. As I lay there, looking up into the darkness of the ceiling, Fresco on his blanket on the floor beside me, Hannah rolled over and put her arm around me. I could feel her body close against mine. "I love you," she said, banishing my nightmares, my fears, all those unwanted voices. "I love you too." We kissed, a gentle, lingering kiss. I was aware of the thick adobe wall between us and the bedroom on the other side not far away. How could we be us in someone else's house? How could we be together here? I thought. Always it took some getting used to, but there was no doubt: it was Hannah who lay beside me, between me and that door to the rest of the world, the rest of the house. It was Hannah who would help us get on the road in the morning, who would make sure we had our coffee, tea, and breakfast packed, though she would take until the last minute to do it while I went out and warmed the car, looked up at the sky, anticipated the day. I hoped there would be snow, wind, and weather, while Hannah, I think, hoped for a day with sun and warmth.

Seven

In the Winter Desert

We woke early the next morning to drive over to the refuge before sunrise. I was surprised at Hannah's willingness to get out of bed quickly. She, like me, was eager to see what the early morning sky might give us during that hour between night and day when the light can be so beautiful. Driving in the blackness of a starlit sky with Fresco curled up on the back seat, I could feel the coolness of the outside and the warmth of Hannah's presence beside me.

As we pulled off the state road and onto the refuge grounds—navigating among the ponds, marshes, and fields for the wintering birds—Hannah turned to me and said, "Let's go to a different place than usual. I know there won't be many birds this year, but I'll look for a spot with a good view of the sky and we can watch the sunrise from there with no other people around."

As I looked out my window, I saw only darkness. "Where are we?" I asked Hannah, feeling disoriented. "We're on the center road," she said. But I could not make it out. I would have to trust her to take us to a good place, which, for me, is more easily said than done. It reminded me of that time when Hannah first started doing all our driving because my eyesight was failing. I had to learn to trust her to stop the car without my also stepping on an imaginary brake on my side to help.

"We're there," Hannah announced suddenly, pulling the car off the road and stopping. "Get out. You'll see."

How could I see in this darkness? I thought. But maybe I could hear. I opened my window and listened for birds but heard nothing.

"There's light at the horizon," Hannah said. "It's got a bit of color in it. Look to your right toward the river and the far mountains."

Stepping out of the car, I looked up at the sky. "I see nothing," I told Hannah, feeling sad.

"Look ahead, to your right, then up," she said. She took my arm, lifted it, and pointed it in the direction of the light.

"I see something," I announced, following my arm, "but I can't see any color."

"Take out your camera with the telephoto lens. See if you can see better with that."

I reached into the car, got my camera, lifted it to my eye, and pointed in the direction Hannah had advised. "It's too dark for the camera," I told her. Then I turned on the back LCD display. It lit up brightly, illumining the night sky as if with daylight, showing a band of light glowing at the horizon, the scene around me taking shape.

We were standing, it seemed, near an observation deck on which people went out in the daytime to see birds on the distant ponds or overhead. There were no birds now, but with my camera I could make out the wooden planks of the deck, the bushes around us, the ponds behind us; the rustle of dry leaves and rushes murmured in my ears.

"Come with me out on the deck," Hannah said, reaching for my hand, knowing I feared taking steps alone in the darkness. "You'll see better from there." She led me as we walked together

up the ramp to the deck, I felt helpless being led but grateful for
having her by my side taking me to where I could see. She had
run ahead first, gone up the ramp, and scouted out the deck for
us, then come back to get me. "My scout," I thought, remembering that Hannah had once told me that, as a child, she had imagined being an Indian scout who could track anything and lead
people ahead, as she did now for me.

Once out on the deck, she put my hand on the top of the
wooden side rail so I could feel the security of knowing where the
edge was and that I would not fall off. She then grasped my
shoulders, turned me around, and pointed me in the direction
of the light at the horizon where the band of brightness against
the dark sky was punctuated by clouds and the shapes of bushes,
and beginning to turn orange. I lifted my camera, adjusted the
settings so the color would be intense enough for me to see, and
zoomed in, aware that, with my naked eye, I would see only faint-
ness. I was amazed.

"There's so much color." I told Hannah.

"I'm glad you can see it. I wasn't sure you could."

I watched, following the clouds moving as the colors changed
from faint red and pink, to a deeper red, then bright orange, and
reddish-orange. The gray clouds overhead were tinged with red
as if they were a striated red umbrella. At the horizon where a
band of translucent orange hit the dark earth, the silhouettes of
rushes, cactus, and a coyote stood forth as if caught in a river of
vibrant, colorful light that brightened and spread as we watched.

"Do you see the red?" Hannah asked. "It's over there. Did you
see the color at the horizon?"

"I see it. It's turning bright orange with some blue."

It was, that morning, surprisingly warm, which I knew pleased
Hannah. I knew she did not like the cold of early mornings. She
usually got so bundled up when we went out in the pre-dawn that
I could hardly find her in her jacket. So the fact that the weather
was balmy for the winter desert was a treat for her. She did not

have to worry about getting frostbite or being blown by strong winds and could stay out longer. I felt moved by her presence, her enthusiasm, her willingness to be out with me at this time of day that I usually felt was mine alone. I had not expected her to be so happy to be out with me. And not only on this morning, but in life. She was with me in life in this same way, I thought, not only here in the desert at dawn. She guided me, led me, helped me to see in ways that extended far beyond my visual blindness.

We spent a good hour on the observation deck watching the sky, getting back in the car to get warm, coming out, going up the ramp to the deck and watching some more. I have pictures from that morning and from a second morning we spent in the same way and a third—those mornings equally colorful, even more so. I was in awe, the sky so spectacular, all the more beautiful because of its simplicity as streaks of color splashed across the dark horizon.

On our third morning as we stood out on the deck, Hannah turned to me. "You brought me here," she said. "You took me here the first time. I remember we were staying in that other bed and breakfast and you left to go over to the refuge by yourself. You didn't know anything about it then. But when you came back, you were happy. You were glowing. You grabbed my hand and said I had to come back with you. You drove me back with you so I could know what you were talking about."

I remembered that first time. I remembered taking Hannah back and showing her the exact spot where I had stood in the sunlight and watched mist rise over the ponds in the refuge, not knowing that I was seeing birds in the distance, while drinking hot coffee, eating a cinnamon bun. I was simply happy, if not well oriented, happy to be out in the morning light, and later happy to bring Hannah back with me.

I had taken Hannah to the refuge then and pointed into the distance, and now Hannah had taken me. Later this morning, we would watch the birds rising as the sun came up, stripping away the darkness, replacing it with bright golden light, and I would take pleasure from that too. But this earlier time in the dark when Hannah guided my hand and my steps so that I could see moved me in a way no brighter light ever could.

We continued south after our days at the refuge, after being sure Hannah had her swims in a local pool and a massage for her back, after we had taken walks, seen the birds, enjoyed the countryside, visited the cemetery where six years before we had gone to honor my mother after she died.

As we sped down the highway toward the open desert, passing small towns, I began to relax. "That hot tub," Hannah gestured as we passed the hot springs town of Truth or Consequences. "Do you remember the first time we had a soak in a spa there? I wish we could stop there now."

That was Hannah, I felt, wanting to fit everything in. But today we needed to make time because we were headed to a place in the southern part of the state where we had never stayed before and we had to pick up groceries on the way.

Several hours later as we drove through an area of vast, dry fields dotted with desert scrub, we approached an intersection where a sign for the "Middle of Nowhere Bar and Grill" used to hang high in the air above the road. We always used to stop to look up at this sign on our trips and bask in the sense of being in the middle of nowhere. But in the years since we first came upon it, the sign had been blown out by desert winds so that now in the rectangle where the bold red lettering on white had been, the space was empty, with only a row of lightbulbs visible, no longer working, but there as if to light up our memories of previous times. The bar and grill was gone, the building that had housed it long boarded up. Still, we stopped for old times' sake. Hannah, Fresco, and I got out of the car and walked around under the vacant sign. "We have been coming here for a while," Hannah said. "We have seen those lightbulbs get broken one by one. I think I can see the craggy Florida mountains in the distance."

We are in the area of the "sky islands," I thought, knowing that my favorite mountain, Big Hatchet, was out there to the west and farther south, rising like an island from a vast desert sea. Some things like the mountain would never change. Some things, like us, would change, though. We had changed over time, I thought. At first when we came on this trip, it was more "Hannah" and "me." Now, it was more "Hannah and me."

At first, there was what she liked, and what I liked. Now we still had those different feelings. For instance, Hannah liked when the weather was warm; she liked to eat plainer food than I did; she liked staying in one spot, not having to drive a lot; she liked getting massages and swimming, and feeling settled and playing her music. I liked feeling constantly on the move, seeing new things, though feeling protected. I liked taking pictures with my camera and going out. I feared being bored, feeling stuck, having self-critical voices set in. Hannah, I think, feared, more centrally, something happening to her physical body—that her back would go out or her stomach become upset. Over the years, I think we had learned that we had to spend more time paying attention to what each of us needed so that Hannah could have days that worked out her way, and I could have times that worked out mine. But it had been hard sometimes, a struggle between us especially in the earlier years, with tears on both sides.

"I want to sit and read," Hannah would tell me, "I don't want to drive. I'm concerned about my back."

"You can read later. It's beautiful light out now."

"You don't listen to me. I feel you don't hear me. I'm invisible to you."

"You're not."

"Well then, show me."

"I hear you. I just feel differently."

I would learn over time, to respond better to what Hannah needed, to plan our trip so that we had extra days, took extra time to do what each of us desired.

"I won't let you be bored," Hannah would say to me more than once. "You always fear you'll be bored, but are you really?"

"No. It's a fear."

"I will take you places. I always do. Remember that."

Our having to settle conflicts between our different needs did not start with my loss of eyesight, but I think it was made more prominent when Hannah began to do all our driving. I remembered, as we rode now through the desert grasslands, how, what seemed a long time ago, I had once driven us. But as we began to travel farther south, Hannah drove us more. It felt like such a far time back that we changed in this way. I almost did not remember the times before, or I remembered them as an adventure—"back when I drove . . . , back when I was that free . . . , back when I was a 'real cowboy girl.'"

Since that time, Hannah had shown me that she did not want my sense of freedom to be lost simply because I could no longer drive, and I hoped I had shown her that I wanted her sense of physical well-being to be always kept intact. But the fears we each had would have to be addressed again and again.

"One chicken or two?" Hannah asked me in the grocery store where we stopped before making our way up the valley to where we would stay for the next few nights.

"Two, I think. They look small." That was my tendency—to encourage us to buy more than what was needed so that we would be sure to have enough, while Hannah preferred to purchase only what was needed. We talked it over, standing in the aisle while Fresco nosed the aromas in the air beside the enticing bags of roast chicken, unaware, perhaps, of the seriousness of our conversation—our concerns with how to take care of each other. We walked off with two chickens, tortillas, and enough groceries to feed us for quite a while.

As we drove up the scenic Mimbres Valley, the air became cooler as we climbed in elevation. Tall Ponderosa pines soon marked the roadside. Turning off the main road, we pulled up to a cottage tucked back in the hills. Opening the front door, Hannah surveyed the interior. "It's one big room," she said, noting that the cottage had a bed near the front door, a living room area, a table for eating, a kitchen area, a very small bath. I was glad to see it had high ceilings with lots of bright light from above and windows on three sides looking out picturesquely on the surrounding woods, where there was a thin layer of snow left over from the day before.

The cottage inside had an elegant feel, was cozy and warm, and nicely appointed with antiques and soft comforters. Still, I was concerned. How would we get along in this single open space? It was going to be a challenge, I thought. At home, we were often apart, protected from each other and possible frictions by having walls between us. My study was at the end of a long hallway, far from Hannah's. We often did things at home in separate physical spaces, careful not to disturb each other. So here, the oneness seemed overwhelming. I yearned to put up a wall—move some chairs, get a plank of wood, make a divider. I noticed an armoire in a corner near the bed. I slid my hand behind it as I walked past it, hoping to find a hidden plywood board, double bed size, with which to build a wall, but no such luck.

I sat down, looked out the window at the hillsides and the snow, and began to feel calm. Then I brought in our bags.

Hannah, of course, started unpacking right away. She has such different habits from me. She unpacks when we get places and puts her things in closets and drawers. I cannot bear the thought of doing that myself. Why put things away if I am only going to leave soon? Why risk the possibility of leaving them behind? It's better to keep everything in my suitcase or duffle. Then I will know where my belongings are, not lose them, not have to merge with yet another place. I will keep myself together more that way, I feel. Yet Hannah does not have these same fears of losing herself to a place we are staying. She seems to have more constancy in her sense of herself.

I staked out an area for my belongings on a couch near the dining table, then turned to help Hannah, who was standing in an alcove at the foot of the bed between the armoire and a dresser. I lifted her suitcase. "Where do you want me to put it?" I asked. "Over here on the chair, where I can get to it easily. I'm going to put what I need in the drawers, but for now, put it up there."

We settled in and, in the end, enjoyed the space immensely and the togetherness it fostered. We took drives and walked in the national forest, taking in the peacefulness. I remembered how, long ago, I had come here alone before I knew Hannah. I had driven up the Mimbres Valley by myself, exploring it at the end of the first year when I taught at the university in Albuquerque. I camped out in the lower part of the valley—in an area I always tried to find again to point it out to Hannah, but I could not find it to show her, possibly because it was behind a place where a mobile home park now stood. Farther up the valley past the cliffs, I had also camped and gotten my car stuck in sand beside a river. A fellow camper had pulled it out with his truck and, in the process, pulled off my back bumper. I was very nervous exploring and camping on my own back then. My inner life was more turbulent. Now, with Hannah, although I had turbulent times, I was much more calm, more reassured. I forgot sometimes that this was a place I had previously come to on my own. Hannah and I had made trips here so often that it seemed ours.

On the second day of our stay in the valley, Hannah, Fresco, and I attended an auction held in a large red barn nearby where they specialized in Western and Native American memorabilia. Walking in the front door, it felt like old times, because Hannah and I had been to this auction on several occasions in years past. I remembered how, the first year we attended, I had felt very conspicuous, not only because I had a guide dog with me, which always called attention to us, but also because I felt people would then see that we were a lesbian couple. Hannah quickly pointed out to me that the two women who were managing the phones and the internet connection seemed also to be a lesbian couple. Still, it was awkward, I felt, having so much attention called to us. I wanted to go places anonymously, to have no one notice me.

As we sat down at a table in the auction, I looked around. We were surrounded by Navajo rugs on the walls and paintings of cowboys and Western scenes, and by Native American and Mexican pottery and jewelry carefully displayed on tables. A lively woman auctioneer stood at a podium up front. I bid on a Navajo rug that Hannah and I both liked and on a few other items. Hannah sat beside me as I raised my hand even though I could not see exactly what the auctioneer was doing, whether someone else had made a bid or not, or whether I was bidding against myself. But she guided me, counseled me, helped me to choose the pieces, told me the colors, put in a vote for her taste about whether a rug or pot was in keeping with what we had in our home or would be a good gift for a friend. I knew this auction was not the kind of event Hannah would come to on her own—the items did not have as much meaning for her—so I especially appreciated her help and her patience.

"Next time you come," the auctioneer said as we stood to leave, "Call first so we can open the gate for you, because we are mostly an online business now. It's changed since before. But we will be happy to let you in."

"Happy to let us in," I thought, pleased by the hospitality, yet also feeling undone—because someone had noticed us. And would there be a next time? I wondered. I tended to treat each moment, each new experience as once and for all. I had felt that way on all of our trips over the years—that each trip might be our last, that we might not come this way again. We were lucky to have been able to make it this time—to have someone at home caring for the pets, to have the money for the flight and lodgings, and I was lucky, most of all, to have Hannah with me, lucky that she had been willing to return with me to New Mexico once again—to be still with me, extending herself in the direction of enjoying what once had been only mine.

If Hannah had her way, I sometimes thought, we would be returning each year, or every other year, to Hawaii or to a tropical island, not to the New Mexico desert in the cold of winter. But I seem to have taken the lead on this, and it seemed part of our arrangement in a profound sense—part of how we worked things out between us. Because after I moved into the city for Hannah—so I could be with her where she had to be—this coming to the desert was, I think, her doing something for me, enabling me to have that part of my life that I missed, that other less urban choice.

I felt sad as we left the forested Mimbres Valley, the quietness, the one-room cottage, but we had places to go. We stayed next in a neighboring town in a house that I liked less well, because it felt more bare and impersonal than the cottage. But it had rooms with walls and a firm bed, and Hannah benefitted from a massage for her back. Then we drove farther south to visit my mountain. There, we walked around in the sunshine, surrounded by cactus, yucca, and vast expanses of arid desert ranchland, with mountains in the distance extending south toward Mexico, Big Hatchet Mountain casting its broad shadow near us. As we walked on a dusty road by its side, looking at the gnarled creosote bushes, the large shapes of the mountains, the sweep of the scrubby land, I thought of all the times we had come here during the past thirteen years. Why did we keep coming back? I wondered. The mountain didn't change that much. Yet there were subtle changes if you looked closely—in the vegetation, the fences, the small-town store nearby that was now boarded up. It was a destination for us, I thought, an adventure we had together. It provided a stillness, a timeout, a feeling of "just the two of us" out where no one else was, or where no one else like us was. The ranchers and Border Patrol were around, and the cattle, but there was a striking sense of open space and of the two of us alone, which I cherished.

I remembered how Teela had been with us the first time Hannah and I came to Big Hatchet. Coming here now with Fresco was a new experience—discovering how he would respond to the smells and the dust, looking at him and missing Teela, but, at the same time, forming a bond with him. It was Hannah, me, and Fresco now, where once we had traveled with "my girl." She was back at home, enjoying her retirement, probably missing Fresco and me, not understanding why we were gone. I would be glad to see her when we returned. I hoped that her memory of my absence would be brief.

I put my arm around Hannah as we walked, heeling Fresco at my side. "Do you miss her?" I asked Hannah. "Do you miss Teela?"

"I do, but I think you miss her more. Remember, you have Fresco now. He's a very good dog. I love him."

"I know, but I miss Teela."

"Come, let's walk up higher on the side of the mountain," Hannah said. "Maybe we will find the windmill we saw the first time."

She knew just how to lift my spirits. I was grateful to her for that, and for coming back here with me so many times—to do something special for me, to make me happy.

That evening as the sun set, we drove farther west to a cabin set out on a dramatic mesa among mountains near the border of New Mexico, Arizona, and Mexico. After we had unloaded our bags in the dark with the help of the grounds manager, we could not get the heat to work. There was a large air conditioning/heating system near the ceiling, but it only emitted cold air. That made sense because during most of the year, this area was extremely hot. But now it was winter, with night fallen, the sky clear and dark, and the temperature beginning to dive to below freezing.

The manager brought us a small heater, apologized, pointed us to blankets, and wished us well. Hannah and I huddled around the heater in the kitchen to eat dinner, then got into the warmest bed in the cold bedroom, piled the blankets high and slept, with Fresco covered up under blankets on the floor beside me.

In the morning, I woke in the dark before sunrise, feeling the cold as soon as I got out of bed, eager to go out to see the light changing in the sky while Hannah slept. I took the little heater into the bathroom, turned it on full blast, washed in cold water, bundled up, grabbed my camera, and stepped outside into the darkness still shivering, questioning why I had ever brought us here.

Outside, to my surprise, it was fortunately beautiful. Spikes of yucca stood forth against a dark sky that blushed blue-gray as the colors began changing over the mountains, the entire desert around me coming to life. I raised my camera to my eyes to watch the colors and to see my surroundings, as I had done before at the refuge with Hannah. Now alone, I wished to tell Hannah about what I was seeing and did so in my mind: "Now it's red, with deep blue, there's a cloud over a mountain peak that is turning crimson, then orange. I will take a picture of it for you. I will show you this wonder that I am seeing while you sleep. I will tell you about how I had to get up in the cold, how I improvised in the bathroom to get washed while freezing. I will tell you because you are here with me even when you are not, and because of all those mornings we have spent together and apart, and all those nights before, all those moments so precious because you have been with me."

Later in the day we would drive again to Big Hatchet and walk among the cactus and yucca. We would return north and visit a small, white church in the countryside on Christmas Eve. There, in the light of luminarias—candles glowing in brown paper bags that lined the stairs up to the church front door—we would join people arriving from a Las Posadas procession singing to those inside and asking for shelter. We were two Jews, two lesbians, strangers accompanied by a guide dog, but in the soft darkness of that night, we were made to feel welcome. Farther up the valley, we would sleep again in the one-room cottage, having become used to the intimate space, dividing it into fictive rooms, and putting pellets in the heating stove. It snowed while we were staying in the cottage, which I liked, and in bed at night, Hannah put her arms around me and held me close. We walked in the snow in the morning, and I valued and cherished, as never before, having her with me in my life.

I have never taken for granted that Hannah would continue to come back with me to New Mexico. I have always treasured our trips and been surprised by the joy she has taken in them, even though we have sometimes had difficulties. Her loving companionship has always felt like a gift to me. And this year it did so especially—maybe because we were older now, more attuned to each other. In the beginning, in the early years, particularly when I first knew Hannah, it felt like "What if": What if we are together? Should we be? Now I felt, "We have been together for so long." Our relationship seemed all the more precious to me because of all that time.

Yet Hannah felt as new to me as she ever did—a new person, a new woman in my life, not me, not the same as me. She was a breath of fresh air, someone who can solve problems, pull me out of my doldrums simply with her presence, her ability to guide me, to say to me: "Take my hand. Now can you see?" "Is that a fear you have, or will it really happen?" "I will take you there. Get your dog. Get Fresco."

On our last day in the cottage when we took our walk in the snow, Hannah fell on an icy patch. It wasn't a big fall, and the soft snow broke it. I reached out my arm to lift her up. She took it, grateful to be by my side and intact. I felt, at that moment, the fragility of our togetherness. I hope I will forever be able to guard that fragility, to help us survive in a good way, to lift her up as she has been lifting me.

Eight

Katie

We have a plant called "Katie." She is now in the living room on a table near the front window, which lets in the most sunlight in our house in shady, foggy San Francisco. I have hidden her behind a larger plant in order to shield her from the drying rays of the bright sun. I am not sure this will be a good spot for her, because my orchid plants on that table do not do very well. But I had to get Katie out of the dining room where she had been thriving, because Sienna, our calico cat, was eating her. There were small holes and nibbles on Katie's leaves and some of Katie's roots were chewed off. Sienna threw them up a few days ago in tell-tale fashion.

Katie was not always a plant. She was our beloved calico-tortoise cat who Hannah gave to me as a present after we had been together for thirteen years. Katie died last spring, one month short of her twenty-second birthday. In caring for her over the years, the bond between Hannah and me grew and deepened as it had not before. Katie was the cat who slept on my pillow every night and lay on my desk beside me as I worked at my computer. She was, as cats go, a "head cat." She always liked to be near my head, ever since she was a tiny kitten. I first met her when she was only a few weeks old. We fostered her litter—her sister, her, and her mother—for the SPCA, and then adopted her when she was big enough. Thus but for four weeks of her twenty-two years, I knew Katie. Hers was a full life, always close to me as I was to her. When Katie died nine months ago, a friend gave Hannah and me a small orchid plant with many lovely, dark purple and white flowers in a shining gray pottery vase. We soon began calling the plant "Katie."

Our friend brought the plant over the very day that Katie died. That evening after dinner as Hannah and I sat at the dining table, we began singing to the plant. We have sung to her now for two hundred and fifty-one days. The homemade song we sing is like a chant. It is the tune we sang to our cat Katie during the last few years of her life each time we gave her fluids to help support her kidneys. We would get the apparatus ready in our bedroom, make the room cozy and warm, hang the fluid bag from the closet door with the new needle attached, through which the fluid would flow.

Then I would place on the bed a tray which had on it a dish full of Katie's favorite wet cat food and a can of fresh food beside it in case she needed more. The idea was to offer her food before her hydration when we first brought her into the bedroom so that she would feel this was a good experience and a nice place to be. I would remove the tray after she had eaten, place Katie carefully on the bed in a box that was made up as a soft cat bed, and start the hydration process, inserting the needle in a pouch under her skin on her back beneath her shoulder blades.

As I did so, and as Hannah monitored the fluid level and steadied the needle, I would pet Katie, restrain her gently, talk to her, and soon start singing. The song was always the same, though with variations, and with taking into account that I do not always carry a tune. Hannah would sometimes join me. Our song, to the tune of "Oh My Darling, Clementine," went like this: "Oh my

Katie, lovey Katie, Katie lovey, lovey do, Oh my Katie, lovey Katie, how I love my Katie do. Katie lovey, lovey Katie, Katie lovey, lovey do." This song would go on for as long as it took to dispense the fluids to Katie, with Hannah looking up at the markings on the fluid bag to know when it was time to stop. I kept petting Katie, especially around her cheeks, which she loved, putting my head close to hers, and rubbing my face against her face, which gave her great comfort and reassurance. Most of the time, she would be purring through the procedure, feeling the closeness.

Then when the proper amount of fluid had been dispensed— one hundred milliliters—Hannah would say, "Done. Needle's out," as she deftly withdrew the long needle and Katie was free to jump out of her box. I quickly took Katie's food tray out of the closet, and, as she sprang from her bed, offered it to her so she could eat right away—a continuation of our way of making the small medical procedures something pleasurable for her. She hungrily lapped up some food. I then opened the bedroom door and Katie would rush out, heading for the kitchen, where she would quickly drink water from the large water bowl on the kitchen floor that served our three cats and three dogs. She was thirsty after that long ordeal—though it really only took a few minutes—and the fact that we had given her subcutaneous fluids did not seem to diminish her desire to drink.

We performed the hydration for Katie, singing to her each time, first every other day, then every day, over a period of two-and-a-half years. The entire procedure, including the preparation of the room and her eating, took about seven minutes, but the time of Katie's actual hydration, when the needle was under her skin, lasted for less than a minute. If the needle came out accidentally during the procedure, we would start over with a new needle, a new feeding, reinitiate the hydration, and sing to her again. Our singing and the petting and rubbing of heads, the closeness between us, was a central connection Hannah and I had with Katie during all that time as we worked to maintain her health and her presence in our lives. We always felt that we were lucky to have Katie, and that this special time in the early morning was worth it, and the least we could do for her.

Singing now to Katie's plant recalls, for me, the warmth of our bedroom, the intimacy we shared, the cat who was so important to me, the feelings and meanings of that time, and the caring nature of our home.

I miss my Katie, miss having her beside me on my desk, miss all the extra work we did to keep her healthy and happy. I miss the mottled tortoise black-and-orange fur of her back, her white calico belly, her white feet, which so often helped me to see her. I would think there was a piece of tissue on the floor, then bend down, and there would be one of Katie's feet glowing gently in the dark. She was quiet and yet she talked. Katie was part Siamese, we think, which may have accounted for her vocalizations—her determined meows, her squawking at me to tell me what she wanted—and perhaps for her long life. Though I do not hear Katie's meows in my mind now, but rather her silence as she sat on my desk, perched, staring at me, the way she sat—still, poised, beautiful, quiet—talking to me with her steadfastness, waiting patiently for me to feed her, to pet her, to put my head close to hers. If I did not respond, did not notice what she was asking, she would reach out her paw and gently pat my shoulder or my face, telling me, "Pay attention to me. I am here. I'm your cat, your Katie."

In the end, Katie finally had a paralysis of her lower body, because of a tumor from lymphoma, and so she had to leave us. Hannah and I gave her medicine to ease her pain in those last few days and we sang to her as we always had. I petted her, drew my head close to hers, rubbed my cheek against her cheek. The night before she left us, she slept, as she always did, on my pillow, surrounding my head. She purred. She was happy there, and I was happy too, to have her, to have her still with me, to have always had her—my head cat, my Katie.

I remember the first time I saw her. A friend who had been visiting us said he had seen a calico kitten in a litter two of our neighbors were fostering for the SPCA. They were moving to Oregon to open a bed and breakfast. If we wanted the kitten, we might take over the fostering. Hannah knew that I missed a previous calico-tortoise cat of mine, Jenny, who had moved with me from New Mexico to California. She had died all-too-soon at age ten. Since that time, I had always wanted another like her. We rushed over to see the litter, went down into the basement, where, in a large cardboard box, we saw the mother, a muted gray calico-tortoise, and a tiny mottled black, orange, and white ball of fur who sped out of the box and flew through the air chasing her tiny orange sister, all the while bumping into things, such that I wondered if she were blind. I must have handled Katie. I know I watched her, and I worried. Would she be healthy, would she be blind, was she okay, would she fill my heart as Jenny had done?

"If you like her," Hannah said to me as we watched the kittens romping, "I would like to give her to you as a gift."

"I would like that very much," I said, grateful for her sensitivity to my needs and not knowing what would next unfold.

Two-and-a-half weeks later, we brought Katie, Buttercup, and Lucy home. I began emptying out my study, where all our cats have been nurtured over the years. Down came the curtains, the cords on the blinds. Out came all my desktop equipment, papers, and pens so that the surfaces would be clear, the closet door closed. In came two litter boxes—a big one for Lucy, the mom, who was still nursing the kittens, and a smaller one for the babies. Out came my work. As I began to watch the little family, I noticed that Katie was an unusually long cat, as was her graceful mother, Lucy, who was both tall for a female cat and long. I also soon noticed that Katie tended to climb up the bookshelves like a monkey would climb, rather than springing up to a shelf, and that when she wanted to get up on my desk, she would first climb to the chair, then climb up onto the desk. I was used to our cats Georgia and Lily, who, even as kittens, simply jumped up to whatever surface they wished to land upon. But Katie climbed, carefully reaching her long arms ahead of her, stretching her body, and then following with her rear legs—as if she was investigating first, then almost pulling herself up. I worried about her. Was something wrong? Was she too long a cat? Would she have a short life? How would the food digest, or pass through, in such a long cat?

With the addition of Katie's family, we now had five cats in our house. Lucy, Katie, and Buttercup were in my study, where the kittens continued their lives of being nurtured, licked, and shown the ropes by their mother. They had litter, three bowls of food, water, toys, sunlight, a rug on the floor. Our two existing adult cats, Georgia and Lily—gentle yet curious gray-striped sisters— were outside the study, not allowed in to disrupt the new cat family. But there was space beneath the closed door wide enough so that a cat could get a paw through to investigate or connect with someone else. I don't think Georgia and Lily swiped often beneath the door, but I did see their little paws come through, and sometimes the kittens tapped back at them. The space in my study was like a cocoon, warm, smelling of food and soft baby cat fur. As I sat with the kittens, particularly when at my desk, I soon noticed that Katie liked to climb from the desk onto my shoulder to settle at my neck close to my head. She was displaying, early on, her nature as a head cat.

One day during the initial period, when the new cat family was in my study and Georgia and Lily outside, I had taken the large litter box from within the room and was carrying it down the back stairs to the basement to change it. Hannah was away for the weekend, so I was alone. Suddenly I found myself tripping down one of the stairs. The litter box flew out of my hands. The litter spread everywhere. I was in tears. This was just too many cats to keep up with. I managed to clean everything up without the smell of cat urine lingering that I so wished to avoid. But in my mind, that moment stands as a reminder of that time when we had more cats than I could easily handle. Yet we wanted them all, loved them all, did much of this so that I could have Katie— finally the calico-tortoise that I had missed when Jenny died, when that part of my past that she represented seemed to die with her—my time in New Mexico, my younger years, my not knowing how to have pets but wanting them nonetheless, my not knowing so many things I felt I later learned.

When I moved to California and met Hannah, she had a scared Siamese cat named Mocha. I had Jenny and my small black dog Geronimo. We gradually merged our lives as we did our cat families. We developed our habits of living together along with our habits of sharing our pets. After both Mocha and Jenny died, we together found Georgia and Lily, two lively orphaned kittens, and I soon developed a fondness for gray stripes. Georgia was a long-haired gray-striped cat, the more intellectual of the two. She would not come when called for food unless it was clear that the food was out. Lily, her sister, was more simple in temperament, short-haired with gray stripes, very active. Katie was to become closer with Georgia than with Lily, but she bonded to them both. At the time Katie came into our lives, Georgia and Lily were six years old and did not understand why a new cat family had suddenly appeared, occupying the space in my study where they, too, as kittens had once played.

Katie, Lucy, and Buttercup lived in my study for two weeks. It was hard to return Lucy and Buttercup to the SPCA when the time came for them to be adopted. I always wished that we had kept Lucy, who was so elegant and a conscientious mother. Hannah wished that we had kept cuddly, little Buttercup. I hope they found good homes. I still wonder about how they fared. It is so hard to give up pets, something once held close. It's hard for me to give up anything, hard to lose—pets, things, people.

At the SPCA, I had to fill out a form for adopting Katie that asked, "Why do you want this cat?" I wrote down, "to enjoy her," surprising myself with my answer, not sure if it was reason enough. Yet it was a statement I kept in my mind ever after, using it to guide me in my attachment to her.

With Lucy and Buttercup no longer with us, Katie and I were alone in my study as our basic relationship began to form. I sat at my computer with my new kitten beside me as she climbed down from my desk onto my lap, then up to my shoulders where she sat at my neck as close to my head as possible. Little Katie, hardly more than a fluffy ball of fur, balanced perfectly there and seemed content. Or she would stay in my lap if I encouraged her, gently resting. I thought it was good to have her close to my body, that it reassured her since her mother and sister were now gone. I liked having her close to me. It seemed to be what she and I both wanted.

As Katie nestled in, I had a clear memory from my life before with Jenny, who had often wanted to be in my lap while I was writing in my study. Back then, I wrote sitting in an armchair with many papers in my lap. I repeatedly lifted Jenny off my lap and put her down on the floor so she would not disrupt my papers. After she died, I regretted putting her down on the ground so often. I did not want to do the same with Katie. She would, I resolved, be near my head, or as close to it as possible, whenever she liked.

Katie was soon allowed to roam free in the house, but she and I continued to spend much time alone in my study with the door closed—because, if it was open, Georgia and Lily would come in and steal Katie's food. They were accustomed to eating in the kitchen at discrete intervals, morning and night, so they would not overeat, but Katie needed her food left out because she was a growing kitten. At first, in order to protect Katie's food while leaving the study door open, I built a cardboard house with a sign on it that said, "Katie's Diner." It had a front door opening made very small so that only Katie could fit inside. However, Georgia quickly learned to enter the diner by putting her head through the door and then raising the entire cardboard structure on her back. Even weighting the little house down with books on top did not stop the two older cats. Katie and I then continued to spend extended time together in my room with the door closed so she could eat undisturbed.

Beautiful Katie lived an extraordinarily long life. When I think back on her time with us, the images merge. It's as if I remember only the beginning and the end. Yet it is also as if she was always there—from the moment I brought her home from the SPCA after leaving Lucy and Buttercup. That day, while covering urine in her litter box, tiny Katie cut her paw pad on a sharp piece of litter so that it bled. Seeing the red blood spurting from her paw, I was dismayed. How could I have let my new kitten be hurt? I wanted her never to be hurt again.

At first when Hannah and I were deciding on Katie's name, we had wanted to call her "de Colores," from the song, because of her striking coloring. We settled on the more conventional "Katie," because both Georgia and Lily had girls' names. But, in our minds, formally, she was "Katie de Colores."

She grew up and into her adult years with Georgia and Lily as her new cat family. With them, she moved from room to room, ate in the kitchen, and settled in, stalked the halls at night carrying stuffed mice, and kept a close eye on us. Lily was always a little afraid of Katie, and Katie wary of Lily, so they kept somewhat apart, but Katie often would rest next to Georgia on our bed, or play with Geronimo on his bed in the kitchen. But her main tie continued to be with me.

Although she was usually calm and serene, Katie was the one of our cats whom we often described to guests as our "scared cat"—because she did not like strangers trying to touch her. If we had a guest with a loud voice, and that guest stood near Katie's food spot in the kitchen while Katie was eating, Katie would jump from her perch on the counter and run from the room. I don't think she was generally scared, but she had a deep wariness and sensitivity to potential threat.

Once during her early years, Katie, my sweet, loving, young cat, who always stayed close to me and seemed to trust me, bit me. Her tail had gotten caught in the swinging door in our dining room. When I went to pull her tail out to release it, she turned around and bit a big hole in my thumb. She was going to protect herself from threat. I think it was not clear to her whether the door was hurting her or I was. We subsequently sealed off that door so it would stay permanently closed and no cat or dog would get caught. And forever after, I watched out for the possibility that Katie might bite me, though she did so only twice more during the many years, not including small warning nips.

Nail trimming time was always a challenge with Katie. She did not like to have her nails cut and would swipe out with her front paws at the eyes of whoever was trying to trim them. At first that was me, when I could see well, and then it was Hannah, with my assistance. I would wrap Katie in a towel and hold her in my lap, firmly grasping her front paws so she could not strike out as Hannah, sitting across from us, gently took each Katie paw and clipped the tip of each nail. After each clip, Katie would yowl loudly as if hurt. I don't think we hurt her, but it was the indignity and something she experienced as a threat. I think that Katie's closeness to me, her patient staying on my desk or by my head, my feeling that she was almost a small furry person, only thinly hid the fact of her keen self-protectiveness, of which she reminded us every so often.

Katie was a very habitual cat. She had things she liked to do over and over. One was that she liked to run down our back stairs from the kitchen into the basement as if it were a great game: "Flee to the basement and see if the person will find you."

She also liked to hide in my closet each night before bed. She would sit in a corner of the closet, poised, perfectly still, waiting for me to reach in and lift her out. She had a particular way she wanted to be lifted, which was by the scruff of her neck like a mother cat would do. If I attempted to lift her out of the dark closet by cradling her in my arms and supporting her bottom, as people normally do with cats, she would yowl, telling me that was the wrong way, until I grabbed her by her scruff instead. She began doing this as a kitten and continued to do it even when she was a full grown nine-and-a-half-pound cat. I often worried that I would hurt her with so much weight dangling from the scruff of her neck, but it never seemed to bother her. After fishing her out of the closet, I would put her on my pillow.

She would lick my face furiously as soon as I came to bed and lay my head down next to hers on the small space that was left as she wrapped her long body around the top of my head. I had to push her little head to the side of mine often because her whiskers tickled me and because she often would not want to stop licking. If in the night, I got up to use the bathroom, she would start the licking again upon my return, greeting me enthusiastically as a mother cat might. Then she would get up and circle my head each time to reposition herself and get comfortable again. When I turned over in the bed, she would consider it time for a new greeting as if we had been suddenly apart. She would get up, circle my head, reposition herself, and give me some serious licking, with her sandpaper tongue. I am amazed that I so valued her place on my pillow over all the years, given that it produced such very active nights. But I truly liked having her there.

Katie's dedicated food spot was on a small counter in the kitchen in front of the microwave, next to the stove. She would climb there from a stool on the floor and sit perched waiting for her food. When she was finished, she would often step carefully onto the middle of the stove, when it was not hot, and delicately sit there cleaning her paws, watching out for intruders. As she got into her later teen years, we did not want to disturb her habits or discourage her eating, so we never bought a new microwave as the old one began to wear out. We also kept our very old avocado green stove that had holes in the top and an oven that was seventy-five degrees off. The newer microwaves being made were deep, rather than tall, and would take up too much space on the counter, not leaving enough room for Katie's food spot. The new gas stoves had grates running all the way across the stove top, with no central flat area where Katie might sit comfortably. Hannah and I kept thinking that Katie would not be with us for much longer, and we would wait to get new appliances. But she lived on, and our kitchen, with its few counters and old stoves, became a testament to her importance in our life.

Katie liked to lie on the dinner table each night, keeping us company while Hannah and I were eating, a furry black and orange table decoration. She would not eat the food off our plates, since I had taught her not to as a kitten. However, she would sometimes drink water from my cup, and she was partial to lettuce, because Georgia had taught her to like lettuce. If I brought a grocery bag into the house that smelled of lettuce, Katie would dig in it for pieces and once stole an entire head. The plastic bag got wrapped around her body as she stuck her head in through the looping handles. She ran away down the hall with it to the bedroom, carrying the big, white bag with a full head of lettuce, a tomato, and a can of soup dangling behind her. I ran after her, knowing she must be scared, and dislodged it. From then on, we never left carry bags out in the house, with their dangerous handles in whose loops cats' heads might get caught, and we emptied bags right away when we brought them in from the grocery.

Katie had Georgia and Lily as her cat companions for nine of her nearly twenty-two years. Georgia died at thirteen and Lily at fourteen. After Lily died, Katie was alone. She seemed so empty. She would sit on her food spot almost all day long, waiting to eat. I wanted to get her new cat friends. Five months later, our search produced two lively kittens, Sienna and Shadow, who would be with Katie for her next twelve-and-a-half years. Sienna is a lovely, classic calico, with patches of orange and black on white—a thoughtful, intelligent cat. Shadow is a muted calico-tortoise—gray, peach, and white—a hunter, interactive, very instinctive. When we brought them home, the two new kittens, sisters, were nurtured in my study, this time with Katie outside. They soon got free roam of the house and became Katie's new cat family. But Katie continued to be primarily attached to me.

As a kitten, Sienna initially wanted to cuddle up to Katie to have her be her cat mother. But Katie swiped at her and pushed her away. The result was that sensitive Sienna, for Katie's entire life, then kept a distance from her. Shadow, however, did not take Katie's batting at her as a discouragement. She kept squirming in and lying down next to Katie, and, in the end, Katie allowed her, so that Shadow could cuddle up and give them both comfort. I was happy that, in Katie's final years, Shadow would sometimes lie beside Katie and would lick Katie's face at night on the bed, with Katie occasionally licking her back.

I am not sure that we needed to get two new cats for Katie so that she would feel less bereft after Georgia and Lily died. Maybe we had to get the two new ones for me. But I felt her aloneness and I wanted her to have cat companionship when Hannah and I were away. It is hard to discern what cats want beyond the basics. Possibly Katie mainly wanted her tie with me and that would have been sufficient. But I don't know. With dogs, it is easier to understand their psychologies.

Katie lived with several generations of dogs in our household, as well as cats. Geronimo, our terrier-poodle, was here when she arrived and was friends with her. He died at age nineteen when she was four-and-a-half. Esperanza came a few months later, a small, lively, black poodle. Four years after that, when Katie was ten, we added Teela, my playful Golden Retriever–yellow Labrador guide dog, because I was losing my eyesight. Teela retired after ten years of work, when Katie was twenty. At that time, Fresco joined us, my second guide dog, a conscientious yellow Labrador. Thus in her last years, our household contained three dogs.

Although Katie had played with Geronimo when she was a kitten, she did not interact with the later dogs. She would walk around them to get to me.

The hardest time Katie and I ever had was a period of two weeks when she was seventeen and needed treatment for a tumor of her thyroid. We took her to a radiation treatment center, where she stayed for three days. When we picked her up, since she was considered too radioactive for human contact, she had to stay in her carry box in the back of the car with no touching or petting by me. When we got her home, she had to be kept in isolation in a room, with no physical contact with us for several days while the radiation was initially leaving her system. We made our bedroom her room, with a litter box, food, and toys, and brief visits to clean the room and to feed her.

Then at night, Hannah and I went downstairs to our basement to sleep in a guest room located below our bedroom. All night long, above my head, Katie paced back and forth and cried. I could hear her little footsteps, and it was heartbreaking. The treatment was saving her life and was not causing her physical pain. Still, I knew it must be terrible for her to be alone, especially at night, without me yet with my being so close. There was no way she could understand radiation. The limited contact continued for two weeks. Then finally when Katie and I were reunited, with much petting, it seemed to make everything all right.

It was always difficult for Katie to go to the vet, which we had to do monthly during her last two years so that she could receive a steroid injection to treat effects of lymphoma. She hated the ride in the car and would yowl loudly in her carrier even while I held it in my lap. I knew she felt scared at the vet, but we were physically together, as we were in the final weeks of her life when I had to give her small pills by hand, wrapping her in a towel and holding her in my lap as I gently placed each pill in her mouth. She trusted me more than I ever expected, and I felt so grateful to have her. It was as if she knew I would take care of her. I think her habits helped her through all these difficulties, for when we got home from the vet each time, she would immediately jump up on her food spot for a feeding and all was well again, the rude interruption forgotten, her normal comforts reinstated.

Looking back on Katie's long life with us as my head cat and my companion, I think often of her pathways in our house, especially her way of approaching my desk. She would, as an adult, always take the long way around—jumping up at the far end of my computer table, then coming around in back of my monitor before emerging near my keyboard, then stepping to the side onto my adjoining desk, where she had a bed. She would take this route even when I tried putting a stool in front of the desk to make a direct climb easier for her. She would also always take the same long route back. I don't know if she insisted on this pathway because it was what she had once done and she tended to repeat things, or if it was because, this way, when she came around and stepped onto the desk, she could have a full view of whether any other cats were in the vicinity. I knew Katie's route well, and because I knew there were many wires and thick cables behind my computer monitor, over the years I gradually added towels as padding on top of the cables to make Katie's route gentler on her small feet, particularly important as she got older.

My desktop: that is Katie's place forever in my mind and where I most miss her. I miss her, of course, from all the places in the house once graced by her presence. I miss her on the cat bed that now sits empty on top of our dresser in the bedroom, where she often took refuge—away from those new kittens, Sienna and Shadow, who might bother her. And my pillow: I miss her on my pillow at night when I go to turn down the covers so that she can get on it and wait for me when suddenly she is no longer there. I do not miss her while sleeping in the night as much as I expected, because of all the extra activity, but I miss her companionship. The other night when Sienna, in unusual fashion, crept onto my pillow and stayed near my head purring, I was reminded of Katie poignantly and felt comforted.

I miss Katie on the little wool rug on top of the record player turntable cover in our living room, where she used to bask in the sun, that now sits empty. High on a shelf, it was a choice spot for her in the evening, as well, because there she could be near my head while I sat in a chair beneath her watching television, my chair pulled up close to the TV screen to aid my eyesight.

I miss Katie in the kitchen on her food spot on the counter next to the microwave where she used to perch. We keep her food spot clear now most of the time, unsure what to put on it in Katie's absence, and as if nothing else should be on that spot but her, which is how we treated it when she was with us—a place of safety for her as well as a place to eat.

I miss her at the dinner table where she lay next to our plates each night. Sometimes Sienna now will lie beside our plates, waiting to be petted, doing what she thinks a cat should do because Katie did it. When we sing to Katie's plant after dinner, I pet Sienna as she lies there. Sometimes she comes up onto the table for petting as soon as she hears Hannah and me start singing. Shadow jumps up and down from the table often if we are not watchful, but she is trying to steal food, not to take Katie's place. When Katie was on the table, Shadow kept away more often, as if she knew it was the elder cat's territory.

I miss the sound of Katie's feet hitting the ground as she jumped down from the dining table or a chair. While our other cats seemed to have more spring in their step when landing, Katie always landed with a thud. I used to worry about that, but she never hurt herself. Probably it was related to her build: she had more weight in her rear quarters. Katie was a beautiful, long, big cat for a female. Because she was our larger cat, we soon began calling Sienna and Shadow our "little cats," which we continued to do even with Katie gone.

I miss the spot in the litter box in the bathroom where Katie used to pee. She always peed right in the middle of the box and did not cover her pee in recent years, so there would be a small tell-tale wet hole, while Sienna and Shadow pee off-center and usually cover. When I clean the litter box now, I look for Katie's spot and am surprised not to find it. I sometimes think I hear footsteps in the bathtub. I pull the shower curtain aside to look in, because Katie liked to get into the tub to drink water in the morning after her breakfast, lapping up what was left from our showers. She liked the privacy of the tub.

In the kitchen, I look up often toward the high cabinets above the stove where young Katie used to climb up to the top and sit there with Georgia and Lily.

There is the space in my closet from which Katie's little head used to peek out, letting me know she was waiting for me to pick her up by the scruff of her neck and place her gently on my pillow.

There is a feeling I have atop my shoulders where once, a long time ago, tiny Katie used to perch. She began doing this when she was but a kitten and continued through many years of her adulthood. I liked to walk around with her draped across my shoulders. I would step to a mirror and I would look at us.

And most of all, I miss Katie on my desk. She picked that surface as hers when she was a kitten, wanting to be close to my head. As she grew bigger and took up more space, I placed a towel, and later a soft cat bed, under a lamp on the right-hand side of my desk so that I could have the center area clear for my work. Katie took to that spot, and, forever after, it was her home base. She liked the warmth of the lamp, the privacy, the protection from the other cats, the closeness to me. When she was in her last months, I covered my entire desk surface with soft towels so that she could stretch out comfortably wherever she wanted to and so that there would be space for Sienna and Shadow to lie with her. My desk, with its softness and warm lamps, became like a hearth in our house that Hannah and I and our other animals centered around as we cared for and kept company with Katie. While I worked at my computer, she was with me, a short arm's length away. I could lean my head over and rub my brow against hers, as I had done for nearly twenty-two years.

When my Katie died, the biggest emptiness I felt was the loss of her presence on my desk, the loss of her constancy, her clear eyes looking over at me, the sense that I was not alone. Sienna and Shadow soon came close and kept me company, for they, too, missed her. I framed a large photo I had taken of Katie and placed it on the wall behind my desk, opposite me so that I could see it as if she were still there. I snapped a picture of Sienna and Shadow lying on the desk on either side of Katie's photo, seeking to have us all together again. I put a colorful Navajo weaving on the area of the desk closest to me where Katie, with her multi-color, used to lie. I propped up a picture of her paw print.

Katie was with me for a very long time. She was a pleasure for me, a constant companion who made me feel less alone, a black and orange decoration for all the surfaces around me. With her white belly and small white feet, she enabled me to see her in the dark. I was her lifeline and she was mine. She insisted on her presence with me, on our bond. I am amazed I became so used to that, as if our closeness made up for something I was missing that I, too, long had wanted. I think that I, like Katie, am some-what scared of people and need the reassuring intimacy with another, the habitual, the favorite things and places, the simple connection.

Katie's plant now sits again on our dining room table. I have moved it back from the living room, where it did not do as well. I have been nursing it, plumping up its leaves. Hannah and I have been singing to it. The plant, the places in the house where Katie once perched stay with me, the memories, the ways Hannah and I have cared for all our animals over the years—Jenny, Mocha, Georgia, Lily, Sienna, Shadow, and Katie, our cats; Geronimo, Esperanza, Teela, and Fresco, our dogs. Our care for them has marked our life together as surely as the love we have given each other. They have filled the spaces of our house, the interstices of our hearts. Katie was here and then gone. She was a gift from Hannah to me back when I needed it. I will never forget the power of that gift.

Katie used to step carefully through the rooms of our house. Especially as she got older, she would hug the walls as she walked down the hallway to avoid ambush from the other cats, and to avoid my stepping on her accidentally. She protected herself; she took care. I want to protect myself, too, not be afraid of protecting, to move through the world with her ease and wariness and with her desire to be close—to have that warmth, that comfort, that reassuring presence, which, for her was me, and for me was her, my head cat, my Katie. I was her Susan and she was my beloved furry friend.

Nine

Attending a Wedding

When Hannah first brought up the subject of Michelle and Jennifer's wedding, "I don't like weddings," I said. "You know I don't believe in marriage. I feel that all the same advantages should go to people as individuals."

"I know," she said, standing in the kitchen, looking at me thoughtfully. I could not see the exact expression on her face, but I knew the feel of it. I felt she wanted me to go with her because it was a wedding of a lesbian couple, and we were a lesbian couple. She could go alone, but it would be different attending with me. I felt in the air a sense of romanticization and of all the conventional sentimentality that surrounds the idea of weddings. I knew that Hannah, like me, was not a big fan of marriage and weddings. We had been together for thirty-two years before we got married, and even then, Hannah liked to refer to that day as our "marriage day," rather than our wedding day, to set it apart from what was normally done.

Though she had mixed feelings, I knew Hannah wanted to attend this wedding, to be surrounded by an aura of love and romance, but, most of all, to be present in support of her friend Michelle.

"Would you like me to go with you?" I asked.

"I would like that very much."

"I will ask a friend to stop in for Teela."

"Were you thinking of staying for dinner?" I asked her later that evening.

"I'm not sure."

"It will be really late if we stay for dinner," I said, feeling I was betraying my reluctance. I wanted to be quickly in and out, to make an appearance, then come home to the privacy of our loving but not long-married life, a life where I would not have to pretend that I believed in marriage.

We went into Hannah's study where I sat beside her as she checked the wedding schedule on her computer.

"It's a formal wedding," she reported, looking at the screen, then over at me. "It's in a church in the country. There is a reception afterward, then dinner and dancing. They want to know what we would like for dinner. Would you like the chicken or the beef, or would you prefer the vegetarian option?"

I balked, not happy about this prospect. "I wouldn't want to have dinner," I said. "We will be there forever. Can we leave after the hors d'oeuvres?"

"I would like the dancing," she mused. "It comes after the dinner."

As we talked, I felt that Hannah would prefer staying for the entire event: the ceremony, the reception, the dinner, and, most especially, the dancing, where there would be live music.

If she were not with me, if she had married someone else, she would be able to stay for dancing, I thought, if she were with someone who liked to dance and who liked the whole idea of weddings. But she had somehow chosen me, a stick in the mud, a not very socially conventional woman, a very private person in some ways.

"How would you feel about not staying for the dinner?" I asked. "The reception can take quite a long time."

"Let me think about that."

We then turned to the project of selecting the gift. "They have registered," Hannah said. "There is a long list of things—dishes, serving ware, pots and pans. You can even contribute to their honeymoon in the Caribbean."

We decided on contributing toward a massage for two while they were on their honeymoon.

This was new ground for me. I knew people registered for dishes and such for wedding presents, but I had never thought of something this experiential.

"There wasn't an option of contributing to a cause in their name," Hannah noted. "I would have liked to have done that."

"You can."

"No, let's do what they want."

I knew that the prospect of a large, formal wedding, the expense, the array of possible gifts while registering, did not appeal to Hannah. It seemed like too great an expenditure of money that might be better used in other ways. But this did not detract from her feelings of looking forward to the event.

"Other people are very different from us. It means a lot to them," I said.

The day of the wedding as we carefully got dressed, Hannah took out of her closet the lovely white shirt she had worn on the day she and I got married. Then she layered a jacket over it. "It's not right for this," I said, looking at her, seeing the length of white. "It's an overshirt and the jacket is too short. But it was perfect for our wedding."

"Oh." She seemed disappointed.

I thought of the shirt I had worn on our marriage day, but it did not seem right either, not dressy enough for this more formal event. I had a feeling, perhaps Hannah did, too, that in going to the wedding of these two friends, we were somehow also going to our wedding, confirming our bond, our treasured intimacy.

As we drove off from the house that afternoon, we were running late. I could hear Hannah mumbling under her breath—irritated with me, I thought, because I had been settling the animals at the last minute and lost track of time, which kept us from leaving sooner. As we headed out of the city and across the bridge, it felt, at first, like a carefree ride to the country. But then we started to get lost. We had missed our exit from the freeway. Hannah was becoming worried. "I always get lost coming over here. We didn't leave enough time," she said, implying, I felt, that it was my fault, and also implying—there was something about her tone that suggested it—that we were going to be late for *our* wedding, not these other people's wedding that could start without us, but ours.

The melody from "Get me to the church on time" rang in my ears as we pulled off the freeway and parked beneath it to assess where we were. After consulting maps, we drove on, taking back roads, still unsure of our route. Hannah grasped the steering wheel tightly, staring straight ahead, as if she could will us to get there on time. I turned to her. "It's not our wedding. We can be late," I said.

"I don't want to be late."

"We won't be late. But I meant, it's not vital."

"It is, I don't like being late. I want Michelle to know that I am there beforehand."

Arriving finally on the grounds of the religious seminary where the wedding would be held, we found ourselves in a naturalistic setting on a steep hillside at the base of a mountain where we were surrounded by bushes and tall trees. I felt as if we were going back in time to a place where sequestered religious men murmured prayers and studied late into the night. Other cars were still pulling in. Hannah breathed a sigh of relief but remained concerned because we had to climb a rock pathway up the hill to reach the chapel.

I let Fresco out of the car and the three of us hurried up the long flight of flagstone steps. Hannah led the way, pointing out irregularities in the stone so that I would not trip. I was almost out of breath upon reaching the top, but fortunately, we were not late. People were gathering outside on a spacious stone patio overlooking the side of the mountain with its bushes and thick greenery. Above us loomed a tall stone bell tower, and beside it was the small church chapel. The tower lent a feeling of importance. The chapel entry seemed dark but inviting.

As we stood on the edge of the crowd looking on, I began to feel cold. I had brought a jacket to put on in the case of cold, which Hannah held for me. At the last wedding we had attended other than our own, I had brought this same jacket, a blue cloth raincoat, because it was the only thing long enough to cover the decorative silk shirt I was wearing that draped down over my pants. It had been so chilly at that previous wedding that I wore the raincoat throughout the service. Hannah had not liked that. She liked it when people could see me dressed up. I had liked feeling I was flaunting my disregard for the whole scene by not seeming to care if I looked terrific. But now, knowing Hannah's wishes, and because I was not very cold, I was happy to leave her carrying my jacket. Still, I felt I did not look dressed up enough, that I never would.

Soon a relative of one of the brides came over to tell us that the ceremony would be starting late. Hannah, Fresco, and I went inside to use the restroom, following a dark stairway that led steeply down as if descending the very side of the mountain. It was then that I began getting anxious about the time. Would Hannah finish in her stall in time? I wondered as I stepped out of mine. I heard music and footsteps overhead, people gathering, going into the chapel upstairs. "I'll meet you up there," I called in a rush to Hannah as I headed for the staircase to climb it with my guide dog, though careful because of the steepness.

"Wait for me," she said. "I want you to be safe."

"I will be safe," I called back.

As I bolted up the stairs with Fresco, I wondered, Why did I now fear being late? I think it was because I wanted to get a front seat so I could see the wedding ceremony as best I could, given the limitations of my eyesight.

At the doorway to the chapel, I stopped, waiting for Hannah. She soon came up the stairs and joined me as we walked into the sanctuary with its polished dark wood pews and high stained-glass windows letting in gentle streams of sunlight. Rich welcoming music was playing on the organ up front. "Turn right here," Hannah said, pointing Fresco and me into a pew. "I think this will be the best place for the dog. There's room for him to lie down."

I was reluctant to turn into the pew toward which she motioned. "I'd like to be closer," I said.

"This is the closest we can get," Hannah noted. "The front rows are reserved for the family. They are beginning to come in. There is less room for Fresco everywhere else."

I sat down hesitantly, looking toward the front. I could not see the altar at all. The inside of the chapel was dark to my eyes and the altar too far away. "Can you see?" I asked Hannah.

"I can."

"What's that in front of us?"

"It's the photographer and the camera. He is set up there to shoot a movie."

"I can't see through him. He is in my way," I said.

"I will change seats with you," she offered.

"Then you won't be able to see."

In front of me, all I saw was darkness and the white shirt of the photographer.

I squirmed in my seat, uneasy. Hannah felt this. "It's the best we're going to be able to do," she said.

Tears welled up inside me. I felt ready to cry. I wanted to stand up, to go to the front, to sit close to the stage where I would be able to see the wedding ceremony.

I held back my tears, my anger at Hannah for putting us here, my disappointment, my desire to urge her to come with me and move forward. I felt that even if the family had reserved the front rows, we could still sit there, because that was where a blind woman should sit—with her guide dog and her lover, the woman she had come with who did not quite understand.

Perhaps I was spoiled, I thought, for I was now used to sitting up front in places. Still, I felt wronged, cheated, constrained by Hannah. I felt I knew better. I wanted us to move forward, but I held it in, though all the while sure that I was indicating to Hannah by my physical presence—by the slant of my body, my looking down, my general uneasiness that I was disappointed, that I didn't like it here in the wrong place, the wrong seats.

The organ began playing the upbeat chords of the processional, announcing the start of the formal ceremony.

"Do you see the flower girl?" Hannah suddenly asked, gently lifting her arm to direct my eyes. "She is coming down the aisle tossing flowers from a basket. She is very small. I think she just sat down on the floor and has turned her basket over, spilling the flowers. She wasn't sure what to do."

I looked quickly toward the aisle and glimpsed a small white dress on the floor, then averted my gaze. I did not want to let Hannah know I saw anything.

"I didn't see it," I lied, though I actually did not see the details.

"The brides are coming down the aisle now. Can you see them?" Hannah said.

I glanced to my left, saw a soft whiteness of clothing. That must be Michelle in her dress, I thought. The woman next to her was in dark clothes. I nodded. "A little," I said, struggling with both what I could and could not see—the blurriness of the two brides, yet their clearly radiant presence.

I sat through the entire ceremony that afternoon, seeing nothing of it. The altar was too far away and the area up front too dark. Most of the time, I averted my gaze, not wanting to be reminded of what I could not see. I pointed my eyes toward the ground so I would feel less acutely my lack of sight, and so I would feel less upset with Hannah for boxing us in, for insisting we sit where I did not want to be. At the same time, I listened.

A woman behind me began mumbling to a person next to her about there being a guide dog in front of them, then explained to the other person what guide dogs did. I heard them whispering and wondered why break the silence surrounding the ceremony? But the distraction relieved some of the tension I felt. It was a familiar occurrence. Often when Fresco and I were out, people talked about us in our presence.

I looked over at Hannah and touched her arm. She nodded as if she had heard. I was beginning to feel closer to her.

Up front on the altar, the minister was speaking, welcoming the guests and addressing the brides. After some words of thankfulness and remarks about the sanctity of marriage, he read a poem about the importance of safeguarding the separateness of the two women—that they should be like two trees standing tall, not in each other's shadow. I thought that the minister, a man, must have chosen this poem, because it sounded very male to me, that two women entering into a marriage would be wanting to join, to be as one, not to stay apart. But those were two sides of the same coin, I knew. Two women can easily feel as one, and so must especially guard their ability to be separate, to stay who they each are. I thought of differences Hannah and I had, how hard we had worked, over time, to feel together in spite of our differences, and how painful it felt sometimes when our differences drew us apart.

A woman with a beautiful voice—the sister of one of the brides—stepped up to the altar and began singing a song of meaning to the new couple. Then the minister asked each of the women what the other brought out in her that she most valued. They gave their responses. "She gives me courage." "She helps me to be persistent." "She brings out the best in me."

As the couple said their vows, Hannah took my hand and held it close to her chest, as if it were us up there getting married. I brought her hand back between us and grasped it firmly, wanting to show her that I was with her. I was feeling calmer now than I had earlier, less caught up in tumultuous inner emotions.

"They're coming back down the aisle," Hannah said suddenly as the two brides whisked by hurriedly past us, Michelle's long, white train sweeping the carpet behind her, Jennifer beside her carrying flowers and smiling.

Hannah and I waited, then followed as the people in the front pews emptied out, walking down the aisle and out of the chapel. Hannah linked her arm in mine as we stepped forward, Fresco heeling by my side. We had not gotten married here today, far from it. I had been on the verge of tears much of the time. My behavior hadn't been anybody's idea of "the best I could make of it."

I was such a failure, I thought. I shouldn't come to these things. They were simply not for me. In my mind, too, I forgave Hannah. I felt bad about having been such a poor sport in relation to her. I felt that this was simply life—sometimes I wouldn't be able to see. Often, I cannot see people sitting across from me at a table or at an event. Why I had become so upset now because of that fact, so angry with Hannah, was still largely a mystery to me. But I think it had to do with issues surrounding taking care. If Hannah failed at one moment—if she faltered in the task—my grief, my upset was extreme. How could I be okay, how could I be happy, how could I be safe if Hannah failed to take care of me as I wished? And though, in fact, she had not failed me, merely put us in what she felt were the best seats, I had felt let down by my best friend.

As we stepped out of the chapel and into the open air, surrounded by the trees and bushes of the mountainside and the blue sky, I turned to Hannah. "I got used to not seeing," I said. "How was it for you? Could you see everything?"

"I could see everything," she said. "But I couldn't hear it. I only heard when her sister sang and when the minister read from the poem. I didn't have my hearing aids with me. I accidentally left them at home. The minister had on one of those headphone microphones and it slipped away from his cheek, so I could only hear words here and there."

"Come with me," I said taking her hand and leading us over to the edge of the flagstone patio where a waist-high stone wall stood just this side of the bushes and trees. "I will tell you what I heard," I said to her, "if you tell me what you saw." And there, as people coming out from the chapel mingled around and the photographer snapped photos, we recounted to each other the bits and pieces of the wedding ceremony, making it whole.

A while later, we proceeded back down the flagstone steps to an area where the reception and dinner would be held. Small, festive tables stood under trees as black-aproned servers walked past with trays of deviled eggs, rolled ham, and spicy crab cakes on toast as the wine and champagne flowed and a band played background music on a terrace nearby. Hannah, Fresco, and I stood at one of the small tables tasting the hors d'oeuvres and sipping the champagne. At one point when Hannah left the table to refill our drinks, a woman—a friend of the two brides—came up to me because, she explained, I had a guide dog with me and so she could introduce herself by talking about the dog. She told me that she was a contributor to an organization that trained service dogs where she lived in Colorado. "I'm not as outgoing as my wife," she said before leaving and after Hannah had returned, "I only came over because I knew I could relate about the dog."

I appreciated her reaching out, but I was taken aback. Her "wife," I thought, wishing I had not heard it. I hoped that Hannah, too, had not liked hearing this word, that we had similar feelings about it, but I was not sure. We stepped over to talk with a small group of other women, also friends of the bridal couple, and they, too, spoke of their wives.

Back at our table, I turned to Hannah. "Wife," I said. "How do you feel about that?"

"It means chattel," she said, leaving me to wonder about the exact meaning of the term, but knowing the sense of it. "It means property," she said, ready to give me a history lesson.

"I prefer 'spouse,'" she added.

"That sounds like 'grouse' to me. I don't like it. I prefer 'partner,'" I said.

At the same time, I remembered how I used to balk at "partner" because it sounded too businesslike. How could they tell that the other woman was not your business partner? I had always before used the word "lover," though feeling very exposed by it. By saying "lover," people would then imagine us in bed, I felt. Still, it conveyed the intimacy, the freedom I felt—that we are lovers, like "free lovers"—that we're not here because of an institution but outside it—free, taking in the open air, carried away on the winds of our spirit to wherever it would take us, on the winds of a temporary romance—here today, gone tomorrow, caught up in the moment, not tied to anything anyone else knew.

But now "partner" sounded better to me than "lover," or if not better, more protected. I was strangely not ready to go back to that earlier time of exposure. Yet I felt there was a truth in the earlier term. Lesbianism was about a private, temporary, fragile space of two women merging into the softness of a "love that dares not speak its name," a forbidden love, a unique, invisible love even now, I thought. No matter how enshrined it might be in marriage and ceremonies, it was still beyond all those words for knowing it that we had.

I looked over at Hannah and at the musicians playing on the terrace not far behind her down a small flight of stairs. In front of them lay a broad cement patio surrounded by plots of grass.

"Do you think that's where the dancing will take place later?" I asked her.

"Yes."

"Do you want to dance? No one else is out there."

"No," she said. "It's too cold. Not now."

I was relieved. It would have been awkward. There was no one else dancing, and, maybe later, they would be dancing inside where it was warmer. And what if we had gone over, who would hold Fresco? Further, I was not someone who wanted to be seen. We would certainly stand out dancing alone.

Still, I wished we had danced, because I thought Hannah would have liked it. She liked music. She liked dancing. I had been such a "pickle," so much not in the spirit of the ceremony in the chapel when I was so irritable about the seats Hannah had chosen for us. I wanted to do something she would like that was in the spirit of a wedding for her.

Then suddenly, in my mind, I saw us there—out in the open in front of the musicians near a stretch of lawn where children were playing. I saw Hannah and me dancing, with Fresco following on his leash by my side. We were holding each other close, dancing slowly in this strange world—ignoring it, not standing out, viewed by only us. No one would see us—none of the other people at the reception up a few stairs munching their hors d'oeuvres and sipping wine, talking about their wives and the bride's dress, talking about being lesbian and gay, talking about the weather. No one would see us but me, and maybe Hannah—Hannah would feel us. I hoped she would feel how committed I was to her, how I cared that she be well, feel good, that she know that even though I was terrible about coming to weddings, I was there in my mind with her and concerned about how she felt—her desire to fit in, her sense of romance, her greater conventionality: she liked roses, she liked champagne. I liked any other flower than a rose. I liked wine instead of champagne. Maybe I got some of that from my mother, who often wanted not to do the expected. But for Hannah, I wanted to be more what was expected—what she expected of me. I tried to live up to that every day, not only on this day of someone else's wedding.

We finished the dancing in my mind and climbed back up the stairs to our table. I was then out of the fantasy and back in the reality I shared with Hannah. "I came with you," I said, looking toward her. "It wasn't our wedding, but I came with you. I'm sorry I was so irritable."

"You're forgiven," she said.

"Are you ready to go home?" I asked.

"I am. I think we have spent enough time. You were right, dinner would have been too long."

Yet I knew that if I had been willing to do it, Hannah would have liked to have stayed for dinner and to have danced afterward when everyone else did—in the right time and place.

I put on my blue coat, preparing to leave. I felt Fresco tugging at my side. Hannah was waiting for me.

We walked back through the crowd of guests, said our good-byes to the brides, their relatives, and the minister, then found our way to the car.

As we began to drive home, I knew we both were thinking about the wedding and about all it raised, and, most importantly, about that earlier wedding—ours—that had occurred four years before when, in spite of my feelings about marriage, and Hannah's, too, we became "spouses for life." That was a very different type of event than this, yet, in some ways, much the same—in terms of the inner emotions involved, in terms of my inner feelings, my reluctance and yet my efforts to embrace, to push away the negatives, to grasp what was good, and in terms of Hannah's steadfast desire to have me with her, to bring me close.

"We got there on time," I said to her as we drove.

"We did. I think Michelle and Jennifer were glad we came."

I reached over and tousled her hair, stroked the back of her neck.

"Are you glad we didn't have a formal wedding?" I asked her.

"I liked our wedding, and I liked that we took the dogs down to the beach afterward."

"Let's do that next week."

"Yes, let's."

Ten

Therapy

She came over to our house to meet with us in our living room. Eva was the psychotherapist Hannah and I had been seeing every two weeks for the past thirteen years and whom we had first seen nearly thirty years ago in the beginning of our relationship. We were now newly back from our trip to New Mexico and I was eager to show her my photos. Always, when we came back from our trip in recent years, we showed Eva our photos, and she would marvel at them—the colors, the sunrises, the broad open space of the desert. She would admire the pictures and convey a sense of how important she thought it was that we took this trip together each year.

This visit from Eva was different than usual. Normally, we met in her office across town. But as of this January, she had retired. We had last seen her in December just prior to taking our trip. She was going to close her office soon and we would not see her anymore for a session. I hadn't been sure, when we left, if we would get along well afterward when we were no longer seeing Eva. Would we get along on our trip? Without her anchor, her advice, her belief in us, her habit of telling us at the end of a session, "Now say something positive you feel about the other," or "You love each other. Remember that."

I always wondered why she thought we loved each other, why that was so important, so obvious. Didn't other couples love each other, too, even couples who split up? But for us, it felt to me like a mystery, a secret revealed, something I hoped was true, said as if it were so.

"We love each other, that's why we get along," I thought. "We love each other, we're going to survive all this." And by "all this" I meant the hard parts, the things we went to Eva to help us with.

I see us in the office where we met with her over those years. I see us driving over, across the San Francisco hills. Hannah would say to me, "What would you like to talk about today, dear?" And I would say, "I don't know. I don't like to plan it in advance. I like to go with what comes up."

Hannah, I knew, liked to plan things in advance. If she had her way, we would discuss and plan a joint strategy every time before meeting with Eva. We would have an agenda and know what to do. Never in all the years we saw Eva did we plan and agree on a course of action in advance before our couples therapy session. I'm not sure if Hannah thinks it would have gone better if we had done so, but I think it went fine as it was.

We would enter the office to meet with Eva after sitting close together on a narrow bench in the waiting room hallway, looking across at a picture of a landscape, beside us a small table lamp wrapped in brown twine, the feeling of the waiting room subdued and intimate. Then Eva would open the door, smile, and welcome us into her inviting office.

I hadn't met Eva before. Hannah had seen her with a previous woman lover and recommended her highly to me. She felt good about Eva even though that prior relationship had broken up. I was particular about psychotherapists. Hannah knew that about me. So I thought Eva must be someone very good indeed if Hannah was introducing her to me.

We first met with Eva soon after Hannah's father died, a loss that I felt had unsettled things between us. I was never quite sure how or why. But I know I felt, "Maybe I'll lose Hannah. It feels like she might not want to be with me anymore." That was in the eighth year of our relationship, five years after we had moved in together. That period is murky in my mind, but I recall feeling things were hard-edged between us, that I was not living up to Hannah's expectations of me.

There was an incident to do with spoons that figured in my mind. I remember going into that first meeting with Eva thinking about how I had just bought two long-handled stainless-steel spoons for us to use in cooking, when really, I thought, one would have been enough, as Hannah had repeatedly advised me. I was feeling guilty about buying the spoons when we walked into the office to meet with Eva.

The office had white walls and tall windows looking out on a side yard, letting in light and giving a feeling of openness. I saw three large, comfortable padded chairs—one for Eva, one for Hannah, and one for me. I felt the coolness of leather and of the space around us as I sat down.

"Hello, I'm glad to meet you," Eva said in a rich voice as welcoming and open and other-concerned as a person's voice could be. I liked her immediately. She was formal, but not too formal. She was a real person interested in helping us, a woman who seemed to me comfortable with a broad range of human emotions, not limited to any one doctrine, but who thought for herself after having her own varied experiences in life. She was also, I felt, comprehending of my own emotional life. From that very first time we met with her, I felt she accepted me, saw me amidst all my emotional pushes and pulls. She saw my emotional reality in an understanding way, took my inner challenges seriously, and I think she respected how I dealt with them. This was unusual for me, for I usually do not feel comprehended well by others.

Eva was also a lesbian, which made me feel she was akin to us. I felt grateful for her graciousness and direct style.

"It's about the spoons," I must have finally said after we had been talking for a while. Hannah looked at me and seemed surprised. This was not a subject prominent in her mind.

I remember that room, I remember the chairs, I remember Hannah sitting not far from me in one of them. I see Eva sitting across from us nodding, receptive. I felt a slight tension between Hannah and me, an uncertainty about what would occur. I know we must have presented some thoughts about ourselves and why we were here. But the exact content of our discussion escapes me.

"See you next week," Eva said when we left.

We walked out of that small building through the narrow tan hallway bathed in the soft light of the table lamp. We stepped down the front stairs onto the sidewalk, and I felt ready to cry. Would it work out? Would Eva be able to help us? Would Hannah still love me? Would we stay together or would we have to split up?

I doubt that Hannah felt the same way. I don't know if she had the prospect of our breaking up very much in her mind. I think the experience was different for each of us. But I know she took my hand. "I love you," she said as we walked down the street toward my car. "We're in this together," she said a few moments later. Or I would like to believe she said that. I know it is what she said—even if not in exactly those words—every single time we left Eva's tucked-away office over the years—no matter how difficult the sessions, no matter my tears, or my attempts to walk out, or the feelings of her own she had presented in a session—the challenges she felt with me—the things I did that upset her, made her feel that I did not "see" her, hear her, or treat her as important.

"I love you. Take my hand," she said. "We'll work it out. I feel better now. Do you feel better?" she asked as we walked.

"I guess so," I said, not knowing for sure, but wanting to feel better, and, in fact, feeling better because she did.

We saw Eva weekly for five months during that first period when we met with her. Her gentle way of having us engage with each other—by first speaking our minds, then listening, then responding thoughtfully to each other—helped settle things between us. Then we did not see her again until twelve years later when I had begun to lose my eyesight and it affected me so that I could no longer drive. Hannah would now have to do all our driving, which raised some difficulties between us, because it threw us together more, made us more interdependent. We had to choose routes together, plan our schedules more in concert, overcome our differences in how we might do things.

I remember I felt very responsible at that time. I felt that my loss of eyesight was causing us problems, so I should initiate, and I suggested to Hannah that we meet with Eva again. By then, she had moved to a different office that was down the hall from the first. There was a couch, a long, low table in front of it. I sat on the couch. Across from me, Hannah sat in a wooden chair with a straight back for support. Eva sat in a larger chair near her. I remember I missed the soft square chairs we had before. After a couple of years, my guide dog Teela was with us and lay on the rug at my feet.

When I think of that second period when we met with Eva, what comes to mind immediately for me is the fact that I cried. I do not usually cry. I have cried when I feel hurt by Hannah, or occasionally when a trying external event happens. I cry in frustration at those times, I think. But with Eva, in that little room with the tall windows and the three of us, I cried in a different way. I cried because I wanted to be understood and because I did not want to be hurting Hannah.

I sometimes felt that Hannah was too hard on me, that she expected me to be perfect for her, expected me to live up to expectations that I often did not know if I could live up to, that I did not even know were there.

In our sessions, Hannah told me that in addition to the pressures she felt from her job, she put great effort into trying to please me, and she very much needed to feel she was good enough, not constantly to feel she was being told she was lacking in relation to me. She needed me to truly see her, to understand the pressures she was under. She felt upset when I did not.

I felt hurt. I did not want to look bad in Eva's eyes. I did not want to hurt Hannah. I struggled to tell "my side of the story." In telling that side, I cried, for I was dredging up deep emotions, even if briefly, and my words came out with much feeling.

I was aware that I did not cry in my own individual psychotherapy sessions, which I had been engaged in for many years, and I did not cry in this way alone with Hannah at home. Why here? Why now? I thought it was Eva—that she was so good in understanding human inner emotional life and in relating to me that I felt I could cry with her, that she would understand.

But I think that it wasn't Eva entirely. It was because Hannah was there. She made it safe for me to cry with Eva and with her. Had I been meeting with Eva alone, I doubt that I would have spoken so often through tears. But with Hannah present to engage me and to puncture my defenses—to prod me, to release me, to be there witnessing, and then to be there when all was said and done—only with her intimate presence and support was I able to speak from my emotions, to delve as deep, to unfold, to burst forth as our earlier therapist had said, like a storm. "Think of her outbursts as a beautiful storm," she had told Hannah back in the first years of our relationship.

But my outbursts now were not the same as before. I wasn't throwing things, I wasn't getting mad at Hannah. I was simply crying, crying because I felt I had been wronged, telling about how I had been upset and how I tried and how I wasn't understood, and how I wanted to be helpful, wanted to be helped, telling about how all of it hurt.

Then I stopped, relieved.

"Thank you," Eva said. "I'm glad you told us that."

She made me feel that I had just said the most wonderful thing in the world and that she was grateful.

Then Hannah would say, "Yes, thank you. I really mean that."

"Now each of you say something good you feel about the other," Eva said before we left. Then we walked down the front stairs and out onto the street.

I think those sessions every two weeks when we met with Eva were a safety valve for Hannah and me. They helped us to talk to each other and try to fix what was going wrong between us. They helped me to stop and show Hannah that I saw her, cared for her, that she was important, that I could let her go as well as go places with her. They helped me correct some of my thoughtless behaviors in relation to Hannah so that she would not feel slighted or hurt. And they helped her, I think, understand me better and accept me, possibly, in part, because Eva did.

But beyond that, I think those sessions were a safety valve because they were a release. All that Hannah had pent up— about her responsibility for driving us, about my needs, about what was wrong in her life that I might have caused—could be aired, though afterward she might say, "I am not being critical of you."

"Then present it to Eva in a way that does not sound critical, that sounds like it's just the way you feel, not a reflection of what I am actually doing. It hurts me to feel I am hurting you."

"I'll try," she said. And then she would begin speaking again, explaining it differently.

That safety valve function, I could feel it tangibly in the air after each of our sessions.

When Eva was about to retire, I feared what would happen when we no longer had the protection of the sessions. I feared that Hannah would keep things pent up, and when they were pent up she would resent me. She would stop being nice to me. Maybe she would reject me. Maybe we would split up. She would abandon me, and then I would abandon her, withdraw or give up. One or the other of the doors to our studies down the long hallway in our house would close.

"Do you love me even after all that?" I would ask Hannah, time and again, on our way home after seeing Eva.

"Yes. Do you love me?"

When I think of how Eva helped us, I hear again, in my mind, things she said to us over the years.

"When that happens, you are each going back to an old place," she would often say to us when Hannah spoke painfully of something I had done that hurt her, and I, in turn, would go back to my own hurts—to feeling that Hannah did not understand me or see my efforts in a positive light.

"Don't go there," Eva would say. "Stop. Take a breath. You have hit a snag."

"Well, if she'll say it without making it seem like my fault," I said.

"Wait," Eva said, holding up her hand.

"I'm ready," Hannah said. "I can try now."

For one of my worst feelings was that I had done something terrible affecting Hannah, that I would be viewed as a bad person by Hannah and Eva. How could I be viewed as okay if I had hurt Hannah so? Then my own hurt would get to be too much and I would want to walk out of the session. More than once, I tried. I got up out of my seat on the couch, Teela stirring at my feet, and began to walk out.

"Don't," Eva and Hannah both said.

"You go on without me. Let her tell you how she feels when I am not here. It's too painful for me to hear." I covered my ears.

"We won't talk when you are not here," Eva said. "It has to be the two of you."

"What can I do to make it easier for you?" Hannah asked, jumping in, so practical, as was her way, wanting to solve a problem between us.

I held back my tears. I sat back down. I would try to stay and listen.

Always that was the hard part for me—being able to hear about what Hannah felt had been hurtful without being overwhelmed by my feeling like a failed person, a poor lover, a phony. How could someone be this lacking and still be in a relationship with a woman she loved?

I sat back. Hannah tried to explain carefully. "When Susan does this: When she comes into my room, when she asked if we can go another place that afternoon and is hurt when I say I am too busy—when she doesn't seem to appreciate the pressures I am under, I feel not seen, and not appreciated for how much I already do. I drive her places she wants to go. She has lost more of her vision now. I have to watch out for her. It's a lot of responsibility. I already do a lot."

"But what about what I do?" I verged on saying, wanting to interrupt, having trouble hearing her at any length. "But what about me? What about my side? I go so many fewer places than before. I don't want to be limited because Hannah is limited, because she has a bad back and so she doesn't like to drive. Then I get limited because of what she can't do. I know it's not true; it's my eyesight that causes this. But I feel that way."

Eva looked toward me when Hannah was through. "Take your time," she said. "But first tell her you understand, you hear what she is saying."

Eva was so even-handed. Always, with her, it was that Hannah would say how she felt and would have to be understood by me as I listened. Then I would get a chance to say my part. Or we would do it in the reverse, with me speaking first. Nothing either of us ever did caused Eva to diverge from her approach of treating us equally.

For Hannah and me, this was often a new thought, because each of us tends to believe that she is right, that the other person is wrong, or has done wrong and should apologize. I think Hannah does this more than I do. She more often feels that she is right and I am wrong when I have hurt her feelings, that it is not equal. Often, outside of a therapy session—both back then and to this day—I like to say to her, "There's two of us. It's got to be both of us that have caused a problem between us. It can't just be me."

She will sometimes reluctantly agree—or at least present the appearance of it—and we will both apologize, making things better. The apology so often goes a long way. Hannah used to have to understand why a problem occurred each time—analyze it and talk it out. But in recent years, she has seemed to me to take it more on faith that both of us contributed. We each hurt the other's feelings. So we each should apologize and maybe we won't have the same problem again.

Maybe it's because of all those years of seeing Eva and our learning to separate out what was hurting each of us in response to the other person. Maybe we each, by now, have a better sense that it's one of those deep-seated fears or injuries from our pasts that comes between us, causing hurt because we are so close.

Maybe that's what Eva meant to say sometimes when she told us, "You love each other, remember that. You are very close. What each of you does affects the other."

I often think about how close we are when I get hurt or upset by a problem between us. "It's because we're close," I tell myself. "What each of us does affects the other. It's not something so terrible."

I recall another thing Eva said that stays with me still. Sometimes I would start to say something in a session, then I would take it back, or start over, lapse into silence again. "Don't take it back," Eva would say. I keep that in mind often when I resist my impulses to articulate a thought or a feeling, when I try to keep it in because I am criticizing it before it gets out.

In our therapy sessions, speaking was often hard for me, both keeping things in and offering them outward.

I remember often sitting in that therapy room thinking, "It's about Hannah. I'm here to listen to her. We're in couples therapy because I've done something wrong, because I'm not a good enough partner, because she has misgivings about me. We're here so we can fix this and so I can act better." I never felt, "We're here because I have complaints about Hannah." I didn't think I had complaints. Or if I did, they were minor. Or worse: they might indicate it was not right for me to be with her. If something was wrong, then it all was wrong. "We're here so I can keep up my side, keep everything together, not let our relationship fall apart," I thought. "And maybe if Hannah understands me better, she will not be so upset by me."

I would listen to Hannah speaking and Eva supporting her and think, maybe somehow this process of discussion will help. I wanted so much to ease things between us, to feel the warmth and closeness I usually felt with Hannah, for the difficulties to recede.

At the start of that second period of seeing Eva, it was my loss of eyesight that brought us to the sessions. But after an initial time, the subject of our meetings with Eva extended far beyond my eyesight and became basically about us—how we interacted, our dependencies on each other, how we helped each other, what we did when things went wrong, what we did together that was good.

I often worried when listening to what Hannah had to say about a problem, wondering if the repeated airings of difficulties was worth it. But I knew Hannah believed in the rational approach of the therapy, that we should not let things go wrong. We should understand them. I might have been more willing to just let things explode sometimes. But I also shared Hannah's desires to have our relationship be good, not a simmering broth of unmet needs—her sense that we should not indirectly act out when we got hurt, but go someplace and talk about how we felt.

I know I was a reluctant talker about myself and how I felt except when I was reacting to Hannah. I have been a reluctant talker about myself in individual psychotherapy sessions as well. I tend to be resistant. I have a hard time letting someone else in to see what I am really feeling or dealing with emotionally. I think Hannah knew that. "Thank you," she said often when we left the session and began walking down the street. "Thank you for telling me how you really feel underneath." That was my reward. I would glow inside when she said it. I was measuring up after all. We were working things out as we should.

Still, dealing with the underlying hurts was difficult.

I was always surprised when there was yet a new problem that Hannah felt we had to discuss every two weeks. I didn't like that she was sometimes afraid to tell me about her complaints or hurts while we were alone at home, that she needed the protection of the session with Eva to do so. But that might just be how it had to be.

Hannah has since told me she feels that one of her most important insights from our time with Eva was that she could tell me what she needed, and I would say, "Yes, I can do that." She did not need to keep it all simmering inside. She could have her needs met from me if she articulated them.

"Both of you think there's not enough to go around," Eva said to us one day, looking over toward Hannah and then me. I thought about that later. The meaning wasn't obvious. It was like what might happen in a family with many children, I thought. It would feel like there were too many and not enough food or resources or love for them all.

We were just two of us. But the thought still might apply. Maybe when Hannah felt I did not see her, she felt I was limited in my resources—that when I was focusing on myself, I didn't have any extra to give to respond to her needs. Similarly, when I felt that she was too busy to help me, or that she was going to be away from me when I wanted her presence, I felt the world would close in, that I would be left abandoned, without resources, bereft, unable to take care of myself. And it wasn't only the feeling of not enough resources to go around from the other person—it was a sense of there being not enough in the universe.

"There's enough to go around," I would sometimes say to myself after that. "This is not the end of the world. There's enough."

Eva's statement seemed to me a particularly female perspective with its concern for nurturance. Maybe where Hannah and I came from, I thought, the limitations of our parents—the limitations of mothering—gave us a sense that there was not enough, that there was scarcity. Maybe we each had felt that growing up—or maybe people in general felt it sometimes.

I thought of Eva's comment more often than I expected to. It had the effect of lifting a darkness, a shroud, a weight, a sense of limitation. The universe wasn't limited. My world wasn't limited. Hannah wasn't inadequate in relation to me, even if, at the moment, I felt it so.

I looked over at Eva after she had spoken, admiring her thought, the way she put it. I felt as if a gust of fresh air had just entered the room as light filtered in through the tall windows.

I looked toward Hannah. Did Eva's comment mean as much to her as it did to me? She looked back at me. I could not tell. But she smiled and looked at me thoughtfully.

"I can," I said. "I can respond to you later when I can't at the time. Can you remember that? I can often do what you need later. But right at that moment, I'm afraid, or I'm hurt. I can't see how I can do it."

I was thinking, right then, of times when Hannah might want to be out at night with friends or stay late down on the campus—and I would be worried about how I would get along without her. How could she leave me just when I needed her? What would I do? I underestimated my own resourcefulness at those times, I thought. I couldn't say yes to her. I couldn't say, "It's fine with me if you go." Instead I said nothing, simply gave her a disapproving look, indicating that it was somehow not all right that she go.

"It's okay," I would say in the end. But I might get upset about it afterward and tell her about it on her return. For I had a habit of thinking that some things would not cause me a problem and only finding out later that they did.

"You have to be careful," I told myself many times. "Don't say it's okay and then suffer the consequences."

"If you go to Berkeley that day," I had to learn to say to Hannah, "then I am going to feel abandoned. What should we do?"

"Maybe if I call you between my events when I'm out . . . ," she began.

We talked about it in a session.

"What if she does that?" Eva asked.

"Okay," I said.

Hannah smiled. She liked to solve things: to have life work out for her as she wanted it to, and, at the same time, to address my fears, my sensitivities.

However, I do not see our sessions with Eva as primarily problem solving about what we should do in a practical way in relating to each other. I remember them as primarily airing the underlying feelings—the slights or hurts that Hannah felt, the reactions or hurts I, too, felt. Then we would tell Eva sometimes about our accomplishments—things we did together, places we went, times when our interactions worked out well, our trip—that big trip, that achievement each year—the trip we took to New Mexico. We would tell her about how we added a guide dog and then a second guide dog to our household, and about how we got married.

"There's enough to go around," Eva had said and I subsequently often said to myself.

"You are close," she had also said.

Hannah and I were close, I knew. But we also felt very separate to me. Maybe some of it is because I often feel locked inside myself. I cannot reach out easily. I am a very internal person. So much goes on inside and I am not sure what to let out, what will make things feel good between Hannah and me.

During our sessions, I was often aware of how Hannah had a very demanding job that put public pressures on her. I had a more limited university position and concentrated on my research and writing, so my pressures were more internal and harder to speak of. When Hannah would sit in the therapy session and talk about the demands of her work in taking care of students or sitting on committees, for instance, I would feel, "But what about me? The demands I feel are more often internal. They are not about external relations or a university structure. But there is a lot of pressure there, too. I have to fight constantly a sense of being a failure, of not living up to conventional expectations of success, and I am doing it more on my own without much outside support. I miss the rewards that you get from an institution."

But Hannah, I knew, shared her rewards, shared her resources, her praise of me—it was because she had the larger institutional position that I could have so much opportunity to do my own work. And always, she read my writing and helped me with it, gave me advice, sharing her expertise. Still, my isolation often made me feel less valuable, less worthy than I wished.

I looked toward Hannah to tell me I was worthy, to tell me I was good. She did that often, and not only about my work, but in her affirmations for who I was.

I thought sometimes about how we each had different political views of what went on in the world around us. While we were both left of center, Hannah was more liberal, I felt, while I was more radical. To an outside observer, our differences might seem minimal, but to me, they loomed large. "Why couldn't she see things as I did?" I thought.

As we sat in the therapy sessions, the ways we were different often struck me. Hannah's speech style, it was different from mine. She was direct, often using currently popular words, while I was more lost in my words sometimes. I was more an "original," Hannah would sometimes say to me—"You are Susi generis."

I thought about how, in our life together, Hannah liked to fit things into a limited time, and I liked to leave time open; how she was always planning the future; how I wanted so much to stay in the present, neither with a past nor a future; how she was practical, and how I wasn't; how I liked to get lost, how she liked to be found. I thought about the different foods we each liked, the different places we liked to go. I wondered how I ever could be with this person who was so unlike me. I felt so unmanageable, so often out of line, feared not measuring up.

I would see our differences, yet see us sitting there together, with Eva sitting across from me near Hannah on the other side of the low coffee table, determined not to let us stray too far apart.

She would turn to Hannah when Hannah was through speaking about an interaction between us, then ask, "What would you like to hear from Susan?"

"I'd like to know she understood what I was saying." Then she would state specifically what she would like me to understand.

And I would repeat it back to her: "That when I walk into the kitchen, you would like to feel that I see you, even if my eyesight is limited. I should try to walk around you, not bump into you."

"I know that you can't always do that," Hannah said. "But it would be nice. What's important to me is that you're thinking of it, that you'll be aware that I'm there. Maybe we can work out some way to get around it—like you saying, 'I'm going toward the refrigerator now.'"

"Okay," I said, resolving that I would check for Hannah's presence and announce my moves in the kitchen more often in the future, resolving to remember to tell Hannah that I saw her, was aware of her, was interested in her day, in her experiences—make my interest, my attention, more explicit than I often did.

Still, I had felt hurt when Hannah said that she felt I did not see her—as she did at other times too—because I felt I did see her, was interested in her. But she didn't feel it. That was the point. I might feel it inside, but she did not feel it. I would have to tell her.

I knew that when I interrupted her telling me about something she did that day, for instance, if I said my opinion or strayed from the subject, it might hurt her because it made her feel I wasn't paying attention to her—that she wasn't important, that she did not exist.

I have tried to improve, and I think the therapy helped highlight the basic theme—that I need to make clear to Hannah that I am interested in her, focused on her, that I care, that she is the center of my universe, at least for that moment in time.

But then what happens to me? I get lost. I so easily get lost. I get lost in the two of us. I get lost in her.

In my way, I think, I have a version of what Hannah has—a sense of disappearing, of being easily not seen. Maybe because we are so close, we disappear into each other. We lose ourselves into our differences—oddly not our similarities, but our differences—how she is not me, how I am not her. She goes to the university when I stay home and work in my study. What's wrong with me, I feel, why am I not her? How can I listen to her—take on her world, be in it, center myself on her—and not feel bad or lacking for who I am? And how can I see her as not lacking because she is not me?

I thought about lesbianism often when faced with the dilemmas of identity raised in our sessions. Maybe Hannah and I were so close because we were both women. We didn't have those other sorts of boundaries between us—the male boundaries, the lines that separate the genders. We were women raised to be supportive of the other person, interactive with the other, merged with the other, feeling for the other, losing oneself. We were women who cared intimately for each other. We were one, and yet not one. We had dreams of nurturance, dreams that we would each be each other's "good mother." It would be heavenly when we were together. It would be peaceful and comforting. It would be perfection.

I sometimes thought back on *The Mirror Dance*, the book I wrote so long ago that was the basis for Hannah's and my first meeting each other that fateful day when I asked her for help with my lesbian community study, and she, curiously, believed that was the reason I had come to her office.

Back then, when I was working on that study, I had to think, in detail, about what made lesbians different. What made a lesbian community different? I had interviewed a therapist who saw quite a few members of that Midwestern lesbian group. She said that it was like a "mirror dance"—the women in their relationships were opposites of each other and yet the same. It was like a dance of sameness and difference. She had observed, and I, too, saw in the community, the fact that the women had idealistic expectations of each other—that here there would be the ideal of perfect nurturance, perfect care, perfect acceptance—and then they felt extreme disappointment when they did not experience perfection.

I thought of some of those findings when I looked at Hannah and me. And I thought further: there was something about us that was so natural, that suggested more. Maybe it's about the vulnerability—the openness to each other—and about the small things, the "under the radarness" of our life together—the ways the small daily details mask so much depth of feeling, and the general invisibility of it all—the deceptiveness, the camouflage in the face of the outer world, the sense of "Now I see you. Now I don't." It was partially a mystery to me still. How are we different? How are we similar? What difference does it make that we are lesbians—two women seeking intimacy with each other, two women going to a therapist to help us be a better couple, to help us get along—to help us to accept, to value, to cherish who we each are—to feel less lonely in the world, more understood, more seen, more touched, more protected, less uncertain about who we are and more confident in our togetherness.

"Now each of you say something you like about the other," Eva said, turning to us.

I looked over at Hannah.

"I like that you take care of me. You take care of our home. I like going places with you," she said.

"You're adorable. I like that you help me. I feel happy when I am with you."

"Do you really feel that?" Hannah asked, as if she had expected less.

"I do."

During the years we saw Eva, much happened in our life outside the therapy sessions. Hannah's mother died. My mother died. Each of us researched and wrote books and taught our classes. Hannah traveled for her work. I stayed home and worked and took care of our pets. We took trips to the coast together, went back East sometimes to see family, and began taking our trip to New Mexico each year with a new sense of commitment. I got my first guide dog, Teela, while we were seeing Eva, and brought her into the session immediately, where Eva and she became fast friends. We brought Esperanza, our little black poodle, into the session once, along with Teela, so Eva could meet her. When Teela retired and I received my second guide dog, Fresco, Hannah and I began coming to Eva's office with two big, beautiful, golden dogs.

When our books came out, we brought them in to Eva. She came to each of our book talks at that time, and we attended one of hers, for she had written a novel.

We brought in photos from our trips to New Mexico. Eva was a painter in part of her life and admired especially the design and the colors. We reported back to her about our trip each time, proud of the ways we had worked things out—so Hannah had "snow days" when she did not have to drive, and I had "running around" days when we could be constantly on the road. Eva enjoyed our trip, enjoyed sharing it with us, made us feel that how we worked things out was important, the problems minor by comparison with the positive experiences we shared. She was there when we left, and there to welcome us back. It was again that feeling of having a safety net—that it's okay to go away, it's okay to come back. It's okay to go away because when we return, Eva will be there, affirming, letting us know that we are good, that we care for each other, that how we care for each other will hold us together.

When I think back on those years of our therapy sessions, I feel again the difficulties I had in listening when Hannah had complaints or felt that I had hurt her feelings. I remember the emotions involved and how I cried, at times, and, through my tears, came to speak.

I remember the more difficult moments—maybe because I was so glad, after the sessions, to have Hannah take my hand and give me a kiss, to have us settle down, back to pushing the distressing feelings away. I remember the difficult times, and I think it's important that they occurred. But what's harder—more invisible, in a way, to remember—is the cloaking feel of that room, and, more importantly, of Eva's presence—who she was for us. She was there providing a place where we could each speak, tell our side of the story. But more than that, she was providing an ambiance that said, time and again, "It's good. You are good together. You love each other. Remember that. You have these 'snags,' these things that don't work out all right. But don't let that undermine you. See it. Say it. Sit with each other. Try to understand where all this comes from. But don't, don't ever let it destroy you."

That faith in us was a faith I never entirely understood—but I believed in Eva, I thought she was talented, knowledgeable, astute.

I believed she must know something I perhaps did not: that the important thing was how we cared for each other—that we cared deeply, cared more than any problem that could come between us, cared more than the hurts, so they could not undermine us.

"Love," Eva used that word. But I never knew quite what that meant. And then I knew it all too well, too deeply. It's an attachment, a deep feeling of—She's here with me. We're together. Our fate is intertwined. The good—all the good that can come from the world to me—and to her—it depends on us together. We're intricately connected. When she walks away from me, my heart hurts. When she looks at me crossly, I hurt. When she comes home with joy in her heart, joy from her day, I am happy too. When she loves, I glow.

I would go through anything, face my fears, be patient or go into action, anything to help her, to befriend her, simply to be with her.

She is my friend.

When Eva came to visit us after she had retired, we were just back from our trip to New Mexico. As we sat with her in the familiarity of our living room, after we had shown her our photos and caught up, she took out a piece of paper on which she had written some thoughts for us to help guide our transition into the future when we would no longer be seeing her.

She was sitting across from me in a wooden rocker, Hannah to my side on the couch. I sat on a chair with Fresco at my feet, Teela had inched over and was now lying close to Eva.

"Here are my wishes for you this year and for many years to come," she began:

Always be grateful for the love you have for each other. It is the greatest gift.

Listen to each other. Remember that she is your friend and wants the best for you. Don't make assumptions. Ask questions.

There will be "snags" but remember that those will pass. Be patient. Those moments are like the changing weather.

Know that you care deeply for each other and always will. Trust your love.

Respect your differences. You chose her for everything she is.

Celebrate the gifts you have been given and have fun!!

Eva then handed to me, and I put in Hannah's hand, a small smooth rock wrapped in a red velvet pouch that she suggested we put in a special place like an altar, where it might help us remember.

That red cloth bag with the smooth black rock inside now sits in our living room on a bookcase under a lamp not far from where Eva sat that day when she visited and gave us her wishes for us.

I wish always to remember them, and I wish to remember Hannah and me sitting across from each other in Eva's secluded office, trying to figure out, time and again, how to do it better—how to be better with each other, how to provide the assurances, the love, we each need. There's no roadmap for this, I thought, as I did often on our travels—no roadmap at all.

It's been five years now since we last saw Eva. Hannah and I talk sometimes about difficult things in the way we did back in our sessions—but only occasionally. More often, we rely on our lessons having been learned long ago. But sometimes still, when things come up that emotionally threaten to divide us—when I fear Hannah's response and she perhaps mine—when our faith in each other fails—"Where's Eva," I think. "I wish we could see Eva again."

And then I hear her, "You love each other. There's enough to go around." I look toward Hannah, reach for her hand. "Let's go in the dining room and talk," I say.

Part IV

Who We Are

Eleven

Are You Two Sisters?

I had just stepped out of a bar in southern New Mexico, near the border of Arizona, New Mexico, and Mexico, in a tiny, isolated desert town. A man followed me out, opening the door for me, offering to help me to my car. "Are you two sisters?" he asked in a challenging tone as I stepped out of the dark bar and into the open air. He had seen me with Hannah inside while she was paying for our lunch in the adjoining restaurant. I heard his question but did not answer, simply headed for the car. My guide dog Fresco was leading me, eager to get there. The man, having seen I was blind when I stumbled a bit and bumped into tables as I made my way out of the dim interior of the bar, now offered to assist me further, following me as I walked across the dusty parking lot. "Do you need some help?" he asked. Then again, "Are you two sisters?" "No," I said to the first question and got into the car hurriedly when I reached it.

Why do people ask if we are sisters? I thought. But more than that, I felt aware of having been asked this question many times before. Often it occurred when Hannah and I were traveling. Did women often travel with their sisters? I wondered. Was that why people asked me about it, or assumed that we were two sisters? I thought at first that could be so. But underneath, I doubted it. I thought it was because we were lesbians, because we both had short hair, because, perhaps, we were familiar with one another—in a casual, intimate way—because we were not wearing makeup or dressy, femme-style clothes. At home sometimes, it had happened, too. A repair person would come to the house to fix the furnace or the garage door and assumed that we were sisters, commenting on it, in fact. Why did they comment? Why did they ask? Why would it matter if we were sisters or not?

I think it's similar to what happens when I am out with my guide dog and the dog is leading me. People ask, "Are you training that dog?" as if it's a question that would settle something more haunting, like, "Are you blind? Or are you sighted like me?"

In this case, the familiar occurrence would be that we were sisters—that would explain us—rather than that we were lesbians. But what do I do, turn around and say to the man in the bar, "No, we're lesbians"? I didn't want to say that because I didn't want to endanger myself. It was broad daylight. We had just had lunch. But it was at a bar and it was in a kind of no man's land out where the range stretches and there are no houses or stores for miles, where the mountains sprawl far into the distance, their huge, looming, dark figures silhouetted like proud majesties, like islands of imposing presence against the broad sky. "Why have some drunk discuss lesbianism with me?" I thought. But I also thought, "Why am I afraid—afraid to tell him what I am, afraid to be a lesbian out in public?" It was 2017, surely a time when people knew what it was, or might be more accepting than in the past when people, usually men, were beaten up in bars for being gay. I wasn't a man, and we were two women, innocuous looking enough to be mistaken for two sisters. Why not have the nerve to say, "No, we're lesbians," looking him in the eye—to the extent I can do that—and seeing what his response would be. Would he strike out at me? Or would he simply stand there and stare? "I see," he would say, or "I thought so." But I kept my back turned to him, said nothing, opened the door of the car and got in.

Hannah came out later and I told her. "He asked if we were sisters," I said.

"What did you tell him?"

"I didn't answer," I said. "I was afraid."

She drove us off quietly, not criticizing me for my cowardice, probably feeling that my not responding was the safe and right thing to do in the circumstance, but also feeling, I thought, "We should be able to do this. We should no longer be afraid of a man in a bar."

As we drove farther south that day, the man's question haunted me, making me think about lesbianism and what it meant to me, about Hannah and me and who we were—our safety, our boundaries, our sense of separateness, our dreams. The surrounding desert landscape stimulated my thoughts as we passed miles and miles of arid ranchland—though it wasn't as denuded as it looked, just more bare than the land we knew back at home. Although my vision is blurry and leaves much out, I could get a general feel for the countryside, the endless, dry fields. Barbed-wire fences stretched into the distance. Scattered cows roamed.

We did not get far enough to see the exotic sheep I had read about, that were on someone's ranch on the way through Arizona. But we did see, and stop at, the Geronimo Monument—a tower of stones reaching toward the sky with a plaque in the middle. I had always wanted to visit this Geronimo monument, so the plain tower of stones by the roadside was a letdown for me, seeing how important Geronimo was in my life. When I lived in New Mexico, I had found a small, spirited, black dog I named Geronimo, after I heard the Michael Martin Murphy song "Geronimo's Cadillac," a slow dirge of a song that would make you feel you were there, driving a long, low Cadillac through the desert, a black Cadillac, with an open roof, a convertible, and with your dog, your little black dog whom you had gotten from the pound.

I had no Geronimo these days. Esperanza, our small, black dog who had succeeded him, was gone too. But Hannah was with me and we were out in the open, going where no man, or no woman, or no women like us had gone before. Many women had come this way, of course, but it always felt like it was just us—on an empty road, moving forward, unsure where the road would take us, headed toward Mexico, or Arizona first and then Mexico, headed toward places where we did not know if we would be safe.

"I think we are no longer in New Mexico," Hannah said after a while. "Do you know where we are?"

"I think we are in Arizona."

"Did you see a sign? I didn't see a sign."

"I don't see very well," I said. "There could have been a sign. I think I saw something far back that said 'Entering Arizona.' It was on the state line road, or where the state line road was crossing the main road. Then the state line road disappeared. Maybe we are going back and forth between Arizona and New Mexico."

"I like to know where I am," Hannah said.

"Yes, I know."

"There's a sign." She pointed. "It says 'Arizona.' It doesn't say, 'Welcome to Arizona,' like the New Mexico signs say."

"Maybe they don't want us there. Maybe they already have enough people in Arizona," I said. "Maybe they are not welcoming. I always feel, in Arizona, that I have to leave quickly, that something bad will happen, like it did that time we stayed in the bed and breakfast across the border and I got food poisoning, an ear infection, and the flu. Do you remember that time?" I asked Hannah.

"Yes. That was a terrible time."

"You went out and got me a salad at the store when I was sick. The woman who ran the bed and breakfast told us they had coatamundis in the trees, scavengers like raccoons. She said to watch out for them because they would attack my guide dog. She had a poodle with long hair and she never cut his hair. I thought that was awful."

"It wasn't a good place," Hannah agreed.

"The next time we were in Arizona, we stayed in the motel in the foothills with the javelinas running around and I hated the mustiness of the motel room and the noise of the fans, so we left early."

"It's always good to come back to New Mexico after Arizona."

"I remember seeing the morning sun glowing over New Mexico, over the broad valley as we drove back, the sun coming from the east, making everything look golden. It was right to go back. 'Goodbye Arizona.'"

Yet here we were in Arizona again, crisscrossing the line, unsure which side we were on: the good place, New Mexico, or the bad place, the threatening, confusing place—Arizona, where they already had enough people and enough business, where they did not exactly welcome you with nice signs.

As we straddled and crossed the line between Arizona and New Mexico, I thought of the border between lesbian and straight, between Hannah's and my intimate world and the larger nonlesbian world around us—how often we moved between the two, how different they were, and yet how that difference was hard to pin down.

Lesbianism was much more hidden than the surrounding nonlesbian world. I had written about it, as had others, in an attempt to celebrate it, to know it, to determine what was "them" and what was "us." But as soon as I thought I had identified the uniqueness of being a lesbian, it seemed to disappear back into the surroundings.

It bothered me that lesbians now got married, that they often wanted to have children—as if that was natural and desirable, as if it made us just like them, as if not having children, not fitting in, was wrong, not now the norm.

I remembered back to when I saw my first lesbian therapist. One day when I finally asked if she was a lesbian, "I am a gay lady," she answered, then not long after that, referring to whether someone we knew was heterosexual—"the breeders," she said, shocking me at the time. I had never heard that word before referring to heterosexual women, and then it was there, "breeders," unapologetically there. I smiled. I told Hannah about it later.

"I've heard the term," she said.

Hannah was often more knowledgeable about these things than me. She had studied lesbian history. I simply had studied the lesbians around me in the present moment, observing them, thinking about it all, thinking about myself and how I was not mainstream even in that group. I remember that when I sent the manuscript of my book *The Mirror Dance* out to the community, one woman wrote to me upset that I was saying bad things about a lesbian community. Why was I doing that rather than emphasizing the good things—like describing how idyllic a community it was, how people really were different there and good to each other? "I did say good things," I told her, "but I'm a sociologist. I have to look for problems, or for what's difficult for people in relation to their group. It's a way I can be helpful."

What I did not say was that is how I myself experienced the lesbian community I had studied. Even though I sought to be part of it, I felt it was not an idyllic place where things were perfect. It was still hard to feel your individual identity in relation to the group. I was aware of feeling like an outsider or marginal even there.

But I was also incredibly moved—by the sense of being among women who had emotional longings for other women, women who had, deep in them, this same need as I did, women who braved the choice of breaking away from the heterosexual world—the world of men and male advantages, of males defining things, the world of a more rough exterior—choosing instead a world where the inner desire for loving and nurturance from another woman could be felt. This was a new world, a different one for me. I studied it. I needed to be part of it. I liked it, even as it scared me, made me feel not entirely part of the dream, suspicious of the idealistic expectations, not just like everyone else even here.

"How do you feel about lesbianism?" I asked Hannah in my mind as we continued on the road toward Douglas, Arizona. "Do you remember the song 'I would go through a desert for you? The thunder is shaking the roof of my car, I would go through a desert for you, and for me'?" I asked her.

"Of course, I know the song," she said. "Cris Williamson."

When I first met Hannah, we would go to "women's concerts," meaning lesbian concerts, and Cris Williamson was one of the singers. Hannah had her records. So did I. In our basement back at home, we have a big Cris Williamson poster showing her standing in the desert among multicolored red and brown cliffs looking off into the distance, a bandana on her forehead, the title of the poster the name of her record *Strange Paradise.* That poster is fading in our basement now, and dusty, but I do not have the heart to take it down and toss it away.

Cris Williamson was in Hannah's and my past, I thought. So much was in our past—a past where the line between lesbian and straight felt much more defined than it did now, a past where I felt lesbianism was something secret I felt proud of, that I alone had discovered.

"Do you remember that bookstore in Berkeley?" I asked Hannah as we continued driving. "Probably you don't. It wasn't there when you moved to California. But I remember it from back when I was in graduate school. It was on a side street in a garage, a woman's bookstore of some sort, or maybe a gay or poetry bookstore."

"I didn't know it," she said.

"I can still see the inside of it in my mind. I went there one day and found a spiral-bound version of the 1960s novel *Patience and Sarah*. It was called *A Place for Us* and it was in a white, wire spiral binding, the old-fashioned kind. I wish I had bought that book then. It was when the author was still calling herself Alma Routsong and I was just discovering lesbianism."

Now here we were, far from that bookstore in time and place, but no less lesbian, no less tied to the unpublished, and to the first published versions of old books, of books that told the truth about us, that impressed me with their boldness.

I remember other books from back then, lesbian novels that seemed illicit, that showed the darker side, "the love that dared not speak its name." I have always loved that phrase. It's how I feel about lesbianism, that the name is hard for me to speak—it's hard now, as it was back then. I still like it being hard to speak, as if that indicates something important about it—that it's vulnerable, an inner part of myself that I dare not have too exposed, that other women, too, I feel, dare not have too exposed. Or else why all this hiding of lesbianism, why all this making it seem "just like everyone else"?

It is hard to generalize. I don't think my lesbianism is the same as everybody else's. I don't know that I am living the dream enough. Maybe that is at the heart of it: the dream—the idyllic female world of loving and acceptance, softness, a woman's breast, a beautiful woman's breast, a drive off into the future— "Thelma and Louise" as lovers—but not sailing off into an abyss like they did in the movie. That was a bad ending, but surely that was the dream—the two women together, the romance, their open-ended adventure as they sped through the desert in their Thunderbird convertible.

Hannah likes to tell people that she and I saw three movies the year *Thelma and Louise* came out, all of them *Thelma and Louise*. For me, it was true. I don't see many movies. Even when I was fully sighted, I did not see many movies. But the ones I see stay in my mind, particularly those about the adventures and intimacies of women.

"Do you know where we are?" I asked Hannah as she drove us through the sprawling desert, her eyes focused on the road. "Are we in Arizona or New Mexico?"

"I'm not sure."

"Do you think I should have answered the man's question?"

Reaching her hand over, she rested it on mine. "It's good to protect yourself sometimes," she said.

As we drove on, the space opened out, the mountains receding farther into the distance, the fields on either side of the road endlessly broad.

"What's in Douglas, Arizona?" Hannah asked me.

"Stores like Walmart. Some old houses. I read about them. They're falling down. Maybe Victorians, left over from the height of the railroad era."

"Let's turn around," she said. "This road goes on forever and it's very bare. Or do you really want to go there?"

Visions of a wonderful place with dilapidated mansions, good Mexican food, and secret finds—Mata Ortiz pottery, maybe old Navajo weavings—images of treasures from my past and treasures from this part of the country loomed before me—all to be found in Douglas. But it wasn't Douglas I was after. It was some dream again, a dream with Hannah.

"I don't think we'll find anything in Douglas," I said finally. "It's not worth going there. I only had a dream."

"You have lots of dreams," she said. "Remember that time when your mother was coming to visit and you thought she should come for two weeks? I had to persuade you that you had a fantasy idea of how great it would be spending time with your mother. One week was more than enough."

Surely she was right. "You're right," I said. "I sometimes have higher expectations than the reality will turn out to be."

I looked around and the dry land seemed so flat as it stretched into nowhere, stretched toward Douglas, Arizona, and nameless places in Mexico. Why were those places in Mexico not on the

Arizona–New Mexico map that I carried in the car? I wondered. I wanted to know the names of the mountains and towns just across the border, but I would have to get another map to find them. Mexico was a land not comprehended by our standard U.S. road maps, I thought. Lesbianism was like that too, not on the map of what was usually seen and known. What should be on the lesbian map? I wondered. In Mexico, on some of my maps, the mountains we see in southern New Mexico—the Hatchets, the Alamo Hueco, the Animas, and the Peloncillos—they become in northern Mexico the Sierra Madres Occidental. But they are part of one contiguous mountain range.

I did not want the mountains to be the same on either side of the border, however. I wanted them to be different in Mexico, more exotic, far away, waiting for me to explore them, waiting like a pristine dream. I wanted lesbianism to be like that too. But would it be a disappointment? What has lesbianism been for me? Is it each of my relationships with different women, or is it my sense of being among women more generally, of lying back, feeling that a world of soft breasts and warm bellies surrounds me, is always there as a potential inviting place where I might go, where I might find true happiness, true comfort?

Then the reality hits—each woman provides only some comfort. There is no all-embracing "all." There is just me, only myself in the end, still seeking the dream, taking comfort in the creation of a fantasy each time. Even with Hannah, I feel I am constantly inventing something to make us feel special, to make us feel right, embroidering the softness of her breasts with all my feelings about female nurturance, with all my desires for a nurturance from a mother I never had, a mother who does not exist—who does not exist in any perfect form but always does as a dream.

"I don't need to go to Douglas," I said to Hannah. "Let's save your driving for places we really want to go, like Big Hatchet Mountain." For I knew that when we drive, it is always a weighing of one alternative of long hours of driving against another, because Hannah has to be careful about driving distances because of her back troubles. But she drives here in the never-ending desert for me, and so that we can go places together—and because, I think she would admit, she likes it now, likes the desert, feels she is here with me in my dreams, sharing those dreams with me, which was not always so. Initially, back long ago before we met, and even at first after we met—the dreams were only mine. But now we have some shared dreams, some places for just the two of us that we feel are special.

Hannah turned the car around on the endless road and we headed north, then got off the black asphalt state road and onto a more private dirt road. The road veered up a hill and to the right, then around to the left and right again, as if circling to get to a place where no one could find us. On either side of the road now were pastures, or what might, in the farthest regions of one's mind once have been pastures—though now they seemed like bare desert—though not entirely barren, each with its own kind of scrub: small plants and grasses whose names I wished I knew. We were surrounded by barbed wire fences that separated the rough, scrubby pastures from us. The road curved, climbed higher. But before it climbed farther, we passed a stretch of land to the side that, Hannah pointed out to me, was marked with street signs on rows of straight streets laid out in a grid stretching off into the desert.

"This was going to be a development," Hannah said. "Someone wanted to build a community here. This is for people who never came."

I was struck by the dream of the open desert, of a space where anything could happen, where anything might be built.

"What would it have been like for those people if they lived here?" I asked Hannah.

"I don't know. They never came. This was someone's dream."

"Would you like to live here?" I asked her.

"No. Would you?"

Probably not, but "Maybe," I thought. "Maybe I would." But not in one of those houses on the bare streets, one of those houses that wasn't really there. The streets were too harsh, too exposed and flat. There might soon be many people living in them. I wouldn't want to live there, I thought, as Hannah and I proceeded up the hill to higher ground.

Then I saw it, perched on the hill, waiting in the sunlight, surrounded by stretches of lower desert extending to mountains in both directions—to the east, where the sun would rise, and in the west, where it would set. There was a smaller house off to one side in a clearing atop the hill, a larger house, though low and hard to see, set back farther, and nothing else. There was a sense of nothing surrounding us but those mountains in the distance and those two low, earthen-colored houses waiting for us. One was the main house, the other a guest house. It was toward the guest house that we were headed.

"I'm glad we came here," Hannah said, getting out of the car in front of the guest house.

I turned and looked toward the magnificent, triangular-shaped mountain behind us. Our vantage point from atop the hill made it look close, as if I could reach out and touch it.

We live in a city, I thought, surrounded by square blocks of cement, surrounded by wooden houses edge to edge, bits of sky. And now we were here among mountains, extended desert as far as the eye could see, surrounded by open space, a bright sky, a broad graveled clearing as if set there simply for us to stand in and look at the mountains. We could pretend they were ours, pretend that we, two women from San Francisco, two lesbians, only recently married, living our own very private life—our own "different" life—we could pretend that we belonged here, were more than just visitors passing through.

Yet we were just that—bringing our lifestyle with us, but passing through—stopping here and there along the way, tasting what it was like—what it was like for others who were not us.

"It's so calm here," Hannah said. "But there's wind. Maybe we'll have a nice sunset."

That was Hannah, I thought, interested in sunsets. She likes sunsets and she likes the moon at night, while I like sunrises. I do not like when the darkness begins, and I never have had a fascination for the moon. Hannah will call me, at home, to come quickly to the window when she sees a full moon in the sky. Here, we didn't need a window. The moon, the sky would be every-where, not in patches like back at home.

We were here in the winter desert, a time I like to travel, be-cause there aren't many other people roaming around. The trees are bare, but I am used to it. I like seeing their singular shapes outlined, whereas trees with leaves on them blend together. We were here in the very southern desert, which, in wintertime, was good, I felt. In winter, there were not many poisonous insects and snakes. They came out in the hot weather. We had a biased view of what life was like here. It was all the more unreal. In the sum-mer, I wanted to remind Hannah, there were snakes and bugs. It wouldn't be pleasant for us.

People who lived here were used to the snakes and insects, however. A woman who was caring for this property had told us, a year ago, that, as a child, she liked collecting insects in a jar. She really liked insects. That was a strange fondness, I had thought. But I figured that if I lived here, I would like them too.

Down below our hill, somewhere in the flatlands, was the man from the bar who had asked me if we were two sisters. I looked over at Hannah as she stood beside me staring at the mountain across from us as if it might move at any moment—change color, change shape—which, in a way it did, but not right now. It changed with the different lights, the weather.

That man down below, what difference might it make to him if we were sisters? Maybe he would imagine us as non-sexual then. If he knew we were lesbians, then he could imagine us sexually. He could go home thinking, "I have met two lesbians."

It was like when I came home from walking with my guide dog and I had met another dog, whose name I asked, and whose breed. Then I could come home and tell Hannah, "I met Roscoe. He's a beagle, two years old." It would add to my repertoire of dogs I knew.

Similarly, if I had told him, we would then be memorable for the man. But meanwhile, I would feel very exposed. Would the man come in the night to get us? Would he say something bad, something naughty? All the images of being attacked or mocked or disparaged, devalued, came to mind for me. So I didn't respond to him. He went back into the bar without knowing who we were.

Did I want to be known? I thought. Yes and no. I wanted not to be seen as merely someone sexual. I didn't want the man imagining me in bed, which is what I thought he would do if I answered his question. But if I didn't answer it, he would see us as two sisters: he would see us as non-sexual. That distinction: why was it so important?

If we were sisters, our travel would be something lighter, I felt—something not as earthshaking, not as radical, not as much constantly a question of who we were—of whether we were getting along well enough, of whether we would still stay together after this, of whether I was good enough to live up to Hannah's expectations of me, Hannah's needs. If we were sisters, we would not be going around hiding it; we would simply say, "My sister."

I know that the expression "sister" can be extended to include many kinds of relationships between women, suggesting an affinity, a common bond, a sisterhood; suggesting something natural, a shared plight, a sense of "being in it together." We were in it together. We had a great deal in common. But we weren't sisters. It wasn't something that could be taken for granted. That was an important difference, I felt. We were not born into our relationship, never to be torn asunder. I know that sisters can have rifts come between them, must make the relationships between them work. They cannot take their relationship for granted. But with us, it was something different—more tentative, more "built," more creating a dream—a dream that would carry us, see us through. With sisters, there is not always this internal question "Is it right that she is my sister? Am I right to be with her?" You just "are." It's a given. But with Hannah and me, it was optional. It was a choice.

"Do you remember back when we first met?" I asked Hannah as she stood beside me gazing at the mountain, the sun gradually lowering in the sky above it.

"Which time were you thinking of?" she asked.

"Back when I first returned to California. Before you knew all my faults."

She lifted her arm and put her hand on my shoulder as we stared toward the impressive Chiricahua mountain peak across from us.

"I'm glad you brought me here," she said.

"Do you think we are sisters?"

"In a way, yes. But no. You're thinking of the man again."

She knew me well. When I got an idea in my head, it was hard to get rid of it.

Shaking my head, as if shaking out the idea, "It's gone," I said. "Go away, man."

"That's right," she said, moving her arm to around my waist. She walked with me and Fresco toward the back of the broad graveled area that spread atop the hill, the two low houses nestled within it. We turned and looked toward the eastern mountains where, in the morning, the sun would rise, where it would be my time, while Hannah was still in bed—my time to see and enjoy the sunrise and the light changing in the sky, hoping to see color.

"Those are your morning mountains," Hannah said. "You see things I never see. Then you tell me about them."

We had our ways, I thought. We had divided the labor somewhat, divided the tasks, divided our special likes and ways. Sisters did that too. But it didn't make us sisters.

I wondered if Hannah thought I shouldn't be doing it—waking up so early in the mornings to see the sunrise, waking up and going out in the dark and cold, staring off to where the first light glowed over the mountain peaks, getting lost sometimes in the dark, pushing myself to see more even when I could not see.

"We do some things sisters don't do," I said.

"Many things," Hannah said. I could hear her smile.

And I thought about the two of us—the things I didn't want the man to know or see. I thought of the large, dark wood-framed bed back in the guest house where we would spend the night. What would happen there? Would it live up to expectations? Would I be a good enough lover?

I did not want to wait. I turned to Hannah and gave her a kiss—a brief non-sister kiss. "I'm happy to be with you," I said. As I did so and felt her body close against mine, I also felt how self-protective we were. We were lesbians and we had to be careful, I thought, even out here with no one else around. I took Hannah's hand as we continued on.

Fresco tugged at his leash. He didn't want to keep up with us as we walked on the graveled path. Fresco has sensitive feet. He doesn't like to walk on pebbles or sharp stones. He lagged behind now, gently tugging me backward, as if I was taking him someplace where no dog should have to go.

"He likes to be careful," Hannah said. "There's nothing wrong with that."

I bent down to check out the gravel on the ground with my hand. It seemed not too sharp. I hoped he would get used to it.

Hannah, Fresco, and I then walked along a ridge that led away from the houses in the clearing. We followed a path bounded, on either side, by desert scrub. As we walked, I looked out at the Chiricahua mountain range on the west, which seemed to go on forever, heading south toward Mexico. We kept moving, but we didn't seem to gain much headway on it. That range—the tall Chiricahua peak and the lower mountains extending north and south from it—were in Arizona. But we were in New Mexico looking from across the border at it, taking it in from a "New Mexico view"—from our particular view as two women, two lesbians, as just us. I was more enamored of mountains than was Hannah, I thought, because they were big and I could see them. But Hannah was interested in them too, felt them magical, especially for us, because this was not our usual life, not something we normally see. Maybe being here felt all the more special because we were lesbians, but I think it would have been special to anyone. Still I think it was especially special to us.

"What do you see?" I asked Hannah as we continued walking along the ridge.

"I see you, dear. You look happy."

"I am. But a little anxious. I worry about whether we are going to have a good time."

"You always worry. There's nothing to worry about. You're with me. We're together. We have all this to ourselves"—she spread her arms wide. "This desert is ours, as far as the eye can see."

I laughed. "As far as your eye can see," I thought, "but also mine" as I gazed at the rugged vegetation blurry in the distance— yucca, dry grasses, low, thorny bushes, an expanse of tumbleweed and brambles, scattered cactus, Soaptree Yucca spires broken off sticking up here and there. All around us was this prickly desert through which we could not walk easily, especially with Fresco's sensitive feet and my limited sight. But we could appreciate it, look out on it, imagine walking through and finding our way back. That would be the hard part: getting back. For I wanted to get off the path and trod through the open desert, find some old shards, some remnants of lives past, something special to take home with us that no one else saw or would find. I wanted to feel I was far away, remote, not on manicured land, not on a path. But I dared not walk cross country now, not with my lack of vision and my dog. Maybe we could do something like that later, if Hannah would lead me.

When the path ended, disappearing into the surrounding desert, we turned around and headed back toward the clearing and the houses. The sun was almost setting now, the late afternoon light shining on the closer mountains, the Peloncillos, making them look golden and soft.

"Look how they are lit up," I said to Hannah, glad to see the bright ochre light reflected on the undulating shapes of the Peloncillo Mountains that bounded the broad desert plain to the east. Now that I see less well, I am always delighted when I am able to enjoy light reflected on mountains, shining on their crevices and dramatic shapes.

The Peloncillos, located in New Mexico, were less tall than the Chiricahuas in Arizona across the way, and, being lower, they were more modest in stature, which felt fitting for us. But there was something about the grandeur of the big Chiricahuas that moved me, felt truly awe-inspiring, even if they were in Arizona. They were in Arizona, but viewed from here, I reminded myself. I didn't have to go into them. I could enjoy them from afar.

As we walked back now on the New Mexico side of the border, the lower mountains felt, if not more like home, at least with their smaller scale, reminiscent of us. I looked around at the vast expanse of scattered brush that extended toward the Peloncillos and thought of Hannah and me.

"We're like the desert," I said to Hannah, "don't you think?"

"I'm not sure what you mean."

"It's the little things. Our life is full of all the little things we do," I said as I looked out over the desert and thought about how we were like the sparsely vegetated landscape that spread before us—more minimal than the mountainous surroundings—how, as women, it was all the little things that mattered. It wasn't only our temperaments. It was our concern for items we each got in the grocery store, for how we each got dressed in the mornings, for all the small details—how to hang a picture in the house. I had a sense that our life was "under the radar," not easily seen by others. We were like the scattered, well-defended plants on the desert floor that blended into the surrounding low-lying plain, indistinguishable when viewed from a distance.

We weren't big and striding through the world—a man holding a door open in a bar and sauntering out, following me, asking invasively if we were sisters, asking intrusively if we were lesbians. We were not asking, not telling, simply standing here on the ridge between two mountain ranges—the Chiricahuas on the west darkening from the sun setting behind them, and the Peloncillos on the east shining a deep golden brown.

Twelve

Private Moments

As we stood looking over at the Chiricahua Mountains in Arizona and at the Peloncillos in New Mexico, entranced to be among them, Hannah turned toward me. "I like it here," she said. "It's so beautiful. It's a privilege to be here." That's how Hannah felt about many things, I thought. We would drive down the coast back at home and she would say, "How lucky we are to live here." Now she was saying much the same thing, "How lucky we are to be here."

Still, I worried. Would we be lucky in five minutes? Would I feel okay later? These moments of specialness between us—between us and the surrounding landscape, between us and our surrounding life—felt rare and transitory. Yet they were so important to me. For with Hannah beside me feeling good, I was saved from my bleak moments, my fears and self-doubts. I felt buoyed by her happiness.

"I love you," I said, wanting not to break the spell of enchantment between us.

Hannah, raising her arm, pointed south. "There's a rosy glow in the distance from the sunset," she said. "Can you see it?"

"No. It's too little and too faint."

"But it's there, and I think I can see a crescent moon," she added.

"Look at it for both of us," I told her as I stared in the opposite direction, toward the Peloncillo Mountains, which I did not have to strain to see.

She could look off at faraway sights and enjoy them, I thought, be in her own unique space. And I had to be separate, apart from her now, marveling at the joy she took in such small, ephemeral things. Hannah was easy to please, I often told myself. A small amount of something that gives her pleasure goes a long way. That was particularly helpful for me to keep in mind when it came to our sexual experiences, I thought. I might feel I was failing to give her pleasure or a significant moment. I had to remind myself that "a little goes a long way," that the pleasure I could give her might be enough, though, of course, I wished to give her much pleasure, to have our intimacies be full and rich.

There it was again—my sense of the invisible, of what the man who had questioned me in the bar did not know, of what I kept from him: Hannah and me in bed, Hannah and me sexual, Hannah and me in our private moments that could not compare to anyone else's, that felt too sensitive to expose, and that raised, at the same time, many larger issues concerning who we were and our place in the world.

We were nearing the end of our walk now, approaching the back of the guest house, a low, earth-toned building with a welcoming feel. "Show me," I said to Hannah as we stood at the back gate. "Show me how I should walk in the morning." For I knew that, in the morning, I would come out in the darkness wanting to walk toward the edge of the scrubby desert to get a good view of the Peloncillo Mountains and the first light before sunrise as it crept up behind them, perhaps producing color. But to do that, I would have to walk in the darkness where I could not see my surroundings or the ground ahead of me. If I stepped too far, I might stumble over the edge of the clearing down an incline into sharp brambles.

"Let's count your steps," Hannah said, taking my hand in hers and leading me forward, Fresco trailing at my side. "Nineteen steps," she counted. Then turning us sideways, "Left fifteen steps. You should have a great view from here." She gestured toward the broad sweep of the mountain range across from us.

I went back to the gate behind the house and practiced: nineteen footsteps forward; fifteen to the left. In the morning, Fresco would not be with me, nor would Hannah. I would be alone in the dark, with my cane and my flashlight. But the flashlight beam did not go far enough to compensate for the inner darkness of my eyesight. Only when I eventually lifted my camera to my eyes, illuminating the scene before me on the back screen, would I be able to see where I was.

"Thank you," I said to Hannah, feeling complete now, feeling helped, feeling that if all else went wrong, there would be a morning tomorrow when I would find my way. But between now and then, there would be the evening. What would happen then? What would the time between us be like? What if I failed to keep up my spirits, failed to do what was right by Hannah, failed to continue living in my dreams?

I walked with Hannah through the back gate and into the guest house, then through the spacious living room, its decorative fireplace high and wide—a central feature in this Southwestern style home built by a technology entrepreneur twelve years before. The living room was comfortable with a plush tan sofa, a wide wooden table in front of it, a deep toned rug. This was the owner's guest house when others visited, while he occupied the main house on the hill set farther back than us, hardly visible from here, empty now since we were the only people visiting this week.

We had stayed on this desert property surrounded by mountains before, but for shorter times. At first, we stayed in a rustic cabin located on a ridge below. The heat and hot water failed to work and the temperature at night hit twenty degrees, so the manager put us up for a second, complimentary night in the guest house. The next year when I inquired, the owner offered us the privilege of staying in the guest house. The owner, who lived back East, had recently bought the sprawling desert estate from the technology entrepreneur, who had gone bankrupt and sold it off at auction.

The guest house was well appointed and more upscale than Hannah and I were used to. I had liked the rustic cabin, even without heat and hot water. But I knew Hannah liked the guest house because it had all the comforts while in the desert: hot water, air conditioning if it were summer, large rooms, a fireplace that worked, a well-equipped kitchen, washer and dryer. These are small details to note—these amenities of a house—but they were important to us because we were trying to find comfort, to share a home, a life. The house was a way we worked it out, a way I tried to please Hannah with my finds.

The guest house had a particularly large master bedroom and, within it, a wide, king-size bed that seemed to me even larger than king size. After glancing toward it, I went out to get our belongings from the car—our bags, jackets, and groceries—and brought them into the house. As I lay our coats and my camera down on the bed, I thought of Hannah and me. We would be sleeping in this broad bed tonight. It was definitely too big for us. There would be far too much room, I thought. On the floor surrounding the bed were several large, colorful rugs—"Navajo style," but not Navajo in fact. They were what I associated with Arizona—taking the more subdued New Mexico colors—the tans, browns, and blacks—and dramatizing them, making them more artificial, more like Arizona in style, I thought—with pastels, bright reds, and bold shapes that leapt from the floor—too bold, too big for Hannah and me. But they were striking, elegant in their way.

The entire room was elegant. In the center was the large bed with dark wooden headboard and footboard, a tan and brown patchwork quilt on top merging into the tan-brownness of the room. This bedroom was the size of three of our rooms back at home, I thought. If you combined my study, our bedroom, and Hannah's study, you could approximate the space of this one room. Our bedroom back at home is small. It fits, at best, a queen-size bed, with a small table on each side of the bed, leaving bare-ly enough room for us to walk around the bed and not step on a dog, or dogs, lying on the floor. But this room had space to spare. A polished wooden dresser sat off to one side under a window that looked out toward the Peloncillo Mountains. A smaller window on the other side let in light above a desk—both ends of the room full of extra space. I laid Hannah's bag on the dresser side of the bed, put my camera on the desk. I looked over at the bed again.

"Come here," I called to Hannah. "I want to ask you some-thing."

"I'm coming," she said, walking into the room.

"What size do you think this bed is?" I asked. "It looks bigger than a king to me."

"Maybe it's an extra-large king," she suggested. "You know about these things. I don't. What matters is that it's firm." With that, she threw herself onto the bed, stretched her hands over her head. "It's a nice firm bed," she said. "It's good for my back."

I looked at her and admired her carefree way of happily toss-ing herself onto the bed. I thought of my back, too, at that mo-ment. I had a sore back because I had injured it hoisting Teela, my first guide dog, up our front stairs when her rear legs no longer worked well. But it wasn't my back I was thinking of as much as of Hannah and me later tonight when we would get into this big bed for sleep, and, as usual, I would think about where we should go—how close, how far apart? The bed was so broad. And would we, or wouldn't we, be sexually involved? Would we caress each other, have a special time between us, or would we have a brief kiss and then roll apart?

That evening, we made ourselves a nice dinner. We lit our Chanukah candles and turned on the lights of the Christmas tree that had been left for us in a corner near the fireplace. It felt odd to me that Hannah was willing to leave the Christmas tree lights on at the same time as the Chanukah candles. But she thought it added more light to the living room. She was, by now, used to the infiltration of Christmas everywhere we went during this early winter season. As long as we lit our candles and said the prayer, and sang the songs, she was pleased. We were Jewish even when surrounded by Christian traditions.

But back when we first met, I thought, she would have turned the Christmas tree lights off, even carted that Christmas tree out into the desert, not wanting it near, not wanting reminders of threats to Jews, feeling them invasive, wanting to feel in a space apart.

We lit the candles, sang two of the songs, and Hannah had us dance—there in the living room, the fire sparkling in the fire-place, the Christmas tree lights on in the corner, the improvised menorah on the black, stone kitchen counter, the candles each standing upright on a piece of custom-cut aluminum foil that we had brought from the store.

As we danced, I was glad to feel Hannah's body close to mine. I felt her softness, her warmth. I thought about our being both Jewish and lesbian—how it divided us from others, made us feel more that we were traveling in our own different world. I thought about the question from the man in the bar and the issues it raised. And I thought about sex: Why was it so haunting—what we do in bed? Why was it so hard to talk about? I was aware of my own sensitivities around sex—how I felt I did not live up to expectations or images in the larger culture, and how I feared exposing my own desires and needs, how it was a challenge to be close to someone else, even with Hannah. I thought of how much I wanted her to feel that I cherished her and loved her deeply.

That night when bedtime came, after the candles had burned down and the fire in the fireplace was almost out—glowing only with remaining embers and hot coals—after the Christmas tree lights were long turned off, and the dishes done, Hannah and I went into the bedroom. I held out my arm toward her as we walked in, as I pulled down the covers, turned back the sheets on the broad bed. There were plenty of pillows. The room was warm. I went into the bathroom to brush my teeth and wash up. Hannah did the same.

"How do you feel about the size of this bed now?" I asked her on her return.

"I like the bed."

"Will you promise to stay close to me? I don't want to lose you in it."

"Of course," she said with much caring, her tone the one in which she always reassured me that I would not lose her, that I would be safe.

"Do you think we need more heat?"

"I think the heat is fine. What about the lights?"

"How about if we leave on the one on the dresser, but turn it down low?" I asked.

Hannah, I knew, usually preferred to have darkness, except if there were candles. She liked candles. However, I liked to see. The darkness scared me, took away from the reality, made it harder for me to have a sense of my surroundings. Then, too, my blindness caused everything to be darker than usual. A lamp on a nightstand simply cast a warm glow, was environmental, not at all harsh. It enabled me to keep in touch with the room outside us, enabled me to feel grounded as I sought to find my way in the interaction between us.

I took off the underpants and tee shirt that I usually wear to bed and got in under the covers. I thought of how people in sex scenes in movies usually take off their clothes piece-by-piece, or have the lover take off the items of clothing one-by-one as part of foreplay. But I liked to get rid of my clothes right away so that, as soon as Hannah was ready, there would then be simply her smooth body against mine, that I would very soon feel her flesh, the warmth of her shape enveloping me, firm against mine, comforting, willing to be with me in this strange bed, this unusual place.

Hannah, however, liked to get in bed with all her night clothes on, which included extra layers in case she got cold. Then I would have to help her take them off one-by-one, fumbling under the covers, never entirely sure how to untangle her legs and arms.

She slid into the bed, though not quite beside me on its broad expanse.

"Come closer," I said.

She scooted toward me.

"Now can we take off your clothes?"

I reached down and first came the shirt over her head, then her sleeping pants.

Then there she was, her nakedness against mine. But it didn't really feel like her nakedness, more her presence, more this moment we shared, a moment all the more precious because it was not every day, not in every place—only sometimes, when we were ready.

I felt the curve of her belly, her breasts against mine as I lay on my back and she came to me, put her face close up against my cheek, lay there for a while.

"It's been a long day," I said. "That man."

"He should only know," she said.

"Why was it so hard to tell him?" I asked.

"Because of this." She gave me a kiss. "And this." She gave me a longer kiss on the neck.

"Stay still for a minute," I said, knowing how much Hannah likes to go into action. Even in bed, she is ready to go, while I take time to get adjusted to her presence, to be comfortable in the moment.

"I feel sometimes this is not what everybody does," I said.

"It's what we do," she answered.

I thought, but did not say: I wonder if I will feel protected enough here—protected not only from threats from the outside, but from feelings that might arise within me concerning how Hannah and I would be close. Would I be able to relax, to let go of my separateness enough to be fully with her?

Hannah rolled over now and I touched her and kissed her breasts. I imagined, in my mind, that I was like a baby, a young girl, a soft inner person symbolically taking nurturance. "Easy," Hannah whispered as I kissed one breast and gently rubbed the other. Then I traced my fingers down her belly, her thighs. I could feel her body warm against me, her hands stroking, feeling for my breasts, my hands stroking hers in turn, feeling her softness, moving down the length of her body as she massaged mine and sought to bring me closer to her.

I felt the challenge of the moment, of inventing our sexual experience anew. What should sex be? How would I know if I, if we, were doing it right enough, lesbian enough, living up to all the expectations that surrounded us in the wider world? How would I know if I was doing well by Hannah, satisfying her desires of me? I only knew that as my lover rolled over and she touched me, her body nestled in with mine, I felt her softness. I looked back on all our years together—what had sex been for us at first? What was it for us now? It had a sweetness now that it did not have at first. It was layered over with all that had passed between us, with all that we had shared.

It was Hannah so close to me—how good her skin felt, how her belly felt against me, how reassuring my sense of her shape. She was totally there, solidly there—reassuring me even as the outside invaded, or threatened to invade. I felt a gentle tenderness in her as I wrapped my arms around her, felt her lying on top of me, her weight like a blanket of firmness, of protection, her breasts soft, reminding me that the nourishment I sought was near.

I was drawn to our closeness, to a sense that I wanted to please her, convey to her how much I cared, prized her, loved her. I wanted her to feel these things through my touch, through my massaging her body on that broad bed, stroking her while holding her in my arms. I wanted her to feel how much I loved her, cared about her, felt we had made our own world, felt protected here in the small space of the two of us, maybe two feet wide, all told—not apart, but holding each other close.

I looked across the room at the lamp gently glowing on the dresser in front of the window, its shades drawn against the outside, against the desert plains below, against that man in the darkened bar. Was he still there? Or was he long gone—back home, where his family was—wondering if we were two sisters or two lesbians? "He had to know," I thought. But, in fact, that night, in that broad bed where we held close, I was soon not thinking of him at all. I was thinking of us—of how we got here. I was thinking that I wanted Hannah to feel that I loved her better than anyone else ever had. She sometimes said so. She said so that night. She praised me, praised my lovemaking, praised our being together, in this bed, so close. I felt her relax. I felt she was pleased. I smiled at her pleasure.

Then she rolled over and turned toward me, petting me, touching my breasts, then moved further below, stroking me gently. I felt her concentration, her care. I pushed away my expectations of who I should be, of whether I was sexual enough. I felt warmed by Hannah against my worries, my fears.

"It's enough," I told myself. "It's enough that you can feel the sweetness going from her to you, feel that in her touch, move into it. It's okay to feel that what surrounds you is open, is constantly threatening to invade, is making you question all the time if you are good enough. It's enough to hold that aside, take just these few moments, that strain of sweetness, that golden ore—the deep resonance of her touch. Prize it. Prize that little time together with her surrounding you." I liked her on top of me, liked her close to me, liked a sense of being almost smothered by her. It kept the world out, kept the man out, kept all that harshness out, those other places.

Could she know how often I fought to be with her without criticism, without constraint or distraction? Could she know how much I sought this tiny space of respite, of relief, and yet held back, often pulled away from it? Yet now we were here. I enjoyed the oneness of us. In my mind, I saw our two bodies intertwined, holding each other in one small part of that broad bed. We were up near the top, about two-thirds of the way over on my side. As we lay together, I felt Hannah falling asleep beside me, resting her chin on my body, my breasts, but firm against me so that I also felt all of her. We were here. We had made it through the day, through our life so far together. The outside world was far off now—those awe-inspiring mountains, those busy places over in Arizona—the places that were not quite ours. I rolled over, taking some space. I gave Hannah a nudge, touching her shoulder with a soft tap.

"Shall we go to sleep now?" I asked her.

"I thought I was asleep," she murmured groggily.

It was odd, I thought, waking her up to ask if she wanted to go to sleep. But I didn't want to go to sleep without her. And I thought I needed to be more separate to go to sleep.

"Go back to sleep, but don't go too far," I told her.

"I won't."

She moved over toward her side a few inches and the two of us slept, Fresco beside me on the floor next to the bed, feeling far away but I knew he was there. Back at home, we have cats on the bed, and we used to have a small dog there too. But here, it was only us—the two of us in this big bed, this big world stretching into endless desert.

In the morning, I woke before Hannah and went out in the dark before sunrise to see the colors changing in the sky above the Peloncillo Mountains. "Nineteen steps forward," I told myself at the back gate, walking ahead, probing the ground with my cane, looking into the darkness. "Now fifteen steps to the left." From there, I thought of Hannah. She had placed me on this spot. I stared into the distance toward where the broad sweep of the mountains should be. Nothing yet. No light to speak of, then a little, then a little more. It was cold. I went inside to get warm, retracing my steps toward the lights of the guest house. I came back out, lifted my camera to assess where I was—took the nineteen steps again, but then I hit the brush, stumbled, and felt the brambles scratching my legs. I came back uphill a few steps, then left the fifteen steps. There I was—in position for the best view.

As I stood in the dark, I watched carefully as a single, thin, dark cloud moved above the two highest mountain peaks across from me. Soon, in a crevice between two closer peaks, I saw a hint of deep red, then a broader patch. It wasn't large but it was a stunning velvet-red and better than no color at all in what promised to be a clear morning light. I watched the small patch of red glow, took a photo of it, studied it through my camera as it brightened, turned orange-red, faded to a coral, then disappeared into the background surrounded by that vast silvery gray sky and the hulking black shapes of the mountains. I felt grateful that Hannah had gotten me here and began to be able to see the ground at my feet without a flashlight, began to be able to see again, my vision less limited now than the night before and in the earlier morning. I imagined Hannah back in bed, felt the chill of dawn.

I walked back to the guest house to take Fresco outside to relieve himself out in front where the sky was brightening. The sun was not yet up, far from being above the horizon, but the general sky was lighter, light enough so that a blind person could find her way.

In the guest house kitchen, I scooped out a bowl of food for Fresco, then left him inside in the living room and walked out again, not wanting to miss any more of the changing light. Grazing the graveled ground with my cane, I headed around toward the front of the low building and stepped to the edge of the clearing.

Across the way, the Chiricahuas in Arizona were waking up. The sun, creeping up behind the Peloncillos in the east, was beginning to throw a deep golden light on the faces of the Chiricahua mountain range, and especially on the massive, triangular-shaped Chiricahua peak that stood opposite me, that loomed larger than the others, dominating the landscape, commanding my view.

The light on the Chiricahuas at this time in the morning was such a deep gold, like the darkest of amber, shining on the huge mountain across from me, highlighting its crevices and rock out-croppings. It was a magnificent, understated, luminous gold I saw that morning that soon would be gone, changing to a lighter gold, then tan, before it faded into shadow. This first color—the depth of it, the uniqueness, the scarcity of it—that it was available to me only at this time of day, and for only a few minutes, and then it would vanish—there was something about it that felt un-matched to me, exhilarating, worth standing out in the cold for, worth every minute of my struggle to be at ease in this strange place where I could not travel alone. Camera to my eyes, I watched the gold on the mountain change from deep amber to a lighter dark gold, then to a rosier gold. I turned around and looked back toward the guest house in which Hannah was sleeping, Fresco perhaps also gone back to sleep. I wanted to share this with Hannah. I wanted her to see it too, but I knew she would rather be in bed asleep.

I tried to follow the road that led downhill from the graveled clearing but stumbled into some brush again at the edge, so intent was I on staring at the mountain across from me as it went through its phases of changing hue. I looked into the distance—there were no clouds in the sky now. I liked it when there were clouds—more drama in the sky, more shadows on the mountains. But this morning, the clarity of the air, the stillness but for the cold and a slight breeze was invigorating. I had a sense of being stopped in time, even as time hastened and seemed too quickly to speed by as the sun steadily rose from behind the Peloncillos on the other side of the guest house and threatened to bask the entire world in light.

When it rose, when it finally rose, the golden color disappeared. The mountain turned a faded tan, then black, in shadow once again, the sun high up now, no longer at an angle, too high to shine with a golden glow on the mountain's face.

I thought of that earlier moment in back of the guest house when I had seen the small patch of red over the Peloncillos, how magical it was, and then how quickly gone. Now the gold light on the Chiricahuas was gone quickly too—a kind of gold that reminded me of the gold before sunset that Hannah and I had seen the evening before when the last rays of sunlight hit the Peloncillos. But the gold on the Chiricahuas this morning occurred before the sun ever came up. Too much light and it disappeared.

Too much light, I thought. The world is often seen with too much light. It displays too much, makes things confusing. Better to see just a little, to see what stands out.

I was fascinated by these plays of light in the desert, as I always was on our trips. I stood gazing across at the mountain, now pale compared with the gold earlier, thinking of Hannah back in bed—thinking of Hannah, always thinking of Hannah. What would I tell her about my morning later? What would I tell her about how I had felt the night before? Did I need to tell her? Was it already shared enough? Had I been a good enough lover? Was I a good enough partner in life?

The night before in bed, Hannah had seemed so content when she rolled over and drifted off into sleep. She had seemed relaxed, as if I was enough, as if I had pleased her, as if she was in the right place—here in this house on the hill—surrounded by desert, by scrub, by mountains, in a bed clearly too big for us, in a house not our own. She was happy here, especially in the sunlight—she liked the sun. She liked the moon and the night stars. For me, they were too far away. I liked the earth, what was right at my feet, the small things I could focus on—the big things too sometimes—the changing of the light, the reflections on these mountain ranges.

I thought about how my vision was murkier now than in years past, making it harder for me to see, harder to take my steps. The glare from the bright light of day was often as blinding for me as the darkness of night. But the vision I had was accompanied by gifts: the gift of being able to see what I could, to appreciate what I could still make out—the broad sweeps of the light even when I could not see individual details; the subtleties of color in the darkness—and to appreciate help from others, from Hannah as she aided me in finding my way. She wasn't out here in this brightness of morning, but she had been very much with me earlier, as she was the night before.

I turned away from the mountain now and headed back toward the house across the graveled clearing, tucking my camera back in its case. Would Hannah be up? What would she be feeling? What would I tell her about my morning?

When I stepped into the house, Hannah was in the kitchen looking out the small window over the sink that, neatly placed, framed a view of the Chiricahuas and, particularly, the impressive mountain peak I had been studying with my camera from outside.

"How was it?" she asked, "How was your morning looking at the sky and the colors?"

"Good," I said. "I found the spot you chose for me. How are you?"

She smiled.

"Did you enjoy last night?" I asked.

"I did." She came close and gave me a kiss. I felt her firmness, her arms around me, felt the protection I had felt the night before. I thought of the two of us and how far we had come, how each day was a new adventure, and each night, how I had these times apart from her, and then we came back together, how much I wished to share my inner life with her—my life when we were separate, my exhilaration in the early morning. And yet, she was a different person—happy to be in bed, to be content in her own ways, to sleep through the best part of the day. I remembered the night before and how she had held me, her body warm, her flesh soft, wrapping herself against me, protecting me from the night, from the stars, from the turbulence within, from all those questions I had about my worth. I thought of her, and of this time between us, as rare, like the patch of red I had seen in the early morning above the Peloncillos, before the deep gold of the Chiricahuas, before anyone else was up.

Thirteen

Careful Steps

I went outside and wandered around with Fresco while Hannah finished breakfast and got dressed. He was getting used to the stones under foot, enjoying the smells of the desert. It was cold out but sunny, everything clear—the mountains glorious in both directions, the desert extending to the Chiricahuas on the west as if they, like the Peloncillos, were near. Coming back in, I told Hannah, "It's beautiful out. The sun is high. What would you like to do today?"

"I'd like to go further into the Chiricahuas," she said.

"Sure, the Chiricahuas," I said, wishing, instead, to stay on the New Mexico side of the border, imagining a trip back to Big Hatchet Mountain farther east.

"We'll go to Big Hatchet tomorrow, I promise," Hannah said, as if reading my mind.

We left our perch on the hill and drove down and across the border into Arizona, climbing up a winding road into a canyon that took us closer and closer to the towering Chiricahua peak we had looked at from afar, that I had seen from the guest house so much earlier that morning cloaked in gold—that now looked brown and red and tan, with huge granite rock faces exposed higher up.

We climbed higher, farther back into the rock-lined canyon, the road narrowing, curving, until we got to a spot with huge boulders atop cliffs on either side—"Cathedral Rocks," they were called—a scenic spot, an entryway into the further mysteries of the canyons cut deeply into this mountain range, stretching back, wooded—with tall trees and gnarled pines jutting from rocks that rose on both sides of a sunken creek that ran along the edge of the road far below.

At the Cathedral Rock entryway we stopped, pulled off the road, then dipped down on a side dirt road into the canyon, heading toward places we did not know and had not been to before—looking for something out of the way, but still in the shadow of the looming boulders, the rock giants. A lone house in the distance out a side road puffed a column of rising smoke near an adjacent cliff. But to the right, the road climbed further. We stopped the car at the base of the climb. I got out with Fresco while Hannah worked on parking the car off the road but not into the thick bushes overgrown on the side.

Fresco wagged his tail, happy to be out, sniffing the air as if he might lead me to wild javelinas or bears, then sniffing the dry grasses at our feet.

"I'm looking forward to this walk," Hannah said, soon joining us, gesturing toward the road ahead as it climbed and curved, making its way up one side of the canyon, thorny plants and cactus at the edges, the sun peering down from between the boulders higher up, brightening everything, almost glaring.

Hannah liked the sun, I knew, and it was good for my sight—better than the dark—but it felt overwhelming to me.

I stared at the road ahead. It was more like a wide path up. There were ruts in it, rough spots, rugged areas I could vaguely see that might be too much for my footing, but most of it seemed smooth enough.

We started up the road, Hannah leading, holding out her hand to me, delighted to be out in the sun in this scenic canyon area. "Cactus," she said suddenly, stopping me, "Stay to your left."

I told Fresco. He didn't seem to notice the command, was intent on sniffing the ground as he guided me. "Rocks, watch for rocks," I told him. "Watch for cactus," as if the words would make sense to him, feeling I was really telling them to myself—and telling them to Hannah—telling her, "Watch out for me."

But it did not need to be said. Hannah always watched out for me, sometimes to a fault, sometimes making me feel like a burden, or too cared for. But I knew she did not mind, or I hoped she didn't. She wanted me to be in good shape, not to fall, to be upright and happy while walking with her, to be sharing the joy she felt.

I could be upright, I knew, but happy—I wasn't sure. This wasn't my element—this open-ended climb on the somewhat wide dirt road, rutted a bit, but smooth enough. I felt a need for more protection. The sun made me feel too exposed, but maybe, I thought, maybe this road will lead to a view, maybe we will get somewhere. The road curved and climbed some more. The cactus around us became larger, more numerous, as if they were giant people on both sides of the path guarding us, welcoming us, accompanying us on our walk and, at the same time, warning us—"Beware. Don't forget your surroundings. Watch your step."

I always had to do that, I felt, "watch my step." Even when with Hannah, even with Fresco—especially with Fresco. With a guide dog, you always watch your step. Walking with the dog emphasizes your self-consciousness. It has caused me to be attentive to all my moves through space because I am sharing them physically with the dog. There are always two of us, consulting about our path, our route, our stops, about obstacles in the way or on the side—here the ruts, the uneven ground, the prickly plants, the cactus beside us, possibly their spines on the road, the rocks in the road.

I was aware of everything, I felt, too aware. I am already very alert. But with Fresco, with being blind—even when I see—I am extremely self-conscious.

And there was Hannah up ahead, taking her steps more quickly than me, happy to be out in the open spaces, climbing the hill, looking for our next view.

She turned back to check with me.

"I'll be okay," I said. "You go ahead."

She stopped farther up the hillside, waiting for me in a grove of huge prickly pear cactus—a forest of them, a colony on both sides of the road, but particularly on the broad uphill side—their large, rounded pads branching outward, making them look like they were statues of people standing together in the sun.

"Isn't this beautiful," Hannah said, looking toward the sky. "I'm in heaven."

"Oh no," I thought. "It's too bright for me." It's too hot—not really hot, but warm now, near noon in the bright sun of winter, the hillside and the cactus blocking the wind, the tan earth reflecting the light, making the air still. I wanted cold suddenly. I wanted dark. I wanted to feel as Hannah did, or to have her feel as I did—that this side of the border, over here in Arizona, in this canyon, this national wildlife area, was not my place. I wanted something else, but I did not know what it was. What did I want when I wanted shelter, when I wanted to be in a different kind of environment than Hannah did?

I looked around at the tall cactus climbing the hillside as if embracing us with their presence, reflecting the sun, casting their shadows in the indirect winter light. At least I could get a picture, I thought. We were stopped. My footing was secure. There had to be something picturesque about cactus. I took out my camera and took a few shots. Later, when I looked at them, the sun was clearly too bright, making the massive cactus look pale by comparison with how they had looked at the time. They looked deep green, almost Irish green with their cream-colored spines sticking out toward us, as they basked in the sun. They looked almost friendly. But I dared not take a step toward them. I knew enough not to trust my depth perception, and not to let Fresco off his leash.

Hannah went farther up the hill to explore around the next curve, then came back. "The road keeps climbing," she said. "We don't have to continue."

"Would you like to?"

"I'm not sure. I think I would like to go back down, take one of the paths that goes lower into the canyon."

"Okay," I said. "But I'm fine to go on farther here if you like. I can manage."

I marveled, at that moment, at how Hannah could keep enjoying a place while I did not. I did not want my discomforts to destroy her mood.

As we stood debating what to do—whether to climb further or turn back and search for a road down below—a woman in a car drove up. It felt strange that someone was driving on this remote road, but I guessed there must be houses or other destinations farther up. She stopped the car, rolling down her window to talk with us. "You might try farther down," she said. "There's a great path going off into the lower canyon back the way you came."

"How do we get there?" Hannah asked, always glad to have specific directions so that she would not feel lost.

The woman pointed and smiled, "Go back down. Turn right, and right again. It will take you to the Double D Ranch. You can walk there. The path circles around. It ends up farther ahead off the main road. But that's quite a few miles. It's more scenic. There's more wildlife."

She looked at us, I felt, in an unusual, very direct way, as if we were friends, as if she knew us, as if we were related. I wondered if she was a lesbian, and if she thought we were lesbian, too. Had she recognized us? Was that why she stopped? But maybe people just stopped out here when they saw strangers walking along a road where strangers did not usually walk. Maybe she wanted to put us in the proper place.

She looked at Fresco. Maybe she likes dogs, I thought. Maybe that was why she stopped—because she saw a guide dog. But people did not always recognize that Fresco was a guide dog. Often they simply saw "dog."

"I take my dogs down there sometimes," she said, as if confirming my thought.

But then again, the degree to which she was friendly made me think, maybe she was a lesbian.

"What do you think?" I asked Hannah after the woman drove off.

"Hard to tell," she said. "People look different around here. A woman can look like a lesbian to us when it's just a Western style."

We retraced our steps back down the sunbaked road, leaving the colony of cactus behind. Then partway to where the car was parked, we turned right, then right again.

"This is more like it," Hannah said, feeling she was now on familiar ground known to lead us somewhere good, not in search of views we might never find.

The road that dipped down into the canyon was narrower and more rutted than the road higher up had been. Hannah walked on ahead to scout it, then came back to tell me, "It's lovely! Follow me."

We walked deeper in, surrounded by tangled brush on both sides of the path, occasional cactus and yucca. I felt the uncertainty of rocks under my feet and grasped Fresco's harness firmly to keep my balance as the path descended and we rounded a bend beside a rock cliff. Hannah reached out her arm to steady me.

"Take my hand," she said. "Let Fresco heel beside you for a minute."

But I didn't want to let go of Fresco's harness handle, and I didn't want to be pulled between them. It was about more than my footing, I thought. I was feeling out of place—too closed in now, while up on the high road toward the cactus colony, I had felt too exposed.

"Is there nowhere in Arizona you'd like to be?" I asked myself. "Probably not," I thought. I felt aware of the fact that my emotional ties were over across the border in New Mexico. Here in Arizona, it was as if I was in a foreign and threatening land—perhaps because it took me away from where I wanted to be, where my dreams lay—from my past with Hannah, and before that when I lived there—dreams of nurturance, adventure, and romance.

I wasn't sure why this lower canyon path seemed so trying, but every step I took felt like it was taking me in the wrong direction—away from New Mexico and farther into Arizona. "How could Hannah like it here?" I thought. How could we be together if she liked roads and paths I did not? What kind of a lesbian couple were we? Why was I not happy out here in the woods, in the desert, heading toward a scenic ranch?

My requirements for being happy, for being content—they so often eluded me.

"Look up," Hannah said.

I did. Above us atop a ranch entry sign, metal figures of a mother javelina with a string of babies behind her were trotting across the scaffold that stretched over the path. "Welcome to the Double D Ranch," the sign said.

As we walked on, we came upon a meadow with trees surrounding it—a greener, more open place. Then I became suddenly tired, as if I was pushing every step. It was the uncertain ground, the ruts, the rocks. But it also was a state of mind.

"The rocks," I said to Hannah. "This spot is beautiful, but the road is too irregular for me. Would you mind if I went back?"

"I'll take you," she said. "I'll go back with you."

"No," I said. "You keep going. I want you to enjoy it here. Fresco will lead me. There are no extra turns. It's pretty simple."

"I'll take you," she offered again.

"No. You stay. We'll go."

Fresco and I then took off, Hannah watching after us, concerned.

"We'll be okay," I called back to her as Fresco began guiding me at a quicker pace than before.

I followed him, tripped after him, tried to watch the sides of the road for cactus, then slowed him down by taking him off his guiding role—not using the harness handle, instead heeling him by my side, holding only the leash, so that I could pay attention to each of my steps and not fall. For when Fresco guides, he takes dog-sized steps around ruts and rocks and stays toward the edge of a path. But my feet are bigger, get caught in the ruts he misses. I don't always like to be walking on the sloped edge of a road where he leads me. So sometimes I guide him, heeling him at my side, even when on treacherous ground. But then I will need to switch back, to grab the harness handle, at times, to get my balance.

We were managing, I thought, as we moved along. It seemed quicker going back. We turned left where I thought we should, then left again. But somehow we were soon far off, not where I felt I was supposed to be. The scrub all around us—the thick bushes and cactus at the edges of the road—looked different and yet the same. I spied a small cactus on my left. I didn't remember seeing that cactus before.

I must have turned left too early, I thought—at that second turn. I stopped, reached down and patted Fresco's head. "Where do you think we are?" I asked him, as if he should know—as if he should know what I was saying, as if he should know how to find our way through this scrub-dotted canyon. He looked at me quizzically.

"Where do you want to go?" he asked, or seemed to ask. "How should I know one of these paths from another?"

I thought he did know, but that he was simply following me. I was the commander. I had told him which turns to take. It was like at home when we got to the end of a block at a curb. I had to tell him whether we were to go straight, left, or right. He shouldn't make that decision for me.

I get lost, I thought. That was life when blind, life even with a guide dog, even in the brightness of day. Back at home, back at the guest house in the early morning, I knew that in the dark, I would have to count my steps, follow my pre-planned route. But out here in the sunlight—in the places where I could see, or thought I could see—the pre-planning, my caution, was not as present. I assumed I could find my way, pick up on visual cues. But how often had that failed me? Very often. And now.

"Let's go back," I said to Fresco, as if he would understand my words. He dutifully turned around with me and we headed back toward the lower reaches of the canyon from which we had come.

Not too much later, Hannah appeared, coming toward us.

"I found you!" she said.

"We got lost," I said.

"It wasn't the same without you," she said.

"Did you enjoy your time?"

"Very much."

We walked together back toward the car, having survived our separateness. I put my hand in Hannah's and let her guide me, having had enough of being on my own. I was stepping more easily over the rocks and the ruts now, feeling Hannah's comforting presence at my side, suddenly aware of how much I had missed her.

As we drove out of the canyon, we stopped along the main road at a visitor center. A man showed us a topographic map and gave me directions to the restroom. He treated us very carefully, I thought. Was that because I was blind, or was it because we were lesbians? Or was it because we were older, though not older than him? Were we seen as two women who might be friends or who might be sisters? Or were we seen as two lesbians among the other people also stopped along the way? I wondered.

"Do you think he thought we were sisters or friends?" I asked Hannah as we stepped out from the visitor center building.

"I have no idea," she said. "Probably he was thinking only about himself, or maybe about the dog. You walk cautiously. People will think you need help."

We drove on down and out of the canyon, the cliffs and tall rocks receding behind us, headed toward a restaurant back across the border in New Mexico where we planned to have lunch. I took a deep breath, feeling we were finally headed in the right direction, feeling the openness, the sweep of a return. Something about Arizona always made me anxious—even with Hannah feeling good, even with directions from a woman who might or might not be a lesbian. I was happy to be on our way back, to a place of new shared dreams with Hannah.

I saw the flatness of the desert plain open out before us as the road curved and descended. We crossed the state line road and then were again in a more arid place—the wide valley from which we had come—not quite home, more sparse, but, for me, more relaxing, more reassuring, not a world center for bird watchers and nature enthusiasts, but a place where people lived, a place less traveled.

We pulled into the parking lot in front of the restaurant, stopping beside an out-of-service gas pump. This restaurant was located just down the road from the bar where, only the day before, I had been confronted by the man who had asked whether Hannah and I were sisters, or whether we were something else yet to be named. I got out of the car, put Fresco's harness on him, and we walked inside.

The restaurant was half general store, the other half assorted tables and booths, with a kitchen in back and the smell of Mexican food—tortillas, burritos, and enchiladas—as well as hamburgers. Fresco and I followed Hannah to a table among the others, where I sat across from her, Fresco at my feet, and looked into the blurry but brightly lit indoor space. I was looking forward to a smothered burrito, which seemed to be a special here.

While we waited for the waitress, questions swirled in my mind: Should we talk, how loudly, and about what? For I was concerned about being overheard. The restaurant seemed to me not very private. I could hear other people's conversations around us—in a booth to my side, and at a couple of tables toward the windows behind me. I didn't want to be noticed. I didn't want to be overheard.

I felt aware of our being two lesbians, feeling that vulnerability I always have when we travel, that sense of being two women in a male or heterosexual world—two women without the protections that I assumed other people could take for granted. Our difference—our choice to live in a female-centered reality—was both invisible and, at the same time, very visible. People might feel it made them uncomfortable or that it was a threat because it implied we rejected men. I feared they might strike out or act aggressively toward us. Being a lesbian, I felt, was an identity to be guarded.

"I'd like to use the restroom," Hannah soon said. As she stood to go over to the counter by the front door to ask where it was, I wondered what the woman at the front desk thought, and what the waitress thought when she saw us. Did they think we were a lesbian couple, or did they think we were just friends, or possibly sisters? Did it even occur to them? Or were they focused on the presence of my guide dog, wondering what that was all about? Or did they not think about us at all?

Was the man who had been in the bar yesterday possibly also in this restaurant? I wondered. Probably not. He was, in my mind, permanently back in the bar. He did not do something as wholesome as have lunch in a regular restaurant. Fortunately, I did not hear his voice coming from any of the tables. But his presence so recently in a place not far from here made me unusually self-conscious.

When I am out by myself, I am similarly self-conscious about how I am seen in public. But when out with Hannah, I am more concerned about the specific question of whether we are seen as a lesbian couple. When I am alone, I often feel that people are seeing me as blind or as training a guide dog for someone who is blind. Thus I have a blind person identity most prominently, at least in my mind. I used to think I was seen as a lesbian most prominently—when not simply seen as a woman, and when not being mistaken for a man. But since the dog has made my blindness more visible, I have felt that my lesbianism disappears more.

In addition, now that I have become older, I often must remind myself that I may be seen as an older woman and therefore in need of assistance, particularly when I am not seen as blind. How I am perceived is a complicated thing to figure out every time I am out. I think of it often—when crossing streets, each time I have an interaction with others—in stores, on sidewalks, in gas stations, when traveling through unknown parts of the country like the desert no less than when in familiar ones.

Thus I feel a loss of my lesbian identity when out alone that has increased in recent years. But when with Hannah, my lesbian identity emerges more. I think it is what everyone sees. And it leaves me feeling very exposed. I want not to give a bad impression of lesbians. I think about how Hannah and I are talking, what we are saying to one another that might be overheard. I think about our physical actions, how we look, how we contrast perhaps with the people around us. At the same time, I want to give a good impression of being a blind person and of how I interact with my dog. People are noticing everything, I feel, and I shrink back from the attention, or the imagined attention, seek refuge in silence, search for niceties, safe topics of conversation to share with Hannah.

I listened in to the conversations around me while Hannah was gone. A man behind me at a table by the window was talking to another man about how he first came to this area twenty years ago to study snakes, then had moved here from Iowa and now kept snakes. A woman came in who was driving a school bus and started talking with the man with the snakes about how she just had time for a hamburger and the school bus was still running. They chatted about their neighbors and how the man with the snakes only sometimes went back to Iowa now to visit.

When Hannah returned, "Ssh," I murmured to her, "listen."

She did, then caught my drift. We needed a safe topic. "What shall we talk about?" I asked her.

"The wall. Can you see that map on the wall?" she asked.

I look toward the wall to my side above a few tables. On it was painted, Hannah told me, a map of the railroad lines in this area with labels noting the historical significance of each line in the development of this part of the Southwest.

"How about if I read the wall to you," she suggested.

"Good," I thought, a safe topic. People will think we are simply tourists. They won't think particular things about us. They won't think about how we are lesbians, or how I am blind, or about our private life. But, of course, they would. Despite my desires not to be noticed, we were being seen, I thought. It had to be a salient difference if that man in the bar had asked about it.

We were two lesbians, sitting at a table in a restaurant–half general store in a small town in New Mexico just across the border from Arizona—at a shiny wood-topped table under bright fluorescent lights—very clearly to be seen. All the other customers, the wait persons, the cook, the woman at the cash register by the front door—they could see we were lesbians—or think that we might be.

"Forget it," I told myself. But I could not.

After our meal, Hannah checked with me. "How about if I go up to the counter and pay," she said, "while you get ready with Fresco and wait for your leftovers?"

I wanted to pay, always liking to perform that gesture of generosity even though the money between us was shared. But Hannah was practical about the time it would take us to do things. "Okay," I said.

I signaled to Fresco to rise from where he was lying stretched out on the floor. He happily put his head in my lap, glad to be up and soon out and about.

I glanced around toward the other people in the restaurant, but couldn't make out much detail beyond lights on the ceiling, other tables blurry around us, a kitchen in a dark window farther back. I looked down at Fresco and felt reassured by his head in my lap, his fur, his devotion. It was simpler to be a dog, I thought. Maybe that is why I liked being seen with him. It was something straightforward for people to see and take in. It was as if, by extension, I was like him too—not a complicated person with many inner struggles, but a person simply relating to her dog.

I got up with Fresco and followed Hannah to the counter by the front glass door of the restaurant where the woman at the register was computing our bill and offering a bag for my leftovers.

"Nice day. Where you from?" she asked.

"San Francisco."

"I haven't been there, but I'd like to. It's a beautiful place."

"This is too," Hannah said.

"Hot in summer," the woman said. "But we like it."

Fresco and I stepped ahead of Hannah toward the front door to go out to the car.

"Beautiful dog," the woman at the counter called out.

It was so often the dog, I thought, that made the bridge—so much easier than lesbianism. But didn't all women have that dream too—somewhere deep inside—that dream of a harboring, an intimacy with another woman that went beyond sisters, that went beyond sex?

"Thanks," I called back to the woman.

"Come again," she said.

Back in the car, I turned to Hannah, the yellow school bus off to the side in an alley behind us still running. "Wow," she said. "That was interesting."

"Good thing you knew some history," I said.

"Why do you think the driver left the bus running?" I asked Hannah.

"I don't know. Maybe the motor doesn't turn on easily. Maybe she has trouble starting the bus, so she just doesn't turn it off."

"Maybe," I said. "Maybe to keep the inside of the bus warm?"

"She sure was talking to the man with the snakes for a while. She didn't seem worried."

"Where was he from?"

"Iowa."

We were talking then about these people we did not know and had not met, though whom we had met, in a way, by overhearing their conversations in the restaurant.

Maybe they felt the same about us. Maybe when back in their cars or outside, or when they next crossed paths with each other— or maybe after we left the restaurant and they were still there, they had said to each other—"You know those two women. I wonder if they were sisters. They were not from around here. Maybe Albuquerque, or Tucson."

"Ready to go?" I asked Hannah, sitting beside her in the car, Fresco curled up on the back seat.

"Definitely. Fasten your seat belt."

As I did so and looked out at the surrounding vast, scrub-dotted fields, I thought of Thelma and Louise riding through the desert in their Thunderbird convertible, the wind blowing their scarves and long hair. I flashed on images of their adventures and ours—ours so much more cautious, more mundane, yet similarly questing, trying to break free, driving ahead in the desert breeze, outrunning the men, outrunning everyone, questing after our particular dreams.

"What next?" I asked Hannah as we drove toward the blue sky on a road carved between the mountains.

"You choose," she said. "Maybe we'll find some interesting history in the local cemetery. We haven't explored that yet."

"And Big Hatchet tomorrow?"

"Yes, tomorrow, I promise."

Fourteen

Border Patrol

We are driving east toward Big Hatchet Mountain. Hannah, at the wheel by my side, looks out intently at the road ahead. I stare out my side window at the Little Hatchet Mountains as we approach them. They are a long band of darkness with jagged peaks bounding the edge of this straight asphalt road. Beyond them, to the south, is the high desert basin that stretches toward Mexico and that once was a large inland sea. All around us is that same basin, extending also to the mountains north, farther away but within sight. We are surrounded, at a distance, by so many mountain ranges it feels otherworldly. The plains around us, the expansive, dry, occasional grassland desert, seems so broad, so wide, protecting us—protecting me from the outside world, from worries I might have elsewhere, from events left behind. We are here, out here, in a vast nothingness. Though only when we first visited was it nothingness to us. At first, when Hannah and I knew this area less well, it seemed endless and untamed, as if we were nowhere. We worried if we would ever return from this place, or if we might get lost in some ditch, some sandy ravine, trapped when the car's tires no longer had traction enough to pull us out of the soft desert earth.

It is scorching here in summer, but not in winter. The plains are inviting, seem almost fertile, full of secrets in their own way—the dry, branchy creosote bushes that once were plump after rains, the red flowers that might, if only briefly, decorate the ocotillo, the leftover yellow fruits of the cholla cactus that throws its spines at you if you come near.

This desert is full of secrets and, for us, full of memories, also secret in their way—tales that fade into the years. "Do you remember?" I ask Hannah as we drive. "Do you remember that time when we stopped off by the side of the road near here to get out and stretch our legs beside the abandoned cattle yard?"

"What happened then?" she asks.

"I saw a man with large binoculars looking south toward the Little Hatchets. I thought he was a bird watcher. I was ready to get out my binoculars to see what he was looking at. But then we realized he wasn't a bird watcher."

"He was a Border Patrol agent."

"Yes. You can tell by their white trucks."

Hannah stared straight ahead, then looked off at the sky to the north on her side of the car. "I remember we stopped to take a picture near here," she said. "I kept trying to get a good picture of a big cloud that was looming over the fields—if you'd call them fields—looming over the desert—very fluffy, almost unreal, spectacular. Those pictures didn't turn out too well."

"Yes, they did," I said as I looked over toward her side and saw again the white cloud, fluffy as it ever was.

"I was trying to get the whole scene in focus," she said, "the fields and mountains as well as the cloud. But it was hard to do. I have a hard time getting the foreground and the background both clear at the same time."

The problem of the "forest and the trees," I thought, knowing I often had difficulty with that too. So I describe everything, or seek to, searching for a larger vision. But I knew I mostly had "trees"—the details of this vast desert, the details of our life together. I had mainly my memories—of the first time Hannah and I came down here to visit Big Hatchet and we tried to find Old Hachita—a ghost town, an abandoned town from the mining era that was south of the road in ten miles or so. Old Hachita was in the foothills of the Little Hatchets. You had to climb a rutted, red dirt road to get there. I remember how scared I was as Hannah turned the car off the main road and started driving up the hillside on the sharply curving road. The ruts seemed wide enough to swallow up our tires. Being scared of heights, and afraid, especially, when I am not the driver, I asked Hannah to turn around, which was a challenging thing to do on the narrow, winding road with nothing, it seemed, on either side but a plunge to down below. But she did it. She turned the car around for me.

There were other times, too, on our travels in the desert when I had asked Hannah to turn the car around when we were climbing some winding road to heights with perilous drop-offs on the side. Once, it was above the border between New Mexico and Colorado. I had asked at a gas station whether it was more scenic to continue driving on the road we were on in New Mexico, or to turn north into Colorado. "Colorado by far," the attendant had said. So we headed up to Colorado. But the road was soon steep, a pass on the side of a mountain, and I could see ice and snow. "I want to go back," I said to Hannah.

"When there's a safe place, I'll turn around," she said.

She turned the car around and we headed back down to New Mexico. I wondered, forever after, what I had missed in Colorado. I imagined the towering snowy mountain peaks that other people saw, other people who were not afraid of heights, who did not turn around. I wondered why Hannah was not afraid like I was. I was glad when we safely maneuvered back down.

Another time, we were in the back country of northern New Mexico, following a narrow forest road that suddenly climbed and seemed to hang on the edge of a cliff, with a precipitous drop-off on the side. I was scared. And this time, there was no turning back. We had to go forward on sharp curves. I had to trust Hannah. I trusted nothing but gravity. I closed my eyes and prayed. I literally prayed, repeating thoughts that asked God to save us, though I do not believe in God and I have almost never prayed. Fortunately, when Hannah said I could open my eyes, we were safe.

The good thing about this desert basin that now surrounded us, I thought, was that it was flat. Unless we climbed the mountains, which mostly had no roads, there would not be perilous edges of cliffs that might scare me.

But Hannah, I knew, had her own kinds of fears, related to the nothingness of the vast desert basin—the way it stretched on down into Mexico, the lack of buildings, of human presence visible to the eye, the occasional barbed-wire fences not entirely penning in the cows. She felt she could easily get lost on the back roads or stuck in sand, and no one would know we were there. It would get cold and dark and we would be stranded. I think she felt additional responsibility for us because she was the driver and physically in charge of getting us back from wherever we might roam during the day. And she was the one with better eyesight. But also, I think, she likes to be more in touch with people and institutions, like universities and towns, than I do. She takes comfort from that, from the connection with the mainstream world, while I take comfort from breaking the connection, from feeling apart.

We were certainly apart down here. Nobody really cared about two women riding along in a small, red SUV with their golden guide dog in the back seat. Nobody much would notice us, I thought. Except, the ranchers might notice if we got on their land, and the Border Patrol agents.

We continued driving on the straight asphalt road, passing the turnoff to Old Hachita, then entered the current town of Hachita, where the general store, to my surprise, was open and freshly painted a dark lime green. The first time we came to Hachita fifteen years ago, the store had been open, and so had a nearby café. There were gas pumps out in front of the store that worked, and near the gas pumps, a sale rack of ponchos made in Mexico blew in the wind. Then in succeeding years, the store had closed—no more ponchos, no more functioning gas pumps. No longer was the café open, or even the bar.

Hachita is a very small desert town, a stop on the way from Arizona to Texas on a road that parallels the place where the railroad tracks used to run. When the railroad faded, as did the mines, the town dwindled, so that it is mostly empty now, marked by a tall brown water tower beside the main crossing of Route 9 with Route 146, which comes down from the interstate farther north. The Hachita Store, which sits at the little-traveled intersection, surrounded by dry, desert fields, had closed and opened again several times since we had begun coming here. It was always a surprise when we arrived. Would the store be open or closed, and, if open, what would it have inside?

At first, this was a pretty well-stocked store, with everything you might want for a trip along Route 9 or for convenience. And it was a community center of sorts. There were video game machines and a lottery machine in the corner by the front window, a coffeemaker, some tables with salt and pepper shakers and sugar on them, waiting for people who might stop by and heat up a hot dog or a burrito. Then it closed, and for years nothing but an empty store sat beside the road—no longer were there gas pumps out front; a sign posted on the glass front door said that "Wednesday" there would be a "community meeting at 8 P.M." But where was the meeting, where was the community center the sign referred to? What month or week was the sign put up? We stopped by and read it but never knew.

I felt sad that the Hachita Store had closed. I missed it. I felt, "What's to become of us? We just found this small town of Hachita, and now it's gone, or threatening to be gone." I'd had a sense that if we needed anything, we could get it at the store. Now, the interior was dark, hidden behind dusty windows, abandoned. Was this really a place to come to anymore—the Big Hatchet Mountain area?

For me, it was. But I worried about Hannah. Would she still want to travel here with me? Would she bring me back without this connection to civilization? The store had a restroom. Now there would be no restroom, only the desert, but so exposed, no big rocks to hide behind in the places where we went, only the open space marked by scattered, spiny shrubs. It would be easy to see us from anywhere—two women squatting among the cactus, cows nearby.

"Do you remember that time after the store had been closed for a few years and we came here and all of a sudden, it was open again?" I asked Hannah as we pulled in today in front of the reopened Hachita Store and considered going in.

"I do," she said. "There were trailers parked over there." She gestured toward a vacant lot adjacent to the asphalt parking area in front of the store.

"Do you recall who was in those trailers?" I asked.

"It was the Border Patrol and workers. They were living in the trailers while they were building the fence between New Mexico and Mexico down in Antelope Wells. They gave the store enough business so it could open again."

"The fence," I thought. I had never seen it. The time we drove down the twenty-nine miles from Big Hatchet to the border at Antelope Wells, I had felt surrounded by a sense of open space, the fields on both sides extending into each other. There was nothing but a stop sign on the road right at the border. If you stepped over it, you were in Mexico. There was no big fence, no wall, only various ranchers' fences in the semi-distance merging into the background of golden-brown dry grasses. I had liked that feeling of open borders, of one land, one country merging into the other, of one desert.

Yet as I had stood and looked off across the border, it felt so different on the other side. It was awe inspiring to me to feel I was seeing across into Mexico, that I had glimpsed another country, particularly this storied one, a country of my imagination—of Spanish-speaking people, Mexican foods, a different way of life, a different culture. Yet the mountains extended as if they were one. I still have the photos I took of the border crossing that day. When I look at them, I see, as I did at the time, a low mountain peak in the near distance on the other side. It still takes my breath away when I see it. "That peak is in Mexico," I tell myself, feeling that makes it mysterious, far away, yet close at hand, somehow magical. I had stood in the sunlight, looking toward the peak and the shimmering land around it and felt fortunate to be viewing it, grateful for the wide open spaces. Ahead of me, the small stop sign sat beside a modest Border Patrol building on the right-hand side of the road.

On that earlier trip, Hannah, my guide dog Teela, and I got out of the car in front of the Port of Entry building, careful to stay on the New Mexico side of the border. I did not want to step accidentally into Mexico and then get arrested or ticketed. A sign high above us near the building said, "Beware, Poisonous Snakes." I looked around suspiciously. My eyesight was fading and I didn't want to step on an unseen snake, or have Teela discover one for me. But it was winter, and the snakes probably were not this near the building. The sign was in Spanish as well as English—"Cuidado Con Viboras"—with a picture of a large snake with a rattle on its tail below bright red lettering warning "Beware." I took a picture of the striking yellow sign, more bold, more big and colorful than any that warned us away from the border. Snakes were more to be feared than anything else in this area, I thought.

Hannah, Teela, and I entered the glass-walled Border Patrol building and asked if we could use a restroom. They didn't have one officially, the agent said, but we could use theirs. We were grateful.

After using the restroom, we left. I was reluctant to depart, not sure if I would ever be back, but expecting I might. But what was there to see—nothing, a border, without much to do. No major traffic crossed this way. There was no one in sight for miles, only the Border Patrol agents in their office looking out their broad windows doing their daily surveillance. As Hannah drove us off, I kept turning around to look back to see what we were leaving behind, getting a view of that peak that was in Mexico beyond the vast plain on the other side that was as bare and brown as it was on the U.S. side. As we headed back toward where we came from, I saw a big green sign looming on the return side of the road. "¡Bienvenidos! Welcome!" it said, "Port Antelope Wells," with a large picture of an antelope displayed up top. "Pride in N.M. Ports." I thought of the "Beware of Snakes" sign across the way, its message more somber and worrisome, warning of danger so close to the border when really there was nothing there—nothing in the landscape to mark a change, but something deep and important nonetheless.

I thought of borders—the invisible borders between Hannah and me and the rest of the world, between us and the straight world, between us and each other, between the world of the sighted and me as blind. All these invisible boundaries separated different cultures. I thought of the landscape, how it held secrets not obvious, how the desert was a map without markings, a road map to be charted by us. I thought of us and of our travels, how we sought out places where we could be ourselves.

Hannah drove us slowly back up the narrow black-topped road from Mexico toward Hachita, passing the shining rock face of Big Hatchet Mountain looming on the east, reflecting the late afternoon sun.

"Do you remember the time we were buzzed by the Border Patrol helicopter?" I asked Hannah now, eleven years later, as we drove south from Hachita again, heading for the open spaces around Big Hatchet.

"Yes, that was unnerving."

"After that, I didn't know if I wanted to come down here anymore."

"It seemed like our privacy was being invaded."

"Yes. I felt like we weren't wanted."

I saw again in my mind that day when we had driven down, the clusters of Soaptree Yucca waving their tall spires at us from the fields beside the road. We passed the main turnoff toward Big Hatchet Mountain and were about to pull into a clearing alongside the road when Hannah noticed men across the way installing additional barbed-wire fences. On our drive down, we had seen them too, stringing the fences and inserting the supports where previously there had not been fences by the road down here. In the clearing where we turned in to park, a man with bulldozing equipment eyed us suspiciously, as if we had no right to be here. Yet we had come here many times before, pulled off the black-topped road to park in a cleared area and walk in on a dirt path close to the mountain, surrounded by scrub, jack rabbits, cactus, cows in the distance. This was public land, aside from the ranches, and usually we were alone. But today, it was not our own space; there was something tense in the air.

We got out of the car. I hooked Teela up and put her harness on in preparation for our walk up near the mountain. When we got to a connecting path where the packed dirt road climbs a small hill, the ruts were so deep that we decided to turn around and instead walk on a side road paralleling the main blacktop. As I started back, a loud buzzing suddenly commanded my attention. I looked up. I could not see well enough to make out the source of the noise, but Hannah could. "It's a helicopter," she said.

"Do you think they could be buzzing us?" I asked.

"I don't think so," she said. "Maybe they are looking for someone illegally crossing."

The helicopter hovered and did not seem to go away.

"I think it's us," Hannah said. "It's coming right over us." She looked up. I followed her gaze. Teela looked up.

"Shall we wave at them?" I said.

"I wouldn't. They might not like that."

I stared up intently and thought I saw a cockpit, perhaps a red body of a plane. "What color is it?" I asked Hannah.

"It's gray, or camouflage. I think they are looking down at us."

I waved, wanting to make us seem friendly, but really wanting to signal them to go away. They spun a few times, hovered a bit longer, then flew off on their way to the next situation that might need their attention.

"That wasn't terrific," I said to Hannah. "I don't like that. It kind of ruins the solitude."

The man with the bulldozer spun his vehicle around and stared again at us, as if he and the helicopter people were in cahoots, as if he was glad for the affirmation of the activity overhead, as if he was saying, "You don't belong here."

"I don't want to be intimidated," I turned and said to Hannah. "I want us to keep walking." Though in my mind, I thought: I don't know. I don't know if I want to be here anymore. Maybe we shouldn't come back here again. Our separateness, my sense of our being someplace special alone where nobody else goes—it feels broken now, invaded. Maybe this border is too busy now, because of the concerns with illegal crossings. Maybe it's not a place for us anymore.

"Maybe we shouldn't come back here in the future," I said out loud to Hannah.

"You can think about that later," she said.

"Let's go for our walk," I said, as I picked up Teela's harness handle and we set out on the side road exposed to the sky that headed us, for a while, south toward Mexico.

As we walked, I thought of the fact that when we were nearer the mountain, we were more hidden; we wouldn't be as easily seen by a helicopter overhead. I wished we were over in that more protected place now. But we were out in the open, the sun bright, the air cool, almost chilly. Hannah had on a winter hat. We came upon a road sign that showed a curve, warning that the straight asphalt road beside us that led toward Mexico would soon take a slight turn. I looked off into the distance using the telephoto lens of my camera and thought I almost could make out the low mountain peak I had seen years earlier when we were at the Port of Entry down in Antelope Wells.

I thought of people who weren't us, who, I suspected, the helicopter was designed to apprehend, migrants who might be coming across these dry fields in the shadow of the mountains. I didn't think there were many people coming across in this area, but maybe the helicopter was part of the new set of tools the Border Patrol was using, tied to an increased desire to stop illegal crossings and contraband.

A concern with illegality had not been very much on my mind during the previous years we had been coming here, though I knew it existed. But it seemed minimal, and apart from us. I had worried that there might be some poor person making his way through the desert who might break into our car when we parked it to walk off toward the mountains. But I thought that any person doing that might, just as likely, be any regular traveler on the road, seeing a car that might have valuables inside. Hannah and I were, after all, women from the city, so we knew to lock our car and hide our valuables when we left it.

Still, I was feeling confused and jolted now, unsettled by the helicopter surveillance.

"Let's get in the car and drive in closer to the mountain," I suggested to Hannah after we had walked a while. "Let's take the road that goes along the back side of Big Hatchet. Maybe they won't buzz us over there."

"I'd like that," she said. "Maybe we will see a nice sunset."

At first when we came to Big Hatchet, no helicopter had buzzed us. No one seemed to be bothered by us. We did see occasional white Border Patrol vehicles, mostly driving the road up from Mexico. Maybe the drivers waved once or twice. Certainly they looked at us in our car. Possibly they looked at our license plate.

"I think they are writing down the number," I remember Hannah saying back then. So we did feel noticed. But primarily I was aware of the fields, the desert, a few ranch vehicles, cows, scrub, distant mountains getting closer and closer as we drove toward them, and the Hachita Store and the little town in the background. The Border Patrol was present but not invasive. Even when they began to stop us by the roadside, there was a carefulness in the manner of the agents.

I remember the first time a Border Patrol truck stopped us. We were coming back up the blacktop from the direction of Mexico, though we had not gone all the way to the Port of Entry. We had only gone around far enough to see the other side of Big Hatchet—the side with the rock face that would glow in the afternoon sun.

We were driving back up when a white Border Patrol truck came up behind us slowly and flashed its lights.

"He's waving us over." Hannah said. "I'm pulling to the side."

She nosed the car over to the shoulder of the road and opened her window.

The Border Patrol agent pulled up next to her in the road, rolled down his window, and politely asked, "What brings you to this area?"

I was stumped, at first, about what to say. So I decided to be honest. "I like this mountain," I said, gesturing toward Big Hatchet on my right. "We come here once a year so I can visit it. I like how it feels to be out here. We live in San Francisco. We teach at a university. We just visit. We walk around. I think it's special here."

He nodded, as if, though odd, that might be true. He smiled.

Hannah said, "Yes, that's why we're here. Do you want to see any documentation?"

"That won't be necessary," he said. "Do you ladies need anything?"

"I have a headache," Hannah said, "but we're okay. We don't need anything."

"Well if you do, just let us know."

He drove off, giving us a small wave.

Afterward, I felt surprisingly glad for his visit—both because I felt we had been given permission to be here, and because I knew that when we came to Big Hatchet, Hannah often tended to become afraid that if we got lost or stuck in the desert, no one would come to help us. She felt we were more in danger as we drove closer in toward the mountain, which we often did on the back side.

I was not worried in the same way, however, because it felt so magical for me to be here. I thought that if we got stuck, some rancher in a truck would come by and find us, since the dirt roads we were driving on went through miles of ranchland that were looked after by the various neighboring ranchers. I also thought we were generally careful where we went. And I liked getting closer and closer to the mountain.

"It's good, don't you think?" I turned and said to Hannah after the agent had gone. "The Border Patrol is watching out for us. If we need anything, they'll help us. You don't have to worry so much anymore."

She gave me a skeptical look. Clearly, being pulled over by a law enforcement agent was not, on the face of it, a welcome experience. I think she was not sure that even the Border Patrol would find us. More likely, I thought, it would be the ranchers.

"If they don't find us, the ranchers will," I offered.

"I have a headache," she said, putting her finger to her temple.

"I had a feeling," I said, "that if I had asked for a band-aid, he would have given us one. We're not alone out here as much as we feel we are."

"Maybe," she said turning the car off the main road and onto the dirt road that led closer to the mountain, the three peaks of Big Hatchet looming before us beyond fields of golden grasses. "But I don't want to stay too long today," she said. "I have a head-ache. I think I am coming down with the flu. But I'll take you. Let's go a little farther, and we'll come back again another day when I'm feeling better."

After that first time, the Border Patrol didn't always stop us. But I was prepared to tell my story. It hadn't been hard. It had seemed odd to say we were here just to visit a mountain that was nowhere and where no one went except people taking care of their cattle and perhaps some individuals illegally crossing. But my explanation wasn't difficult for me to give. I felt it made us seem innocuous. I rarely feel innocuous—in fact, just the oppo-site. Always, I feel, as I did at that time, "But we're lesbians. We don't believe in police or Border Patrol apprehending people coming over the border and what they sometimes do to them. We don't, or I don't, believe in strict lines between countries, in mili-tary, in wars and fighting." I had all the prejudices that people often do against nationalistic marshaling of brute strength. And here I was feeling that the Border Patrol agents were our friends and should be·reassuring to Hannah.

After that incident of being stopped by the side of the road, I did feel much better about Border Patrol agents, at least those in this area. We were different from them, I knew. We were two women intimate with one another. We taught at a university. We represented views not the same as theirs. But maybe we were not that far apart, simply occupying different spaces, different insti-tutional structures, different lives.

There was this polite border between us and them, I thought. I didn't, in practice, have to deal with a border between my own and another country, like the Border Patrol agents did down at Antelope Wells. But I did have to deal with a border between me and others, between me and people with other lives. I was concerned about the border between Hannah and me as a couple and the outside world. I didn't like strangers stepping over it. We weren't an open borderless country when it came to relating to the outside.

It was all too complex to think about, to settle once and for all, or on one day here.

"Let's head on back now," I said to Hannah as the sun began to set and the winds came up and the wails of coyotes began to fill the air. We turned the car around and headed back toward Hachita and north as darkness fell. I reached for Hannah's hand, glad for her comforting presence beside me. I glanced behind us toward Teela, who lay stretched out on the back seat, and felt the reassurance of our private world.

The next year when we visited Big Hatchet, I was surprised that no one stopped us as we drove farther along Route 9. We were very close to the border. It ran almost alongside the road on the stretch just east of Hachita. We hadn't driven this far on Route 9 before. We usually headed directly south to go down to Big Hatchet. But over here, the land opened out even more expansively. A wide desert plain extended beside us backed by a line of distant mountains. Looking out at that plain, we were looking into Mexico.

As one after another white Border Patrol van passed us by on the road, "Why aren't they stopping us?" I asked Hannah. "We aren't driving the same car as before."

"I don't know," she said. "Maybe they have more important things to do. Maybe we don't look threatening."

"Maybe because we are driving a Candy Apple Red SUV," I said, very aware, as I always am, of the details of our rental car. This one had a big spare tire on the back also in a covering of Candy Apple Red. It was brighter than the usual red car, and had started out very shiny, so much so that a man in a truck, earlier in our trip, had stopped beside us in a supermarket parking lot, opened his window, and called out, "Great car!" Compliments like that made me feel part of things. We were different, and stood out, but people still could be friendly.

I looked over at Hannah who was navigating the road while surveying the broad fields to our right, the white vans passing by, the sense of endless blacktop in front of us.

"How about if we turn back soon?" she said.

"Too many white cars? Too close to Mexico?"

"Yes. I would rather go see our mountain."

As we turned in on the side dirt road heading toward the back of Big Hatchet, the air felt cool and clear. A stillness surrounded us, a sense of remove from the road and vehicles miles away. We turned right on a farther dirt road cutting through the fields of brush and the remains of cow patties, then rounded a bend heading closer in. "They're in our spot," I said suddenly to Hannah.

"I see them," she said.

A white van sat in a clearing beside a lone tree. A discarded huge black truck tire lay beside it. The driver of the van sat in the front seat focusing on something on the seat next to him. He didn't seem to be paying any attention to us.

"I guess we just continue," Hannah said.

"Yes, keep driving."

As we headed on, I thought of how often we had stopped in that clearing, how if the Border Patrol van had not been there, we would have pulled in, parked the car, and walked, for a while, on the road, surrounded by the cactus, tarbush, and silence; how sometimes when we came upon stray cows and steers in this area, Hannah would worry that they might charge us or that we would scare the cattle. This wasn't a spot way up close to the mountain, where we would often go, continuing on, but it was one of our spots, one of our stopping places.

"The agent didn't bother us," I said as we drove, feeling that was odd. "He didn't stop us. He didn't ask what we were doing here."

"Probably he had been notified of our plates," Hannah said. "Or maybe we're just not that important."

"I don't like it," I said. "They're all around. We just don't notice them."

"I don't like it either. But forget them. Focus on us. We're here. Look around."

I looked toward the hulking shape of the two peaks of the mountain that seemed to envelop each other ahead of us.

"Let's go farther. Let's head toward the windmill," I said, wishing to find us a more protected place.

The following year, when the Border Patrol buzzed us with their helicopter, it felt like the last straw. As Hannah and I drove back from our time at the mountain that day, she turned to me— "Next time," she said, "I want you to call first."

"Call the Border Patrol?"

"Yes. Tell them we're coming."

"Then maybe they won't send the helicopter after us?"

"That, and I will feel better if someone knows we are out here. Anything could happen to us. I have been wanting you to do that for a long time."

The next year, I called the Border Patrol local office before we set out for Big Hatchet from where we were staying farther north.

"I want to let you know we will be in the Big Hatchet area today," I said. "We're two women. We're from San Francisco. We teach at a university. Each year about this time, we come and visit the mountain. I am legally blind. We travel with my guide dog. Would you like our license plate number?"

"Thank you," the supervisor said. "And the make of the car would be helpful too."

I gave him both.

"What time do you expect to arrive and to leave?"

How could I know exactly when? I thought. So much was up to chance out here.

"We'll be coming around 11 A.M.," I said, "leaving about 5 or soon after sunset."

"I'll tell my men."

"Another thing. Last year when we were in the area, we were buzzed with a helicopter. Could you ask them not to do that?"

"Sure. I'll tell them. Thank you for calling."

"I did it," I said to Hannah after hanging up the phone, surprising myself that I had actually made the call. Often Hannah asks me to do things that I would never think of doing on my own. And this was one of them.

"He was nice about it. He thanked me."

"I thank you too," she said.

In the next few years, the Border Patrol did not stop us. I called each day before we set out, gave them our car make and license plate number. And each time, the local manager politely said, "I'll tell my men."

Still, I questioned whether we should go back, especially that first year after the helicopter incident. Maybe I had been to Big Hatchet enough now. Maybe it was getting boring, I thought. Maybe it was too much like a war zone; there was too much Border Patrol activity.

The year after the helicopter buzzed us, for instance, as we were returning from our day at the mountain, we pulled the car to the side of the wide dirt road that runs along the back of it, surrounded by miles of scrub, tan earth and scrawny bushes, grasses waving golden in the sun. I got out of the car and was standing at the edge of the road watching the gold color glinting off the grasses, waiting for the sun to set. Maybe there would be some orange color over Big Hatchet later, I thought, some cloud that might turn pink in the afterglow. But the sky above the mountain was clear.

I began walking along the edge of the road, my camera with its telephoto aimed at the various desert plants, wanting to keep some images of the yucca with their tall spires and the gnarled cactus as a remembrance, wanting to stay here, to savor the scene, to be uninterrupted before we left.

"Get back in the car," Hannah called suddenly. "Step over to the side. They're coming!"

"Who's coming?" I called into the wind, quickly stepping off the road, to the side, and up into a place among the yucca. As I looked over toward the sandy dirt road, a white van with a tall radio tower atop it began to approach. Standing next to the tower in the open back of the van was a Border Patrol agent dressed in camouflage.

I raced back to the car and got in beside Hannah.

The van with the tower pulled up alongside us. "How are you doing?" the driver asked through his open window. "Do you need anything?"

"We're fine," Hannah said. "We don't need anything. We're going to watch the sunset."

"Nice," the driver said with a thoughtful manner and a relaxed smile.

I looked over my shoulder back at the radio tower. I assumed it was for transmitting and capturing signals to aid in the Border Patrol's efforts to know who was in the desert around us or near, or on, the mountain and what they were doing.

I didn't think it was tracking us.

The young man in the van standing next to the tower waved. The agents were always friendly now, often asked if we needed anything. But this was the first time I had seen a radio tower atop one of the trucks. The driver of the van with the tower on his vehicle pulled forward, then drove on. He was followed by another white van without a radio tower, then, a few moments later by two white trucks. The drivers slowed and waved as they passed us.

It was nearing 5 P.M. They had probably seen us earlier in the day, I thought, noted down our license plate, been told not to bother us by the supervisor back in the local office, and gone about their business. But it haunted me that they had been hiding in the desert in the nearby fields, or been somewhere farther off where we did not see them, been there all along as we walked out here, pretending it was just us.

"It's just us now," I said to Hannah after they drove off. "I think maybe this is the end of their shift. Maybe between this and the next shift, we'll be alone here to watch the sunset."

"Maybe," she said.

In my mind, I see us during those years after we began calling the Border Patrol before we set out, and during that earlier period when their presence was becoming more obvious. They were part of the landscape as much as the dry brush, the tall, elegant ocotillo, the little groups of cows that had somehow strayed from the herd.

I see us one memorable day when we had driven in closer to the mountain and walked on a path that led east toward the Mexican border, which was out of view but not, in fact, very far away. The boundary with Mexico was closer here on the north side of the mountain heading east than when we drove south along the face of Big Hatchet toward Antelope Wells. But the border must be more impassible here, I thought. The dark shape of the three peaks of the mountain were glistening on our right, fields for cattle on our left—though always it was unclear to me how the cattle found much of sustenance in that dry scrub and the wispy, scattered grasses.

We walked that day around a cattle guard, the sun shining on the rocky ground at our feet, then climbed toward a windmill we had not visited for quite a while. I remembered when we first came upon that windmill fifteen years before—back when Teela was first with me and everything was special, everything was new—back when we first discovered Big Hatchet after a long drive south.

Today near the windmill, Hannah, Fresco, and I stopped. "Where is it?" I asked Hannah after we had climbed the rocky path up, passed the cement water storage tank dry as it could be.

"It's ahead of you," she said, pointing forward.

"I can't see it," I said. "I can't see any windmill."

"It's there," she said. "There's a solar panel on the ground in front of it."

I looked down at the ground at the shiny surface of several small, square solar plates, then up. A metal scaffolding rose next to the solar plaques. But on top of the A-shaped scaffolding, the windmill was gnarled. It had lost its wooden paddles. Where once they had proudly spread out in a circle to catch and transport the wind, making it into energy, making it strong, now there was only a center piece of bent steel—misshapen, high in the air, the wind hitting it, not sure what to do.

"Like us," I thought, not sure what to do in this vast terrain, this world of others than ourselves, this world both like us and not like us—where people went about on their other duties, only sometimes taking notice of us, yet wanting to know if we were going to be there.

It had been a long time since we had been coming to Big Hatchet, I thought—since we had last climbed up to see the windmill. It wasn't a long time in terms of Hannah's and my entire relationship with each other. But it was a long time nonetheless. That time spanned the period since I had begun to lose my eyesight and since I had begun traveling with a guide dog. It spanned a lot of Hannah's and my getting to know each other, learning to travel, to go off together—learning how to work things out. Hannah had taken me back here to Big Hatchet year after year—except when one of our pets at home was sick or dying and needed our help. We had skipped two of the years among the fifteen. But we had experienced this extended, solitary desert over all those years even so.

"Our windmill," I said to Hannah. "It's gone, or pretty gone. It's sad."

"They're both here," she said. "They're using solar power now, but the windmill is still here. Remember that. Notice that. Both the old and the new survive. Times change. Our experiences change. But we have each other." She came close and gave me a kiss.

I returned her kiss and felt her softness, the shape of her body against mine. I looked over her shoulder at the desert and thought of us.

"Remember that time you posed me by the ocotillo with the windmill in the background?" I said. "You posed me with Teela for a picture. I still have that picture."

"Yes," she said. "Let's see if we can find the spot."

I scampered up the hill, with Fresco by my side, searching for the tall ocotillo from before. There was no one obvious plant. Ocotillos here were few and far between. Then there it was, a scrawny remnant, maybe what was left of the original, or perhaps one of its seedlings.

"It's thin, but maybe it's this one." I pointed.

We didn't take a picture of it, of me with Fresco in the same place as when Hannah had photographed Teela and me years earlier—the tall ocotillo waving its fronds behind us, the windmill in the background, the broad desert below us stretching out into the distance, the bordering mountain ranges keeping nothing out, but marking the plain, marking the space, the land turning yellow in the afternoon sun.

Hannah and I had grown to prize the late afternoon light out here at Big Hatchet, I thought. It turned everything gold. It hit the grasses and shrubs, hit our faces, hit my golden dogs, made us feel special to be here—at a remove, not bothered, not in our usual spots, our usual haunts, not in the city, not surrounded by others, by white trucks or cattle ranchers or helicopters. Now we were here only with each other. I put my arm around Hannah's shoulder. She came close, slipping her arm around my waist as we stood looking out. A world was far below and at a distance in the outstretched desert. Close by, I felt the quiet surrounding us, saw the land bathed in gold, and treasured my memories of other times—some more peaceful than others, perhaps. But really all of them were peaceful. The only rough parts that mattered were those that might disrupt the life between us. And we were here now out at Big Hatchet—out in the desert where few people went, or cared to go, other than the ranchers, the hunters, the Border Patrol, the occasional hikers and migrants. But this space wasn't theirs. It was ours. Wherever we went, we were in our own space together. The outside world, it was just that—outside. It intruded sometimes, unsettling us. But we didn't let it destroy us even when it entered in sometimes over our boundaries.

"Focus on us," I remembered Hannah had said that time I bemoaned the presence of the white Border Patrol van in "our spot" in the clearing near the cattle. "Focus on us. We're here. We're together."

I thought about how she had so often helped me keep the world out, helped me keep disturbing thoughts at bay, helped me feel more settled and reassured within myself, took me places even if they were foreign to her, places where I could feel at a remove. She was magical to me, somehow unexpected. She was practical yet happy to go on new adventures with me. I took her hand as the three of us walked down the rocky path on the side of the mountain, then along the back road toward our car.

We drove out that day through the small town of Hachita with the store that was only sometimes open and the bar that had closed and not opened again, and we stopped in at the Hachita Store. I bought a tube of toothpaste and a frozen burrito before we went on our way. Just before we pulled out of the parking lot, a woman clerk from inside came out to ask if I wanted water for my dog. She disappeared and returned with a large, white mixing bowl full of fresh water from the hose outside.

"Wouldn't want him thirsty," she said. "I like dogs."

"Thank you," I said, wondering what she saw when she looked at us: two women, traveling, friends, or lovers? One had a dog.

"Let's head out," I said to Hannah.

With my toothpaste, burrito, and some memories of an earlier time, we drove on, heading back west toward other borders with other meanings, and other places we might call our own.

"It was a good day, don't you think?" I said to Hannah as the setting sun shone on the fields beside us, turning them a bright straw-colored tan, lighting the land as if it were a shining sea.

"A very good day," she said. "With you, all of them are good."

Fifteen

Looking Back

We pulled the car off to the side of a small back road leading inland from the sea, in a spot where high grasses lined a clearing glistening in the sun. Beside the opening, a broad metal gate was swung back, making the narrow dirt road ahead seem inviting but private. Maybe it led to someone's house, I thought. Maybe we were not supposed to go on it.

"I don't know about this," Hannah said, getting out of the car. "I don't like to trespass. There's no sign telling us whether this is a public road or not."

"The gate is open," I said. "If someone doesn't want us there, they can come and tell us to leave."

I liked the sense of the road being unmarked, though I knew Hannah liked to have things be defined, to know exactly where she was.

"Let's walk on it," I said. I opened the back door of the car. Fresco jumped out. I put his harness on him. Hannah and I took up our bags and we started out.

The sun was filtering through the branches of the tall trees all around us that lined both sides of the road, bringing with it the spirit of the ocean not far away, though here, in the woods in the shadow of the coastal mountains, we felt in a separate world.

The road quickly dipped down to a spot where a wooden bridge crossed an adjacent creek. I stepped carefully following Fresco, following Hannah. I looked over at her. She was sparkling just like the sunlight on the earth, reminding me of how much I loved her, of her brightness for me, her guiding spirit in my life.

As we walked, the road began to climb. On one side of us was a hill rising from the ravine in which we were proceeding. On the other side of the soft dirt road was a drop-off to a swiftly running creek sunken deep below, its waters gurgling and racing, making a rich whooshing sound I heard against the gentle rustling of the trees. The air felt clear and crisp with a touch of the wetness that seeped through the earth and trickled down the hillside to my left in places. The new spring growth—the green sprouts and shoots beside the path—freshly damp, alive and vibrant—made this particular walk feel like a new beginning, a fresh start, an adventure.

As we walked, we talked, as if this dreamlike road demanded looking back.

"Do you remember," I asked Hannah, "that time when we first went to the beach down the coast just after we met?"

"And you made us chicken sandwiches?"

"Yes, that time."

"I think the beach was somewhere in this area, maybe where this creek lets out at the shore."

"I remember playing Frisbee on that beach," she said.

"I remember the hippie school bus parked by the side of the road in front of the restaurant with the blue windows while we were waiting at the gas pumps across from the ocean to get gas. I wanted us to travel around in a bus like that, a bus that could be our entire home."

"We don't exactly have a bus," she said. "But we have each other. Wherever we go together, it's our home."

"Now watch out!" she announced suddenly. "Follow close behind me. There's a puddle coming up in a pothole on your left."
I stared ahead, but the damp earth in front of me looked all the
same, shining with the wetness of the previous day's rain and with
the indentations of tire tracks on both sides of a raised center section. I stepped quickly behind Hannah as Fresco neatly avoided
the deep mud puddle. We continued that way for a while, hopping
back and forth between mud puddles in the road. "It's kind of
fun," I said, though it was somewhat tense. I was not always sure if
I was missing a puddle. "I just stepped into one," I told Hannah.
"Be careful," she called back to me. When the road evened out,
we resumed our conversation.

"Do you remember our first trip to New Mexico?" I asked her.

"You took me to see every ex-lover you ever had."

"Most of them, yes. But I think I missed one."

"And when we moved in together, remember my boxes?"

"You left them in the guest room unpacked for a very long
time."

"But we made it. We finally began living together. It took
three years."

"That seems like a short time now, but it felt long then."

"Do you remember that time your mother first came to visit?"
I asked her. "She didn't approve of me initially. But I liked that
she had a sense of humor."

"And your mother?"

"She liked you right away," I said. "You were the daughter she
never had."

"I'm small and Jewish, and I know how to talk to people."

"You do. You have a lot of tact."

"It's stage presence. Both my parents liked the theater."

"You never met my father," I reflected. "I wish you had. He
would have liked you. He was a historian. He liked to collect old
documents, like you do. Do you know, he didn't approve of my
marriage to Joel? He thought Joel was probably gay."

"And he was."

"But at the time, neither he nor I knew. We were being hetero-sexual, doing what was expected."

"Are you glad you chose me?" Hannah asked.

"Definitely. I can't imagine being with anyone else." I looked over at her and smiled. "I also sometimes have a hard time understanding you because you are different from me."

"You mean I like things to make sense?"

"Yes. But you feel you have a monopoly on reality. You always think you know best what is real or true. You think that when I disagree with you, I am wrong, that I don't understand how things work."

"Sometimes you don't."

"Remember Esperita."

"You were right about that. Esperanza loved that floppy, stuffed dog that you found for her in the grocery store. I didn't think she needed it. But you were sure she would love it."

"Do you think often about our wedding day?" I asked her.

"I prefer to call it our 'marriage day.'"

"Sometimes I do too. Did you ever really think, before then, that we needed to get married?"

"No. I thought we were doing fine as we were. I got used to not being married, to being just us, 'domestic partners.'"

"I never liked that expression much. It doesn't summarize us," I said.

"Nothing does. Financially, it was good to be domestic partners, and financially, it was an advantage for us to get married."

"Yes, I know. But I still feel. . . ."

"I know how you feel. All the same advantages should go to people as individuals."

"I wasn't sure how I would survive our marriage day, so much ritual, and City Hall, and people being interested and wishing us well."

"I liked that."

"I liked our trip down the coast afterward, our honeymoon."

"It wasn't really a honeymoon."

"For me it was. I liked going with the dogs. I miss Esperanza."

"I know you do."

"I want a puppy. I really want a little black dog again."

"Not now. I feel it's too much for me now."

"Maybe kittens?"

"Yes. When kitten season comes, we'll look. There should be many of them then."

"I can't wait."

I looked up at the tall trees, felt the breeze. Kitten season was almost here. It was spring, a time of new beginnings. Our time has always been the fall though, I thought and said aloud to Hannah.

"Because that was when we met. It's also the season when we started to go to New Mexico."

"I remember how, the first time we went, the chamisa made you sneeze. You had terrible allergies."

"But I did it for you dear. I wanted to know about your life."

"And now the trip is more ours. It's something we do together that's unusual for us."

"Eva encouraged us," Hannah said. "She affirmed how important the trip was for our relationship. She always liked to hear about our travels afterward."

"I miss Eva."

"I do too."

"Did you think when we first saw Eva that we might break up?" I asked her.

"I don't know that I did. I thought we needed help, or I needed help. You were a lot to handle."

"Things weren't going smoothly."

"I like them to go smoothly. You're right."

I thought of how much Hannah "smoothed" our lives, not liking outbursts, friction, problems unsolved between us. She liked, instead, a sense of the two of us together, almost taking each other for granted, giving each other space, though that was hard sometimes; it was hard to be together and yet separate, to be like each other and yet different.

"I remember when I first met you, you had your Siamese cat, Mocha, and I had my calico Jenny," I said as we continued walking. "Mocha was a very scared cat."

"But she was a good mouser. I got her when I lived alone in my apartment and I had a mouse. Mocha caught it. I was terrified of mice."

"I brought Jenny with me from New Mexico along with my dog Geronimo."

"Then when they died, we got all these other animals."

"I like having a lot of animals," I said.

"Sometimes it's too much though, when they are sick."

"We had three dogs and three cats after I got Fresco and we still had Teela and Esperanza."

"That was quite a household."

"And now it's just you, me, and Fresco. I feel lonely sometimes with just the three of us. It was very hard for me when Sienna and Shadow died this winter. We lost five of our animals in four years. It makes me sad. I miss them all."

Hannah stepped toward me and put her arm around me. "Keep walking," she said. "There will be more."

"Remember your tenure case, soon after we met?"

"My tenure case," she said gravely.

"It's still there in a way."

"Yes, it is."

"But you've shown them. You worked hard."

"I couldn't have done it without you. You helped me."

"I tried to."

"Remember your response to *The Mirror Dance* when I first showed it to you?" I asked.

"You had no grammar. Someone had to point that out to you eventually."

"I have only a little more grammar now. But yes, it helps. Still, I don't organize my writing in a way that you always think makes sense."

"It makes sense in its way. It's just not always my way. I'm your biggest fan."

"And I'm yours."

"When we walk on a road like this," she said, "I feel it's like when we go to New Mexico. It's an adventure, just us, not working, just experiencing something together, looking around."

"I like going places with you," she added. "You stay home a lot."

"I do. It's a warm, nurturant place for me where I work and keep company with the animals. We took care of Katie at home for a long time doing the hydration."

"We always take care of our animals. You care for them well."

"I like to do it."

"You make our house beautiful. You make everything beautiful."

"You take care of me."

"I try."

"Do you think we'll reach the end of this road?" I asked her as the meandering road began to climb more steeply toward a grove of spectacular redwoods ahead of us.

"It depends, maybe not on this walk," she said. "We'll go as far as it's comfortable for us. It's pretty now, don't you think, just us, and the freshness after the rains?"

"Many puddles. But yes, the greens are very green."

As we walked on, taking in the scenery, I marveled at the rushing stream, the edges of the road that dropped straight down. I enjoyed being together, letting Fresco sniff the low grasses, hearing the sounds of birds. I thought of how important the remove was for us, the sense of being in our own private world. I thought of Hannah's steadiness beside me. Eventually, we turned around and headed back. As we retraced our steps down the hill,

Hannah pointed out particular plants beside the road that she wanted to make sure I could see.

"Look to your right," she said suddenly. "What's that growing next to the yellow bush near you? It looks like something we once had in our yard, with the lilac-colored flowers."

"Ceanothus," I recalled, bending over to see it up close.

"Now look down. See where that stream of water, that rivulet, is flowing at the base of the hillside."

I followed her pointing finger toward some little blue flowers low to the ground on spikes of green. I squatted down with Fresco to study them more carefully. "They're forget-me-nots, I think. They grow all around the streams down here. They come out in the early spring. I like them."

"I thought you would."

Eyeing the stream of blue, I thought about the name of these flowers, how they wanted us not to forget them, just as I wanted not to forget my times with Hannah.

"What's that?" she pointed to a cluster of tall grasses with their heads curled up.

"Fiddlehead fern," I said, as if it were obvious.

Farther down the hill, in a patch of sunlight, Hannah raised her arms in joy, cupping her hands in front of her as if to catch something.

"Butterflies," she said. "Baby butterflies."

"What color are they?"

"White, I think. Maybe yellow."

"Any orange?"

"Maybe a little."

"Maybe they'll be monarchs?"

"Maybe."

I wished I knew more about butterflies. But I knew I was thinking not so much about them as about my life with Hannah and about my sight. I couldn't see the butterflies. I could only ask after them and admire Hannah's joy, her sense of discovery, her carefree arms in the air—the fact that she often could see what I could not. Among the major experiences that had marked our time together, my loss of sight certainly had to be one of them— like her tenure case in the early years, like our moving in togeth- er, our trips to New Mexico—during which, each year, I came to be aware of how much further my blindness had progressed, and of how much more I depended on Hannah to be my eyes, and more than that—to be close to me, to be my guide, my light, to bolster all of me.

I held out my arms, looking at Hannah ahead of me down the hill as if she, like the butterflies, would suddenly fly up.

She turned around. "Did you see them?" she asked.

I smiled. "I saw something. Maybe a yellow one."

"I'll take a picture of it for you. Then when you get home, you can see it on your computer." She took out her cell phone camera.

That evening when we got home, we looked up the name of the road we had so joyfully walked upon that day. Sitting in the dining room, Hannah took out her phone. "It says the name of that road is 'Old Woman's Creek Road.' It's not on all the maps though."

"Really?" I said. "Do you think it's named for an old woman, or is it an 'old' meaning 'former' Woman's Creek Road? Roads are sometimes called 'old' when a new road takes their place."

"It doesn't say," she noted. "Maybe it's named for an old wo- man who used to live there."

Still, I thought the name of this road was saying something about us. We were "old women" now in a way. I didn't feel old. But I knew Hannah and I were far older now than when we first met. It made sense that we might find a road called "Old Woman's Creek Road" just when we were in need of new beginnings. The creek—the swiftly rushing creek fed by fresh waters from high above—loomed in my mind. It seemed fitting that we would fol- low a road named for such a creek, for movement in space and time, fresh waters, circulating waters, heard through the wind on a bright sunny day.

A few weeks later, we went again to Old Woman's Creek Road, to see if it was really there, and to see if it still seemed as magical the second time around. It did. There were puddles again in the tire tracks. We started off on our walk, thinking now less of our past together than of what the future might hold. Somewhere midway into our walk, a blue truck came up the lonely road behind us. I heard its wheels on the gravel laid in the potholes and felt surprised that someone else was here—so much had I begun to think of this as a road on which only we traveled.

The approaching truck slowed and pulled over. "Howdy," the driver, a man in his mid-forties, scruffy as the truck, said. "Nice to see people with a dog out here. I hope the dog is enjoying the road."

"We love it," said Hannah.

"I'm on my way home from work," he said.

"You live up there at the end?"

"I do."

"Do you know why this is called 'Old Woman's Creek Road'?" I asked.

"They say there used to be an old woman who lived in a cabin at the far end up top. I don't know. I never met her. But she could have lived there."

"Do you think it was once an old logging road?"

"Could be. Don't know. You ladies enjoy yourselves now," he said.

I looked over at Hannah as he drove off, his vintage blue truck disappearing around a corner where the redwoods towered over the sunken stream.

"Maybe there's an old woman there we should meet," I smiled at her.

"We are the old women," she said.

"Not all that old."

"No, not all that old." She came close beside me and gestured toward the open space. "What matters is that this is our road," she said, "a place for us to walk and feel together."

That night, as on many before, I snuggled up to Hannah in bed. Dreams of new kittens, dreams of new roads, dreams of Hannah's soft body, her presence beside me, close to me, surrounding me, rich with her love; memories of old roads we had taken, paths through woods and cactus and yucca; memories of Border Patrol agents and other people's weddings; thoughts about how I didn't like to be called a wife filled my mind. I saw again the two "Baggie-tie brides" that danced atop our wedding cake.

I remembered the first time I had met Hannah in her office and wondered if she was a lesbian, then brought myself to ask directly. I had thoughts about how much we shared, teaching our courses, helping each other understand the larger world around us, going to the grocery store, making our dinners, going to the beaches, making our house our home.

I remembered the time when I had first attended a gay pride march with Hannah and watched the Dykes on Bikes zoom by. I had visions of us in bed in strange places, the neighbors at a distance through thick adobe walls; visions of my once throwing a coffee cup when I was upset, of Hannah making clear to me she wanted no more of that; visions of meeting her, small as she appeared in many an airport waiting room or in a parking lot; visions of watching after her as she left me to go off to teach her classes on campus; visions of her coming back to me, taking Teela and me into the car, driving us home from work, driving us other places. I remembered planning our trips—to New Mexico, to the beach, even to Hawaii once—hot as it was, finally an island paradise. I had visions of cleaning up after our many animals, of Teela and Fresco and Esperanza—of back when we had two golden guide dogs and one little black one; back when we had our cat Katie as well as Sienna and Shadow—all of us huddled in the bedroom at night, keeping each other warm. I had visions of years that went by quickly and slowly, visions of a future yet to unfold. I thought of tomorrow and the days to come.

I saw again the morning when I had gone out and viewed the glorious, velvet-red sunrise in the desert while Hannah was still asleep. Sometimes we had to be apart. But often we were together. I thought of Hannah's decency, her honesty, her arms around me, her seeing me, seeing us through it all. There was a firmness there. She was not letting me go.

The morning after our second visit to Old Woman's Creek Road, I rolled over in bed, gave Hannah a kiss, and tousled her hair.

"I wrote something," I told her. "It's a story about two women. They're something like us."

"Will I like it?" she asked.

"I hope so."

"I'll like it," she said.

Afterword

On Writing
Are You Two Sisters?

Because I am a sociologist, trained in the traditions of participant observation and ethnomethodology, I always think it is a good idea to tell the reader something about the method of a study and how it evolved. While no explanation can be complete, it can give some sense of the sources, motivation, and goals of the researcher or author.

The first story I wrote for *Are You Two Sisters?* was about a cat, Katie, who had lived with Hannah and me for almost twenty-two years. As I wrote about our caring for Katie, I felt that I was talking, more fundamentally, about Hannah's and my relationship with each other, how it had changed over time, how animals—our pets and two guide dogs—had figured in our life together, and about the caring nature of our home. I had previously written about my bond with my guide dog Teela, and this focus on a human-animal relationship seemed a natural next step. It did not occur to me at the time, though it did soon after, that it may have been easier for me to tell a story of our connection with a cat than to speak more directly of our relationship with each other, which felt very private. My Katie story now sits in the middle of this book as Chapter 8, a quiet reminder, at least for me, of the ways a lesbian intimacy may often appear as background, or be partially hidden, belying its importance.

Desiring to experiment further, I wondered what it would be like to confront the nature of a lesbian intimacy more directly. The "Early Memories" chapter followed as I looked back and tried to re-create, in my mind, the time Hannah and I had first met. What could I learn and share with others from looking at our beginnings? What themes might emerge? As I wrote, what came back to me especially was our identity as lesbians, two women who had, some years earlier, made the choice to seek their most intimate and nurturing moments with other women. I thought of our feelings of apartness from the larger heterosexual world. The challenges of female intimacy started to become foremost in my mind. I remember when I got to the end of that chapter and described attending our first gay pride march together the year we met—"If I include this," I thought, "Hannah will like it." I knew Hannah appreciated political representations of reality, and I wanted very much for her to like my work.

As I wrote, from the very beginning, I had in mind, "What would Hannah think?"—Hannah being a stand-in for the real-life woman whose experience I was also drawing upon. I kept asking myself, Am I representing our life in a way that is kind enough, true enough, full enough to incorporate some of her sense of reality as well? Am I making clear that this is only my view, though it is of a shared experience? Am I creating a representation of reality that is not harsh, but gentle, as I wished our relationship to be—and gentle even when I might be discussing difficult things—like my initial fears about getting involved with Hannah because she reminded me too much of my familial past?

But somehow working out those nuances of representation—how to portray the two of us although viewed from only one, and how to take into account how the other might feel—seemed worth it. I sensed a rare opportunity to explore issues of lesbianism and intimacies between women further than I had initially in *The Mirror Dance*, where I had dealt with similar issues, but in the context of a lesbian community.

After finishing "Early Memories" and showing it to Hannah and to a good friend who always reads my drafts, I felt an affirmation for at least this start. "Are you brave enough?" I remember my friend asking after reading the chapter, and I knew what she meant: "Am I brave enough to continue writing in this intimate manner in exploring the life of a lesbian couple?" I wasn't sure. It seemed presumptuous. But I felt a desire to take it on. I thought of other lesbian couples I had known and how I always wondered about their life behind the scenes. Ours would not be the same as theirs, but it was a reality I knew well.

I had started in sociology by interviewing others for my studies. Over time, my narratives concerning gender, sexuality, and disability had become more personal, or autoethnographic, drawing from my own experiences. Perhaps now I could extend the self-reflective approach I developed in my previous work to explore the emotional dilemmas—particularly the ambiguities, the unspoken and seemingly minor challenges, the pushes and pulls, the contradictions and the joys of a lesbian intimacy.

One of those conflicting pulls led to the next chapter, "The Pull of the Past," which describes our first long road trip together when Hannah and I traveled to New Mexico, where I had previously taught and where I now introduced her to old friends and lovers and to the desert landscape I had so enjoyed. As I wrote this chapter, I remembered how that trip had helped me pull myself into the present with Hannah and to detach from a past where she was not yet so central in my life. It was a deeply emotional chapter for me and, at the same time, a liberating one. After writing it, I felt able to commit more fully to the task of representing the journey of Hannah and me in my writing. We had a past we had broken away from to be with each other. We had a present that felt to me somehow daring.

As the subsequent chapters unfolded, each focusing on a shared experience that might be fruitful to explore in my search for insights revealing of a lesbian intimacy, I faced certain challenges. First was that of setting the scene. I wanted the reader to feel physically present with us in particular situations as I sought, within them, to explore issues important in our relationship. I would describe desert landscapes or rooms in houses, trips down the coast, or in San Francisco City Hall, hoping to make the scene feel tangible enough so the reader could share in, and reflect on, the experience along with me. Second was the challenge of representing both members of the couple in a natural way. For that purpose, I increasingly turned to the use of dialog. I often heard our voices in my mind as I wrote—the ways Hannah said or may have said things, my own style of response. I especially wanted to give a feel for Hannah through her speech, since so much of the storytelling came from within myself. Third was the challenge of selection: Which of all our experiences should I present in detail? Here I had to proceed intuitively, following an internal sense of direction, guided by particular themes. Still, as I wrote, I found myself constantly aware of a need to protect the very experiences I wished to describe. For just as Hannah and I felt a need to safeguard ourselves as lesbians in the outer world, I felt a need to protect us in my writing. What could I say that sheltered our relationship at the same time as I revealed it?

Several themes repeatedly came to mind for me as I wrote. These concerned the navigation of identity—between Hannah and me and between us as a couple and the outside world. I repeatedly found myself articulating differences between us as individuals, desiring to show how our differences arose and how important it was that we acknowledge them in a way that allowed us each to keep a sense of separate identity. In a parallel fashion, I saw themes of our need to differentiate ourselves as lesbians in a larger world, where we often felt we had to blend in to protect our safety. I thought about how our gender socialization led to such blending in, emphasizing female traits of deference to the other. I saw our needs for sanctuary—for us to find ways to affirm and treasure our relationship and each other in a society where a female couple was not the norm and where our life felt less prescribed by roles than it might be for a heterosexual couple.

In each of the chapters, I focused on specific aspects of these themes. In "Our Marriage Day," I confronted issues of conformity to convention and Hannah's and my feelings of ambivalence toward heterosexual institutions. In "Down the Coast," I pursued that theme further and was able to review, in a loving way, our history over our previous thirty-two years. In "On the Road Again" and "In the Winter Desert," I explored how my increasing blindness influenced our relationship over time. I confronted differences between Hannah and me in detail in "Moving In" and later in the "Therapy" chapter, where I also emphasized the importance for us of external support. In "Attending a Wedding," I revisited themes of conformity to heterosexual convention and introduced potential differences with other lesbian couples.

Finally, in a series of chapters on "Who We Are" drawing from a journey in the New Mexico desert, I focused on challenges of carving out space to be ourselves. In "Are You Two Sisters?" I dramatized our feelings of vulnerability as we traveled in a largely heterosexual environment. In "Private Moments," I turned to themes of sanctuary and intimate sexuality. In "Careful Steps," I examined our cautions, while in "Border Patrol," I sought to illustrate the invisible boundaries both within us and between us and the outside world as we traveled. In "Looking Back," my two characters review their larger journey while walking on a road aptly named "Old Woman's Creek Road."

When I began writing *Are You Two Sisters?* I had been losing my eyesight for some time. It worsened during the five years while I was working on the study so that increasingly I had to rely on the voice in my computer to speak my words aloud to me. I think that this process of listening as I wrote resulted in both a more emotional flow in my narratives than might have occurred were I guided by my visual sight, and a deeper concern for how things felt. It also affected how Hannah and I reviewed my work. In previous studies, Hannah had always read my drafts on paper as I wrote them, giving me her advice and editorial suggestions. For this ethnography, I did not want her doing a critical reading at first, because I was afraid she might be too worried about how "Hannah"—her fictional other—was portrayed and that she might correct my grammar before I was ready for that. Therefore I planned to read the text of each chapter aloud to her, for I wanted to share the experience and get her feedback.

I felt that I had to reassure her, from the start, that if she was bothered by certain things I described and wanted them omitted or changed, she should tell me and I would abide by her wishes, or perhaps explain further why I felt something was important to include. Fortunately for me, Hannah was very supportive of the goals of my project from the start, and when she had sensitivities and requested omissions or changes, given time, I could accommodate them. It also helped that while I was writing my drafts, I showed each chapter to several outside readers whom I trusted so that I would have an external perspective as well. For it was important for me, and for Hannah, to know "What would this text read like for someone who was not us?" I often asked my outside readers whether they felt I was portraying Hannah sensitively enough, and whether I was revealing too much or too little about us, especially in certain more intimate passages.

A curious thing happened while I was reading my chapters aloud to Hannah. At first, we enjoyed them together as the action and scenes unfolded. We would laugh at the humorous parts, remember the moments from our past, feel part of the dialog I had created as if, indeed, it were "us." I began by reading aloud to her from paper printed with very large bold letters so that I could make out my words even if haltingly. Very soon,

I could no longer read from the printed page because of interfering glare and my increasing loss of detailed vision. I turned to reading to Hannah from print enlarged on my iPad. I remember sitting in our dining room, reading the chapters to her, holding the iPad up to my eyes, and Hannah saying, "This is much better. Your trouble reading from the paper was getting in the way." After reading from the iPad for a while, my ability to make out the letters there failed too. So I brought Hannah into my study where I sat at my computer and read aloud to her from the letters in reverse colors on the screen, but that text very quickly faded from my view as well, and my reading out loud became halting.

"It's getting in the way again," I remember Hannah said. "Would you trust me to read on paper by myself?"

I immediately felt worried. "If you promise not to change things," I told her. "If there's something you're sensitive about, okay. But don't change my grammar yet."

Hannah then read the last few chapters on paper, kept her word, and gave me enthusiastic responses. Eventually she would give me her editorial suggestions on each chapter as we went through the entire manuscript in detail, but only after all the chapters were done, the entire story told.

Thus, because it consistently followed my intuitions, I think this ethnography is truly mine. If Hannah were to tell our story, it would be her version—more would be said here, less there. The reader would get a more full sense of Hannah's internal perspective. However, I think the narrative is also indelibly Hannah's, reflecting her involvement not only in the past that I have represented, but in the very forming of my telling about it.

Often as I read aloud to Hannah, she would say after a story ended, "That's exactly how it was, exactly what happened. You've really captured it." And she would say it with a smile, as if that pleased her. I would usually respond, "But it's a fiction. I made it up. That's not exactly what happened. It's a version."

"I know," she would say. "But it's exactly how I remember it." That seemed to me the highest compliment. It meant that my "fiction" was not too far off.

In the beginning, I had wanted Hannah to like my work. Chapter by chapter, she assured me that she did. In the very last chapter, I tell her that I have written a story: "It's about two women. They're something like us." She responds by generously reassuring me that she will like it. That type of exchange occurred often while I was completing this ethnography. I would print out my most recent chapter, hand it to Hannah, and say, "I hope you'll like it." "I'll like it," she would answer. And then she did. "And I have a few suggestions," she would add. "You don't have to take them. But maybe you might." The story of my writing this book thus mirrors the story presented in it.

During the time I was working on this study and sharing it with Hannah, I often felt an insularity or sense of aloneness about our couple. I was trying to describe us, but that was often hard for me to do when viewing us from within. I soon found myself turning to external landscapes—especially those of the New Mexico desert in the later chapters—to help me illuminate the nature of our intimacy. When I looked out at these external landscapes, I found I was then able to use features of them to reflect back on features of us. In part for that reason, external landscapes figure prominently in many of the chapters. I often felt as if I had a third character along with me as I was writing. Sometimes it was a desert landscape, at other times a coastal one, or perhaps a visit from someone's mother, or a visit to the space of a grocery store in which the two of us were buying a chicken and my guide dog Fresco was nosing the air. In describing our relationship with that external space, I was then better able to gain perspective on us. As I wrote, I kept telling myself, "You have you and Hannah, and you have a third party. You think of it as the landscape, but really it is the outside world in which you both travel."

That point brings me back to a central theme of *Are You Two Sisters?* More than anything else, for me this is a book about "self and other"—about the sensitive and vulnerable internal space of each individual and, in this case, of two lesbian women—and the external space of the "other" in which they move and live. Their interaction with the broader world affects their intimacy with each other, and their intimacy with each other sometimes affects the world. I hope the reader will bring her own interpretations to the text, enjoy and learn from my stories, and perhaps see herself reflected in them.

For further discussion of the relationship of *Are You Two Sisters?* both to my prior work and to important literature in the fields of gender, sexuality, and disability studies, and ethnographic method, please see the Bibliographic Notes. I am grateful to the scholars and authors who have come before me and to those currently seeking, in their research and writing, to represent social realities in new ways. *Are You Two Sisters?* is intended as a contribution to that effort.

Bibliographic Notes

Are You Two Sisters? *The Journey of a Lesbian Couple* extends themes of gender, identity, disability, and vision explored in my prior books: *Come, Let Me Guide You: A Life Shared with a Guide Dog* (West Lafayette, IN: Purdue University Press, 2015); *Traveling Blind: Adventures in Vision with a Guide Dog by My Side* (West Lafayette, IN: Purdue University Press, 2010); *Things No Longer There: A Memoir of Losing Sight and Finding Vision* (Madison: University of Wisconsin Press, 2005); *The Family Silver: Essays on Relationships among Women* (Berkeley: University of California Press, 1996); *Social Science and the Self: Personal Essays on an Art Form* (New Brunswick, NJ: Rutgers University Press, 1991); *The Mirror Dance: Identity in a Women's Community* (Philadelphia: Temple University Press, 1983); and *Hip Capitalism* (Beverly Hills, CA: Sage Publications, 1979).

I explain my use of a personal approach to ethnography in *Social Science and the Self: Personal Essays on an Art Form* (New Brunswick, NJ: Rutgers University Press, 1991) and further discuss it in "The Art of the Intimate Narrative," in *Come, Let Me Guide You* (West Lafayette, IN: Purdue University Press, 2015): 183–198. See also Krieger, "Beyond 'Subjectivity': The Use of the Self in Social Science,"

Qualitative Sociology 8, no. 4 (1985): 309–324. I discuss my use of fictional devices within sociology in "Fiction and Social Science," *Studies in Symbolic Interaction* 5 (1984): 269–286, included in *The Mirror Dance* (Philadelphia: Temple University Press, 1983) as an Appendix, 173–199. I also explore these issues in "Research and the Construction of a Text," *Studies in Symbolic Interaction* 2 (1979): 167–187. I reflect on central themes of *The Mirror Dance* in *"The Mirror Dance* Revisited," *Journal of Lesbian Studies* 9, nos. 1–2 (2005): 1–9, and review early studies of lesbian communities in "Lesbian Identity and Community: Recent Social Science Literature," *Signs: Journal of Women in Culture and Society* 8, no. 1 (1982): 91–108.

In developing the ideas presented in *Are You Two Sisters?* I am indebted to literature in the fields of feminist, gender, and sexuality studies, disability studies, and ethnographic method. This literature provides both a context for the current work and suggests further valuable perspectives.

Lesbian Studies

Most importantly, I have been influenced by prior scholarship and popular writings on lesbian community and identity. Particularly formative for me have been those writings published between 1970 and 2000 when the subject of separate female relationships was being explored with the goal of making lesbianism more understandable, acceptable, and visible. Important works in this area both from that period and more recently include Sara Ahmed, *Living a Feminist Life* (Durham, NC: Duke University Press, 2017); Dorothy Allison, *Skin: Talking about Sex, Class and Literature* (Ithaca, NY: Firebrand, 1994); Gloria Anzaldúa, *Borderlands/La Frontera: The New Mestiza* (San Francisco: Aunt Lute, 1987; 4th ed., 2012); Gloria Anzaldúa and AnaLouise Keating, *The Gloria Anzaldúa Reader* (Durham, NC: Duke University Press, 2009); June Arnold, *The Cook and the Carpenter: A Novel by the Carpenter* (Plainfield, VT: Daughters, Inc., 1973; New York: New York University Press, 1995); Dawn Atkins, ed., *Looking*

Queer: Body Image and Identity in Lesbian, Bisexual, Gay, and Transgender Communities (New York: Haworth Press, 1998).

See also Niharika Banerjea, Kath Browne, Eduarda Ferreira, Marta Olasik, and Julie Podmore, eds., *Lesbian Feminism: Essays Opposing Global Heteropatriarchies* (London: Zed Books, 2019); Judith Barrington, ed., *An Intimate Wilderness: Lesbian Writers on Sexuality* (Portland, OR: Eighth Mountain Press, 1991); Evelyn Blackwood and Saskia Wieringa, eds., *Female Desires: Same-Sex Relations and Transgender Practices across Cultures* (New York: Columbia University Press, 1999); Lucy Jane Bledsoe, ed., *Lesbian Travels: A Literary Companion* (San Francisco: Whereabouts Press, 1998); Susie Bright, *Big Sex, Little Death: A Memoir* (Berkeley, CA: Seal Press, 2011); Rita Mae Brown, *Rubyfruit Jungle: A Novel* (Plainfield, VT: Daughters, Inc., 1973; New York: Bantam, 2015); Terry Castle, *The Apparitional Lesbian: Female Homosexuality and Modern Culture* (New York: Columbia University Press, 1993); Rachel Hope Cleves, *Charity and Sylvia: A Same-Sex Marriage in Early America* (New York: Oxford University Press, 2014); D. Merilee Clunis and G. Dorsey Green, *Lesbian Couples: A Guide to Creating Healthy Relationships* (Emeryville, CA: Seal Press, 1988; 4th ed., 2005).

Further relevant lesbian works include Jeanne Cordova, *When We Were Outlaws: A Memoir of Love and Revolution* (Midway, FL: Spinsters Ink, 2011); Trudy Darty and Sandee Potter, eds., *Women-Identified Women* (Palo Alto, CA: Mayfield Publishing Company, 1984); Lisa Diamond, *Sexual Fluidity: Understanding Women's Love and Desire* (Cambridge: Harvard University Press, 2008); Kerryn Drysdale, *Intimate Investments in Drag King Cultures: The Rise and Fall of a Lesbian Social Scene* (Cham, Switzerland: Palgrave Macmillan, 2019); Elana Dykewoman, *Riverfinger Women: A Novel* (Plainfield, VT: Daughters, Inc., 1974; Tallahassee, FL: Naiad Press, 1992); Lillian Faderman, *Naked in the Promised Land: A Memoir* (New York: Houghton Mifflin, 2003; London: Bloomsbury Reader, 2020), *Odd Girls and Twilight Lovers: A History of Lesbian Life in Twentieth-Century America* (New York: Columbia University Press, 1991; reprint ed., 2012), and *Sur-*

passing the Love of Men: Romantic Friendship and Love between Women from the Renaissance to the Present (New York: Morrow, 1981; New York: Harper, 1998); Leslie Feinberg, *Stone Butch Blues* (New York: Firebrand Books, 1993).

See also Estelle B. Freedman, Barbara C. Gelpi, Susan L. Johnson, and Kathleen M. Weston, eds., *The Lesbian Issue: Essays from Signs* (Chicago: University of Chicago Press, 1985); Marilyn Frye, *The Politics of Reality: Essays in Feminist Theory* (Freedom, CA: The Crossing Press, 1983) and *Willful Virgin: Essays in Feminism, 1976–1992* (Freedom, CA: The Crossing Press, 1992); Marcia M. Gallo, *Different Daughters: A History of the Daughters of Bilitis and the Birth of the Lesbian Rights Movement* (New York: Carroll and Graf, 2006); Linda Garber, ed., *Tilting the Tower: Lesbians, Teaching, Queer Subjects* (New York: Routledge, 1994); Judy Grahn, *The Judy Grahn Reader* (San Francisco: Aunt Lute Books, 2009); Barbara Grier (Gene Damon) and Coletta Reid, eds., *The Lavender Herring: Lesbian Essays from the Ladder* (Baltimore, MD: Diana Press, 1976); Lauren Jae Gutterman, *Her Neighbor's Wife: A History of Lesbian Desire within Marriage* (Philadelphia: University of Pennsylvania Press, 2019); Jack Halberstam, *Female Masculinity* (Durham, NC: Duke University Press, 1998; 20th anniv. ed., 2018); Marny Hall, *The Lesbian Love Companion: How to Survive Everything from Heartthrob to Heartbreak* (New York: HarperOne, 1998).

Additional valuable writings are Sandra Harding, *Whose Science? Whose Knowledge? Thinking from Women's Lives* (Ithaca, NY: Cornell University Press, 1991); Sarah Lucia Hoagland and Julia Penelope, eds., *For Lesbians Only: A Separatist Anthology* (London: Onlywomen Press, 1988); Amber L. Hollibaugh, *My Dangerous Desires: A Queer Girl Dreaming Her Way Home* (Durham NC: Duke University Press, 2000); Karla Jay, ed., *Dyke Life: A Celebration of the Lesbian Experience* (New York: Basic Books, 1995); Karol L. Jensen, *Lesbian Epiphanies: Women Coming Out in Later Life* (New York: Harrington Park Press, 1999); Susan E. Johnson, *Staying Power: Long Term Lesbian Couples* (Tallahassee, FL: Naiad Press, 1990); Jill Johnston, *Lesbian Nation: The Feminist Solution* (New York: Simon and Schuster, 1973); Michele

Kort and Audrey Bilger, eds., *Here Come the Brides! Reflections on Lesbian Love and Marriage* (Berkeley, CA: Seal Press, 2012); Joan Laird, ed., *Lesbians and Lesbian Families: Reflections on Theory and Practice* (New York: Columbia University Press, 1999); Elizabeth Lapovsky Kennedy and Madeline D. Davis, *Boots of Leather, Slippers of Gold: The History of a Lesbian Community* (New York: Routledge, 1993); Joan Larkin, ed., *A Woman Like That: Lesbian and Bisexual Writers Tell Their Coming Out Stories* (New York: Avon Books, 1999).

For further explorations, see Ellen Lewin, ed., *Inventing Lesbian Cultures in America* (Boston: Beacon Press, 1996); Sasha Gregory Lewis, *Sunday's Women: A Report on Lesbian Life Today* (Boston: Beacon Press, 1979); Audre Lorde, *I Am Your Sister: Black Women Organizing across Sexualities* (New York: Kitchen Table: Women of Color Press, 1985), *Sister Outsider: Essays and Speeches* (Freedom, CA: Crossing Press, 1984; Berkeley, CA: Crossing Press, 2007), and *Zami: A New Spelling of My Name* (Trumansburgh, NY: The Crossing Press, 1983); Del Martin and Phyllis Lyon, *Lesbian/Woman* (San Francisco, CA: Glide Publications, 1972; Volcano, CA: Volcano Press, 1991); Isabel Miller, *Patience and Sarah* (New York: Fawcett, 1985), originally published as *A Place for Us* (New York: McGraw Hill Book Co., 1969); Beth Mintz and Esther D. Rothblum, eds., *Lesbians in Academia: Degrees of Freedom* (New York: Routledge, 1997); Lisa C. Moore, ed., *Does Your Mama Know? An Anthology of Black Lesbian Coming Out Stories* (Decatur, GA: RedBone Press, 1997); Mignon R. Moore, *Invisible Families: Gay Identities, Relationships, and Motherhood among Black Women* (Berkeley: University of California Press, 2011).

See also Cherríe Moraga, *Waiting in the Wings: Portrait of a Queer Motherhood* (Ithaca, NY: Firebrand Books, 1997) and *Native Country of the Heart: A Memoir* (New York: Farrar, Straus and Giroux, 2019); Cherríe Moraga and Gloria Anzaldúa, eds., *This Bridge Called My Back: Radical Writings by Women of Color* (Watertown, MA: Persephone Press, 1981; New York: State University of New York Press, 2015); Bonnie J. Morris, *The Disappearing L: Erasure of Lesbian Spaces and Culture* (New York: State University of New York Press, 2017) and *Eden Built by Eves: The Culture of Women's Music Festivals* (Los Angeles:

Alyson Books, 1999); Joan Nestle, *A Restricted Country* (Ithaca, NY: Firebrand Books, 1987) and Joan Nestle, ed., *The Persistent Desire: A Femme-Butch Reader* (Boston: Alyson Publications, 1992); Esther Newton, *Cherry Grove, Fire Island: Sixty Years in America's First Gay and Lesbian Town* (Boston: Beacon, Press, 1993; Durham, NC: Duke University Press, 2014) and *My Butch Career: A Memoir* (Durham, NC: Duke University Press, 2018); Joanne Passet, *Indomitable: The Life of Barbara Grier* (Tallahassee, FL: Bella Books, 2016).

Further influential contributions are Adrienne Rich, *The Dream of a Common Language, Poems 1974–1977* (New York: W. W. Norton, 1978), *Blood, Bread, and Poetry: Selected Prose 1979–1985* (New York: W. W. Norton, 1986), and *Essential Essays: Culture, Politics, and the Art of Poetry*, ed. Sandra M. Gilbert (New York: W. W. Norton, 2018); Christine M. Robinson, *The Web: Social Control in a Lesbian Community* (Lanham, MD: University Press of America, 2008); Esther D. Rothblum and Kathleen A. Brehony, eds., *Boston Marriages: Romantic but Asexual Relationships among Contemporary Lesbians* (Amherst: University of Massachusetts Press, 1993); Jane Rule, *Lesbian Images* (New York: Doubleday and Company, 1975) and *This Is Not For You* (New York: McCall, 1970; London, Ontario: Insomniac Press, 2005); Leila J. Rupp, *Sapphistries: A Global History of Love between Women* (New York: New York University Press, 2011); Cheela Romain Smith, Giovanna Capone, and Xequina Berber, eds., *Dispatches from Lesbian America* (Fairfield, CA: Bedazzled Ink Publishing, 2017).

See also Arlene Stein, ed., *Sisters, Sexperts, Queers: Beyond the Lesbian Nation* (New York: Plume/Penguin, 1993); Donna M. Tanner, *The Lesbian Couple* (Lexington, MA: Lexington Books, 1978); Carla Trujillo, ed., *Chicana Lesbians: The Girls Our Mothers Warned Us About* (Berkeley, CA: Third Woman Press, 1991); Lindsy Van Gelder and Pamela Robin Brandt, *The Girls Next Door: Into the Heart of Lesbian America* (New York: Simon and Schuster, 1996); Jacqueline S. Weinstock and Esther D. Rothblum, eds., *Lesbian Ex-lovers: The Really Long-Term Relationships* (New York: Harrington Park Press, 2004); Jacqueline S. Weinstock and Esther D. Rothblum, eds., *Lesbian Friendships: For Ourselves and Each Other* (New York: New York University Press, 1996); Erin O. White, *Given Up for You: A Memoir of Love, Belonging, and Belief* (Madison: University of Wisconsin Press, 2018); Deborah Goleman Wolf, *The Lesbian Community* (Berkeley: University of California Press, 1979); Susan J. Wolfe and Julia Penelope Stanley, eds., *The Coming Out Stories* (Watertown, MA: Persephone Press, 1980) and the revised 2nd ed. by Julia Penelope and Susan J. Wolfe, *The Original Coming Out Stories* (Freedom, CA: The Crossing Press, 1989); Bonnie Zimmerman and Toni A. H. McNaron, eds., *The New Lesbian Studies: Into the Twenty-First Century* (New York: The Feminist Press at the City University of New York, 1996).

Important periodicals focusing on lesbian issues include the *Journal of Lesbian Studies*, 1997–present; *Conditions*, 1977–1990; *Sinister Wisdom*, 1976–present; *The Ladder*, 1956–1972; and *Lesbian Connection*, 1974–present.

Queer and Gay Studies

I am also grateful for writings in the broader field of queer and gay studies in which attention to intimate relationships between women and alliances between women and men are often salient. These works have extended their theoretical and empirical reach in recent years and raised valuable questions concerning the complexity and fluidity of sexual and gender identities. Significant works in this group that provide context for the current study include Henry Abelove, Michèle Aina Barale, and David M. Halperin, eds., *The Lesbian and Gay Studies Reader* (New York: Routledge, 1993); Jonathan F. Alexander, Deborah T. Meem, and Michelle A. Gibson, *Finding Out: An Introduction to LGBTQ Studies*, 4th ed. (Thousand Oaks, CA: SAGE Publications, 2020); Samantha Allen, *Real Queer America: LGBT Stories from Red States* (New York: Little, Brown and Company, 2019); Brett Beemyn, ed., *Queer Studies: A Lesbian, Gay, Bisexual, and Transgender Anthology* (New York: New York University Press, 1996); Allan Bérubé, *Coming Out under Fire: The History of Gay Men and Women in World War II*, 20th anniv. ed. (Chapel Hill: University of North Carolina Press, 2010).

See also Chris Brickell and Judith Collard, eds., *Queer Objects* (New Brunswick, NJ: Rutgers University Press, 2019); Michael Bronski, *A Queer History of the United States* (Boston: Beacon Press, 2012); Judith Butler, *Gender Trouble: Feminism and the Subversion of Identity* (New York: Routledge, 1999); Robert J. Corber and Stephen Valocchi, eds., *Queer Studies: An Interdisciplinary Reader* (New York: Wiley-Blackwell, 2003); Katherine Crawford-Lackey and Megan E. Springate, eds., *Identities and Place: Changing Labels and Intersectional Communities of LGBTQ and Two-Spirit People in the United States* (New York: Berghahn Books, 2020); John D'Emilio, *In a New Century: Essays on Queer History, Politics, and Community Life* (Madison: University of Wisconsin Press, 2014) and *Sexual Politics, Sexual Communities: The Making of a Homosexual Minority in the United States, 1940–1970* (Chicago: University of Chicago Press, 1998); Martin Duberman, ed., *A Queer World: The Center for Lesbian and Gay Studies Reader* (New York: New York University Press, 1997) and *Stonewall: The Definitive Story of the LGBTQ Rights Uprising That Changed America*, rev. ed. (New York: Plume, 2019); Monalesia Earle, *Writing Queer Women of Color: Representation and Misdirection in Contemporary Fiction and Graphic Narratives* (Jefferson, NC: MacFarland, 2019).

Further influential works in queer and gay studies are Lillian Faderman, *The Gay Revolution: The Story of the Struggle* (New York: Simon and Schuster, 2015); Larry Gross and James Woods, eds., *The Columbia Reader on Lesbians and Gay Men in Media, Society, and Politics* (New York: Columbia University Press, 1999); Judith Halberstam, *The Queer Art of Failure* (Durham, NC: Duke University Press, 2011); Donald E. Hall, Annamarie Jagose, Andrea Bebell, and Susan Potter, eds., *The Routledge Queer Studies Reader* (New York: Routledge, 2013); Lisa Henderson, *Love and Money: Queers, Class, and Cultural Production* (New York: New York University Press, 2013); Stephen Hicks, *Lesbian, Gay and Queer Parenting: Families, Intimacies, Genealogies* (New York: Palgrave Macmillan, 2011); Debra Hope, ed., *Contemporary Perspectives on Lesbian, Gay, and Bisexual Identities* (New York: Springer, 2009); Annamarie Jagose, *Queer Theory: An Introduction* (New York: New York University Press, 1997).

Additional significant works include E. Patrick Johnson, *Sweet Tea: Black Gay Men of the South* (Chapel Hill: University of North Carolina Press, 2011); E. Patrick Johnson and Mae G. Henderson, eds., *Black Queer Studies: A Critical Anthology* (Durham, NC: Duke University Press, 2005); Jonathan Ned Katz, *The Invention of Heterosexuality* (New York: Dutton, 1995); Heather Love, *Feeling Backward: Loss and the Politics of Queer History* (Cambridge, MA: Harvard University Press, 2007); Armistead Maupin, *Logical Family: A Memoir* (London: Doubleday, 2017; New York: Harper Perennial, 2018); Hannah McCann and Whitney Monaghan, *Queer Theory Now: From Foundations to Futures* (London: Red Globe Press, 2019); Joan Nestle and John Preston, eds., *Sister and Brother: Lesbians and Gay Men Write about Their Lives Together* (San Francisco, CA: HarperSanFrancisco, 1994); New York Public Library and Jason Baumann, eds., *The Stonewall Reader* (New York: Penguin Books, 2019); Thomas Piontek, *Queering Gay and Lesbian Studies* (Urbana: University of Illinois Press, 2006); Uriel Quesada, Letitia Gomez, and Salvador Vidal-Ortiz, eds., *Queer Brown Voices: Personal Narratives of Latina/o LGBT Activism* (Austin: University of Texas Press, 2015).

See also Juana María Rodríguez, *Queer Latinidad: Identity Practices, Discursive Spaces* (New York: New York University Press, 2003); Gayle Rubin, *Deviations: A Gayle Rubin Reader* (Durham, NC: Duke University Press, 2011); Leila J. Rupp, *A Desired Past: A Short History of Same-Sex Love in America* (Chicago: University of Chicago Press, 2002); Leila J. Rupp and Susan K. Freeman, eds., *Understanding and Teaching U.S. Lesbian, Gay, Bisexual, and Transgender History*, 2nd ed. (Madison: University of Wisconsin Press, 2017); Leila J. Rupp and Verta Taylor, *Drag Queens at the 801 Cabaret* (Chicago: University of Chicago Press, 2015); Hugh Ryan, *When Brooklyn Was Queer: A History* (New York: St. Martin's Press, 2019); Marilyn Schuster, *A Queer Love Story: The Letters of Jane Rule and Rick Bébout* (Vancouver, Canada: University of British Columbia Press, 2007); Eve Kosofsky Sedgwick, *Epistemology of the Closet* (Berkeley: University of California Press, 1990); Kathryn Bond Stockton, *Beautiful Bottom, Beautiful Shame: Where "Black" Meets "Queer"* (Durham, NC: Duke University Press, 2006).

For further valuable ideas, see Rodger Streitmatter, *Outlaw Marriages: The Hidden Histories of Fifteen Extraordinary Same-Sex Couples* (Boston: Beacon Press, 2012); Nikki Sullivan, *A Critical Introduction to Queer Theory* (New York: New York University Press, 2003); Mattilda Bernstein Sycamore, ed., *That's Revolting! Queer Strategies for Resisting Assimilation*, rev. ed. (Brooklyn, NY: Soft Skull Press, 2008); Michael Warner, ed., *Fear of a Queer Planet* (Minneapolis: University of Minnesota Press, 1993); Vera Whisman, *Queer by Choice: Lesbians, Gay Men, and the Politics of Identity* (New York: Routledge, 1996); Jason Whitesel, *Fat Gay Men: Girth, Mirth, and the Politics of Stigma* (New York: New York University Press, 2014); Robert Williams and Ted Gideonse, eds., *From Boys to Men: Gay Men Write about Growing Up* (New York: Carroll and Graf, 2006).

Transgender Studies

I have benefited, as well, from the perspectives on gender and identity emerging from the field of transgender studies, which has challenged many traditional notions about the fixedness of identity and called attention to the importance of individual choice. Significant works in this area include Caspar J. Baldwin, *Not Just a Tomboy: A Trans Masculine Memoir* (London: Jessica Kingsley Publishers, 2019); Genny Beemyn and Susan R. Rankin, *The Lives of Transgender People* (New York: Columbia University Press, 2011); Anne L. Boedecker, *The Transgender Guidebook: Keys to a Successful Transition* (Scotts Valley, CA: CreateSpace Independent Publishing Platform, 2011); Kate Bornstein, *Gender Outlaw: On Men, Women, and the Rest of Us* (New York: Routledge, 1994); Jennifer Finny Boylan, *She's Not There: A Life in Two Genders* (New York: Broadway Books, 2013); Heath Fogg Davis, *Beyond Trans: Does Gender Matter?* (New York: New York University Press, 2017); Morty Diamond, ed., *Trans/Love: Radical Sex, Love and Relationships beyond the Gender Binary* (San Francisco: Manic D Press, 2011).

See also Laura Erickson-Schroth, ed., *Trans Bodies, Trans Selves: A Resource for the Transgender Community* (New York: Oxford University Press, 2014); Laura Erikson-Schroth and Laura Jacobs, *"You're *in the Wrong Bathroom!": And 20 Other Myths and Misconceptions about Transgender and Gender-Nonconforming People* (Boston: Beacon Press, 2017); Leslie Feinberg, *Trans Liberation: Beyond Pink or Blue* (Boston: Beacon Press, 1999); Ardel Haefele-Thomas, *Introduction to Transgender Studies* (New York: Harrington Park Press, 2019); Alex Iantaffi and Meg-John Barker, *Life Isn't Binary: On Being Both, Beyond, and In-between* (London: Jessica Kingsley Publishers, 2019); Janet Mock, *Redefining Realness: My Path to Womanhood, Identity, Love and So Much More* (New York: Atria Books, 2014); Julie L. Nagoshi, Craig T. Nagoshi, and Stephan/ie Brzuzy, *Gender and Sexual Identity: Transcending Feminist and Queer Theory* (New York: Springer, 2014); Ruth Pearce, Igi Moon, Kat Gupta, and Deborah Lynn Steinberg, eds., *The Emergence of Trans: Cultures, Politics, and Everyday Lives* (New York: Routledge, 2020).

Further valuable works include Micah Rajunov and A. Scott Duane, eds., *Nonbinary: Memoirs of Gender and Identity* (New York: Columbia University Press, 2019); Deborah Rudacille, *The Riddle of Gender: Science, Activism, and Transgender Rights* (New York: Pantheon, 2005); Gayle Salamon, *Assuming a Body: Transgender and Rhetorics of Materiality* (New York: Columbia University Press, 2010); Julia Serano, *Whipping Girl: A Transsexual Woman on Sexism and the Scapegoating of Femininity*, 2nd ed. (Berkeley: Seal Press, 2016); Jackson Wright Shultz, *Trans/Portraits: Voices from Transgender Communities* (Hanover, NH: Dartmouth College Press, 2015); Susan Stryker, *Transgender History: The Roots of Today's Revolution*, 2nd ed. (New York: Seal Press, 2017); Susan Stryker and Aren Aizura, eds., *The Transgender Studies Reader 2* (New York: Routledge, 2013); Brynn Tannehill, *Everything You Ever Wanted to Know about Trans (but Were Afraid to Ask)* (London: Jessica Kingsley Publishers, 2018); Ann Travers, *The Trans Generation: How Trans Kids (and Their Parents) Are Creating a Gender Revolution* (New York: New York University Press, 2018).

Additional significant writings are David Valentine, *Imagining Transgender: An Ethnography of a Category* (Durham, NC: Duke University Press, 2007); Reid Vanderburgh, *Transition and Beyond: Observations on Gender Identity* (Portland, OR: Reid Vanderburgh, 2017);

Norah Vincent, *Self-Made Man: One Woman's Journey into Manhood and Back Again* (New York: Viking, 2006); María-Amelia Viteri, *Desbordes: Translating Racial, Ethnic, Sexual, and Gender Identities across the Americas* (New York: State University of New York Press, 2015).

Disability Studies

I owe a great debt to insights gleaned from the disability studies literature, and, particularly, the writings on women and disabilities. This literature raises important questions about the role of gender in affecting experience, and, like the literature on lesbianism, often highlights themes of caring, nurturance, and self-acceptance. I am particularly grateful for accounts dealing with blindness and vision loss, for example: Sally Hobart Alexander, *Do You Remember the Color Blue?: And Other Questions Kids Ask about Blindness* (New York: Viking, 2000); Belo Miguel Cipriani, *Blind: A Memoir* (Tucson, AZ: Wheatmark, 2016); Hannah Fairbairn, *When You Can't Believe Your Eyes: Vision Loss and Personal Recovery* (Springfield, IL: Charles C. Thomas, 2019); Mara Faulkner, *Going Blind: A Memoir* (Albany: State University of New York Press, 2009); Beth Finke, *Long Time, No See* (Champaign: University of Illinois Press, 2003).

See also Gili Hammer, *Blindness through the Looking Glass: The Performance of Blindness, Gender, and the Sensory Body* (Ann Arbor: University of Michigan Press, 2019); Nicole C. Kear, *Now I See You: A Memoir* (New York: St. Martin's Press, 2014); Georgina Kleege, *Sight Unseen* (New Haven: Yale University Press, 1999); Stephen Kuusisto, *Planet of the Blind: A Memoir* (New York: Delta, 1998); Rod Michalko, *The Two-in-One: Walking with Smokie, Walking with Blindness* (Philadelphia: Temple University Press, 1998) and *The Mystery of the Eye and the Shadow of Blindness* (Toronto, Canada: University of Toronto Press, 1998); Frances Lief Neer, *Dancing in the Dark: A Guide to Living with Blindness and Visual Impairment* (San Francisco, CA: Wildstar Publishing, 1994); Beth Omansky, *Borderlands of Blindness* (Boulder, CO: Lynne Rienner Publishers, 2011); Laurie Rubin, *Do You Dream in Color?: Insights from a Girl without Sight* (New York: Seven Stories Press, 2012).

Significant works from the broader disability studies field that have influenced my thinking include Elizabeth Barnes, *The Minority Body: A Theory of Disability* (New York: Oxford University Press, 2016); Katherine Bouton, *Shouting Won't Help: Why I—and 50 Million Other Americans—Can't Hear You* (New York: Sarah Crichton Books/Farrar, Straus, and Giroux, 2013); Victoria A. Brownworth and Susan Raffo, eds., *Restricted Access: Lesbians on Disability* (Seattle, WA: Seal Press, 1999); Eli Clare, *Exile and Pride: Disability, Queerness, and Liberation* (Cambridge: South End Press, 1999; Durham, NC: Duke University Press, 2015); Barb Cook and Michelle Garnett, eds., *Spectrum Women: Walking to the Beat of Autism* (London: Jessica Kingsley Publishers, 2018); Lennard J. Davis, ed., *The Disability Studies Reader* (New York: Routledge, 2016); Elizabeth J. Donaldson, ed., *Literatures of Madness: Disability Studies and Mental Health* (Cham, Switzerland: Palgrave Macmillan, 2018).

See also Katie Ellis, Rosemarie Garland-Thomson, Mike Kent, and Rachel Robertson, eds., *Manifestos for the Future of Critical Disability Studies* (New York: Routledge, 2019) and *Interdisciplinary Approaches to Disability: Looking Towards the Future* (New York: Routledge, 2019); Mary Felstiner, *Out of Joint: A Private and Public Story of Arthritis* (Lincoln: University of Nebraska Press, 2005); Kenny Fries, ed., *Staring Back: The Disability Experience from the Inside Out* (New York: Plume/Penguin, 1997); Eileen Garvin, *How to Be a Sister: A Love Story with a Twist of Autism* (New York: The Experiment, 2010); Kim Q. Hall, ed., *Feminist Disability Studies* (Bloomington: Indiana University Press, 2011); Sarah Hendrickx, *Women and Girls with Autism Spectrum Disorder: Understanding Life Experiences from Early Childhood to Old Age* (London: Jessica Kingsley Publishers, 2015); Judith Heumann and Kristen Joiner, *Being Heumann: An Unrepentant Memoir of a Disability Rights Activist* (Boston: Beacon Press, 2020); Kay Redfield Jamison, *An Unquiet Mind: A Memoir of Moods and Madness* (New York: Vintage, 1997); Michelle Jarman, Leila Monaghan, and Alison

Quaggin Harkin, eds., *Barriers and Belonging: Personal Narratives of Disability* (Philadelphia: Temple University Press, 2017).

Further valuable writings are Harriet McBryde Johnson, *Too Late to Die Young: Nearly True Tales from a Life* (New York: Henry Holt, 2005); Alison Kafer, *Feminist, Queer, Crip* (Bloomington: Indiana University Press, 2013); Heather Kuttai, *Maternity Rolls: Pregnancy, Childbirth and Disability* (Black Point, Nova Scotia, Canada: Fernwood Publishing, 2010); Simi Linton, *My Body Politic: A Memoir* (Ann Arbor: University of Michigan Press, 2006); Raymond Luczak, ed., *QDA: A Queer Disability Anthology* (Minneapolis, MN: Squares and Rebels, 2015); Nancy Mairs, *Waist High in the World: A Life among the Nondisabled* (Boston: Beacon Press, 1996); Robert McRuer, *Crip Theory: Cultural Signs of Queerness and Disability* (New York: New York University Press, 2006); Susannah B. Mintz, *Unruly Bodies: Life Writing by Women with Disabilities* (Chapel Hill: The University of North Carolina Press, 2007); Lorna Moorhead, *Coffee in the Cereal: The First Year with Multiple Sclerosis* (Oxnard, CA: Pathfinder Publishing, 2003); Milo W. Obourn, *Disabled Futures: A Framework for Radical Inclusion* (Philadelphia: Temple University Press, 2020).

Additional useful perspectives appear in Leah Lakshmi Piepzna-Samarasinha, *Care Work: Dreaming Disability Justice* (Vancouver, Canada: Arsenal Pulp Press, 2018); Harilyn Rousso, *Don't Call Me Inspirational: A Disabled Feminist Talks Back* (Philadelphia: Temple University Press, 2013); Elyn R. Saks, *The Center Cannot Hold: My Journey through Madness* (New York: Hyperion, 2007); Marsha Saxton and Florence Howe, eds., *With Wings: An Anthology of Literature by and about Women with Disabilities* (New York: The Feminist Press at the City University of New York, 1987); Tobin Anthony Siebers, *Disability Theory* (Ann Arbor: University of Michigan Press, 2008); Rebekah Taussig, *Sitting Pretty: The View from My Ordinary Resilient Disabled Body* (New York: HarperCollins, 2020); Shelley Tremain, ed., *Pushing the Limits: Disabled Dykes Produce Culture* (Ontario, Canada: Women's Press, 1996); Susan Wendell, *The Rejected Body: Feminist Philosophical Reflections on Disability* (New York: Routledge, 1996); Daniel J. Wilson and Jeffrey A. Brune, eds., *Disability and Passing: Blurring the Lines of Identity* (Philadelphia: Temple University Press, 2013); Alice Wong, ed., *Disability Visibility: First-Person Stories from the Twenty-First Century* (New York: Vintage, 2020); Caitlin Wood, ed., *Criptiques* (Portland, OR: May Day Publishing, 2014).

Ethnographic Method

Discussions of ethnography that both explain and provide context for my use of a personal and "everyday life" approach to sociological narrative have been extremely important to the development of my work. I am deeply grateful to scholars who have explored issues of subjectivity, positionality, and alternative methods of representation. Their valuable works include Tony E. Adams, Stacy Holman Jones, and Carolyn Ellis, *Autoethnography* (New York: Oxford University Press, 2015); Stephen Andrew, *Searching for an Autoethnographic Ethic* (New York: Routledge, 2017); Angelika Bammer and Ruth-Ellen Boetcher Joeres, eds., *The Future of Scholarly Writing: Critical Interventions* (New York: Palgrave Macmillan, 2015); Arthur P. Bochner and Carolyn Ellis, *Evocative Autoethnography: Writing Lives and Telling Stories* (New York: Routledge, 2016); Matt Brim and Amin Ghaziani, eds., "Queer Methods," Special Issue, *Women's Studies Quarterly* 44, nos. 3–4 (2016); Kath Browne and Catherine J. Nash, eds., *Queer Methods and Methodologies: Intersecting Queer Theories and Social Science Research* (New York: Routledge, 2016); Heewon Chang, *Creating a Multivocal Self: Autoethnography as Method* (New York: Routledge, 2017); Peter Collins and Anselma Gallinat, eds., *The Ethnographic Self as Resource: Writing Memory and Experience into Ethnography* (New York: Berghahn Books, 2013).

See also D'Lane Compton, Tey Meadow, and Kristen Schilt, eds., *Other, Please Specify: Queer Methods in Sociology* (Oakland: University of California Press, 2018); Dána-Ain Davis and Christa Craven, *Feminist Ethnography: Thinking through Methodologies, Challenges, and Possibilities* (Lanham, MD: Rowman and Littlefield, 2016); Norman K. Denzin, *Interpretive Autoethnography* (Los Angeles: SAGE Publications, 2013); Marjorie Devault, *Liberating Method: Feminism and Social*

Research (Philadelphia: Temple University Press, 1999); Carolyn Ellis, *Final Negotiations: A Story of Love, Loss, and Chronic Illness* (Philadelphia: Temple University Press, 2018), *Revision: Autoethnographic Reflections on Life and Work* (Walnut Creek, CA: Left Coast Press, 2009; New York: Routledge, 2020), and "Telling Secrets, Revealing Lives: Relational Ethics in Research with Intimate Others," *Qualitative Inquiry* 13, no. 1 (2007): 3–29; Amin Ghaziani and Matt Brim, eds., *Imagining Queer Methods* (New York: New York University Press, 2019); Martyn Hammersley and Paul Atkinson, *Ethnography: Principles in Practice*, 4th ed. (New York: Routledge, 2019).

Further valuable discussions appear in Sherick A. Hughes and Julie L. Pennington, *Autoethnography: Process, Product, and Possibility for Critical Social Research* (Los Angeles: SAGE Publications, 2016); Ellen Lewin and William L. Leap, eds., *Out in the Field: Reflections of Lesbian and Gay Anthropologists* (Urbana: University of Illinois Press, 1996); Mary Jo Maynes, Jennifer L. Pierce, and Barbara Laslett, *Telling Stories: The Use of Personal Narratives in the Social Sciences and History* (Ithaca: Cornell University Press, 2008); Tessa Muncey, *Creating Autoethnographies* (Thousand Oaks, CA: SAGE, 2010); Robert J. Nash, *Liberating Scholarly Writing: The Power of Personal Narrative* (New York: Teachers College Press, 2004; Charlotte, NC: Information Age Publishing, 2019); Laurel Richardson, *Fields of Play: Constructing an Academic Life* (New Brunswick, NJ: Rutgers University Press, 1997) and *Writing Strategies: Reaching Diverse Audiences* (Los Angeles: SAGE Publications, 1990); Jo Woodiwiss, Kate Smith, and Kelly Lockwood, eds., *Feminist Narrative Research: Opportunities and Challenges* (London: Palgrave Macmillan, 2017).

I am also indebted to reflections on narrative and storytelling by writers, particularly Judith Barrington, *Writing the Memoir: From Truth to Art*, 2nd ed. (Portland: Eighth Mountain Press, 2002); Joan Didion, *Slouching Towards Bethlehem* (New York: Farrar, Straus and Giroux, 1968; New York: Picador Modern Classics, 2017); Vivian Gornick, *The Situation and the Story: The Art of Personal Narrative* (New York: Farrar, Straus and Giroux, 2002); Nancy Mairs, *Voice Lessons: On Becoming a Woman Writer* (Boston: Beacon Press, 1994); Ann

Patchett, *This Is the Story of a Happy Marriage* (New York: Harper, 2013); Gloria Steinem, *My Life on the Road* (New York: Random House, 2015); Amy Tan, *Where the Past Begins: A Writer's Memoir* (New York: Ecco Books, 2017).

Topical References

Valuable perspectives on the southern New Mexico border area in which some of the stories in this book take place include Philip Connors, *Fire Season: Field Notes from a Wilderness Lookout* (New York: Ecco, 2011); Kelly Lytle Hernandez, *Migra! A History of the U.S. Border Patrol* (Berkeley: University of California Press, 2010); George Hilliard, *Adios Hachita: Stories of a New Mexico Town* (Silver City, NM: High Lonesome Books, 1998); Julian Lim, *Porous Borders: Multiracial Migrations and the Law in the U.S.-Mexico Borderlands* (Chapel Hill: University of North Carolina Press, 2020); Sandra Day O'Connor, *Lazy B: Growing up on a Cattle Ranch in the American Southwest* (New York: Random House, 2003); Carol Smith, *To Animas with Love: A History* (Dexter, MI: Thomson-Shore, 2009); Rachel St. John, *Line in the Sand: A History of the Western U.S.-Mexico Border* (Princeton: Princeton University Press, 2011); Samuel Truett, *Fugitive Landscapes: The Forgotten History of the U.S.-Mexico Borderlands* (New Haven: Yale University Press, 2006); Susan J. Tweit, *Barren, Wild, and Worthless: Living in the Chihuahuan Desert* (Albuquerque: University of New Mexico Press, 1995).

See also, for geology and plants, Carolyn Dodson and Robert DeWitt Ivey, *A Guide to Plants of the Northern Chihuahuan Desert* (Albuquerque: University of New Mexico Press, 2012); Bob Julyan, *Wild Guide: Passport to New Mexico Wilderness* (Albuquerque: New Mexico Wilderness Alliance, 2020); Robert Julyan and Carl Smith, *The Mountains of New Mexico* (Albuquerque: University of New Mexico Press, 2006). For the Arizona borderland mountains, see William Ascarza, *Chiricahua Mountains: History and Nature* (Charleston, SC: The History Press, 2014); Wynne Brown and Reed Peters, eds., *Cave Creek Canyon: Revealing the Heart of Arizona's Chiricahua Mountains*

(Rodeo, NM: ECCO Wear and Publishing 2014); Ken Lamberton and Jeff Garton, *Chiricahua Mountains: Bridging the Borders of Wildness* (Tucson: University of Arizona Press, 2003); Richard Shelton, *Going Back to Bisbee* (Tucson: University of Arizona Press, 1992).

The Cris Williamson lyrics referred to in Chapter 4 are from "Shooting Star," *The Changer and the Changed*, Olivia Records, 1975. The phrase "the love that dare not speak its name," referred to in Chapters 9 and 11, is from a poem by Alfred Douglas, "Two Loves," *The Chameleon* (Oxford, England, 1894), subsequently popularized by Oscar Wilde in his 1895 indecency trial; see Richard Ellmann, *Oscar Wilde* (New York: Vintage, 1988).

Susan Krieger is a sociologist, writer, and Research Fellow at the Clayman Institute for Gender Research, Stanford University. Her prior books include *The Mirror Dance: Identity in a Women's Community* (Temple), *Social Science and the Self: Personal Essays on an Art Form*, *The Family Silver: Essays on Relationships among Women*, *Things No Longer There: A Memoir of Losing Sight and Finding Vision*, *Traveling Blind: Adventures in Vision with a Guide Dog by My Side*, and *Come Let Me Guide You: A Life Shared with a Guide Dog.*